AF646902

INDO-PAK WAR 1971

Reminiscences of Air Warriors

INDO-PAK WAR 1971

Reminiscences of Air Warriors

Foreword by

Air Chief Marshal VR Chaudhari PVSM AVSM VM ADC

Edited by

Air Marshal Jagjeet Singh PVSM VSM (Retd)

Group Captain Shailendra Mohan (Retd)

Marshal of the
Air Force Arjan Singh &
Mrs Arjan Singh Trust

PENTAGON PRESS LLP

AIR FORCE ASSOCIATION

INDO-PAK WAR 1971
Reminiscences of Air Warriors

Edited by ***Air Marshal Jagjeet Singh PVSM VSM (Retd)***
Group Captain Shailendra Mohan (Retd)

ISBN 978-93-90095-50-6

First Published in 2022

Copyright © Air Force Association (AFA)

All rights reserved. No part of this publication may be reproduced, stored in a retrieval system, or transmitted in any form or by any means, electronic, mechanical, photocopying, recording or otherwise, without the prior written permission of the AFA.

email: afaheadoffice@gmail.com
website: www.afa-india.org

DISCLAIMER: The views expressed in the articles published in this book are solely those of the authors. Neither the Air Force Association nor the editors bear any responsibility for their authenticity and accuracy.

Published by
PENTAGON PRESS LLP
206, Peacock Lane, Shahpur Jat,
New Delhi-110049
Phones: 011-64706243, 26491568
Telefax: 011-26490600
email: rajan@pentagonpress.in
website: www.pentagonpress.in

Printed at Aegean Offset Printers, Greater Noida, U.P.

Dedicated to
all the Air Warriors of
1971 Indo-Pak War,
particularly to those who sacrificed their lives
in the service of the nation.

* * *

A lamp doesn't speak.
It introduces itself through its light.
Likewise, achievers need not talk about themselves.
They will be automatically known because of their achievements.

"Dedicated to the Achievers of 1971 War".

AIR FORCE ASSOCIATION

The Air Force Association (AFA) came into being on 15 Sep 1980. The initiative of establishing AFA was taken by the late Marshal of the Air Force Arjan Singh. Late Air Chief Marshal PC Lal was its first President and late Air Cmde Amrit Lal Saigal was the first Secretary.

AFA is registered under the Societies Registration Act 1860. The Association has 20 branches spread all over the country. It also has two branches abroad, one each in UK and Australia. The Head Office of AFA is located at New Delhi. It constitutes of a Governing Council (Central) and an Executive Committee (Central) for its management.

It is one of the five associations of Air Veterans duly recognised by the Ministry of Defence. It is an apolitical body established to look after the welfare of Air Veterans and their families. It acts as an interface between the Air Veterans and various Government agencies like Service Head Quarters, Ministry of Defence, ECHS and Kendriya Sainik Board etc.

The Association helps its members in resolving their pension, medical and other service related issues. It also manages various scholarships sponsored by the members and other individuals/ organisations. These scholarships are for the wards of serving and retired Air Force and DSC personnel for pursuing professional and non-professional courses. It also gives financial assistance to certain needy air veterans and widows based on merit.

In the year 2004, Marshal of the Air Force Arjan Singh and Mrs Arjan Singh established a trust with their personal savings to look after the welfare of the Air Veterans and their families. The functioning of the Trust is also managed by Air Force Association.

To keep the members updated on the service and other issues of general nature affecting them, the Association publishes a bi-annual magazine AFA News (Eagle's Eye). The Association has its own Website and Facebook account which act as an interface between the association and its members.

The Association is headed by the most recently retired Chief of the Air Staff as its President.

Contents

वायु सेनाध्यक्ष
CHIEF OF THE AIR STAFF
★★★★

एयर चीफ मार्शल वी आर चौधरी
प वि से मे अ वि से मे वा से मे ए डी सी
Air Chief Marshal VR Chaudhari
PVSM AVSM VM ADC

Tel : (011) Off : 23012517
Res : 23017300
Fax : 23018853

वायु सेना मुख्यालय
नई दिल्ली - 110011
Air Headquarters
New Delhi - 110011

FOREWORD

1. India won a historic war against Pakistan 50 years ago on 16th of December 1971 which led to the creation of a new independent sovereign nation - Bangladesh, ending an oppressive and tyrannical domination of West Pakistan over East Pakistan. The nation is celebrating "50 Glorious Years" of the historical victory by declaring this year as the "Swarnim Vijay Varsh". The Indian Air Force had played a pivotal role in the liberation of Bangladesh by defeating the Pakistan Air Force in East Pakistan and achieving total air superiority. This in turn, facilitated the ground forces to march towards Dhaka without any fear of an attack from the skies. Tangail para drop and the attack on Governor's Residence hastened the fall of Dhaka and forced the surrender of 93,000 Pakistani soldiers, the biggest such surrender after World War II, across the world.

2. The initiative taken by the Air Force Association in bringing out this book carrying authentic accounts of the events as reminisced by authors who had actively participated in operations is highly commendable.

3. This book is being released to commemorate the "Swarnim Vijay Diwas" and I am quite sanguine that it will be well received by Air Veterans, Air War Historians, Service Personnel and Academia to get a first hand account of the role played by Indian Air Force in the War of 1971.

4. I congratulate the editors for ably editing this book and the Air Force Association for publishing it.

Jai Hind!

Air Chief Marshal
Chief of the Air staff

17 December 2021

The Concept

Air Chief Marshal BS Dhanoa PVSM AVSM YSM VM (Retd)

This year is being celebrated as the Swarnim Vijay Varsh to commemorate our victory in the Indo-Pak War of 1971. I wish to congratulate all those Air Warriors who were a part of those magnificent operations that led to the liberation of Bangladesh. The entire nation is proud of them.

IAF's prominent role in the 1971 War significantly contributed to the spectacular victory and attainment of our Politico-Military Objectives. Several books have been written on the IAF's role in this war at the macro-level, starting with the wonderful memoirs penned down by the then Chief of the Air Staff, Late Air Chief Marshal PC Lal in his book, "My Years with the IAF". Thereafter, many more books have been published to commemorate the Golden Jubilee Celebrations of this war.

IAF conducted one of the most successful Airborne Ops missions in East Pakistan post World War ll. We also cannot, of course, forget the first Heli-borne operation, both during day and night, that was ever conducted in our history which led to positioning of thousands of troops at the doorsteps of Dacca.

We, at the Air Force Association, felt that there existed a paramount requirement to pass on the narrative as experienced personally by participants in this war for the benefit of succeeding generations of Air Warriors so that they might gainfully utilise this invaluable experience in the times to come. It was also important that the facts be recorded to challenge any unsubstantiated claims of loose writings, especially in social media, which might diminish our superb contribution and undermine the role of IAF in the 1971 war.

Therefore, it was proposed that Air Force Association should publish a book titled "Indo-Pak War 1971: Reminiscences of Air Warriors" which would carry experiences of Air Veterans who participated in the war. I discussed this with Air Chief Marshal RKS Bhadauria, the then CAS, who is now the President of AFA. He graciously accepted the proposal.

The Air Veterans were requested to send in their articles by 31st July 2021 so that the book could be published well in time for its release during the "Golden Jubilee" celebrations. The articles could carry battle accounts, meaningful personal contributions or even remembrances of friends who did not make it back. Hence these articles do not touch upon much of strategic issues. Usually, such books carry writings about the aircrew, but I felt that the Air Warriors across the spectrum should contribute. With that background, we went ahead and asked all the veterans to send their experiences irrespective of Rank, Branch/Trade. Thus, the book carries articles by air warriors of all the branches and trades. The response has been overwhelming.

The book is now in your hands. I want to congratulate the editors for their tireless efforts in bringing out this book in time for the Swarnim Vijay Diwas celebrations.

MESSAGE

Air Chief Marshal RKS Bhadauria PVSM AVSM VM (Retd)

The fourteen-day Indo-Pak war of 1971 has been acknowledged as one of the most decisive conflicts in recent history, and its outcome was the creation of Bangladesh. During this conflict, the IAF brilliantly demonstrated the application of strategic and tactical air power through its carefully planned and executed air campaign across the realm of air operations. The effect of these operations was to make short work of the PAF contingent in East Pakistan and force the PAF in the west to stay within their airspace and carry out only hit and run attacks. Air to ground operations by the IAF were closely coordinated with the Indian Army, and either destroyed or bypassed many Pakistani strongholds in the East. Well-conceived air drop and heli-lift operations enabled the Indian Army to leapfrog the many riverine obstacles and reach the doorstep of Dhaka in less than ten days of fighting. In the west, the IAF dominated a numerically matched PAF and decisively blunted enemy thrusts at Chhamb, Shakargarh and Hussainiwala. The devastation wrought by IAF Hunters on enemy armour at Longewala has become the stuff of legends. Carefully crafted strategic attacks against enemy harbours, oil and gas reserves and rail arteries brought Pakistan as a nation to its knees.

The execution of these plans was in the hands of Air Warriors who were amongst the most courageous, dedicated and committed warriors that this country has ever seen. Their dogged stubbornness to carry out their missions to find and engage well-hidden targets often led them to carry out multiple passes at low height and speeds knowing fully well that this left them vulnerable to enemy fire. Our victory, although emphatic, came at great cost. In the highest traditions of jointmanship, the vast majority of IAF losses and casualties were while carrying out air to ground missions in aid of ground forces.

I am very happy that we have finally been able to tell the stories of these great men who risked their lives for a just cause in the highest traditions of the Indian Armed Forces. I am sure that these stories will be read by the present and future generations with great interest and hope this collection of first-hand accounts will be cherished by many for years to come. I commend the editors for their efforts to bring out this book on this historical occasion.

PREFACE

The genesis of the Indo-Pak War of 1971 and the birth of an independent and sovereign Bangladesh can be traced back to the landslide victory of Sheikh Mujibur Rahman's Awami League Party in the 1970 general elections of Pakistan. His party won a clear majority in the National Assembly of Pakistan by winning 167 of 169 seats in the elections in the East Pakistan out of a total of 300 seats in the National Assembly. Zulfiqar Ali Bhutto's Pakistan People's Party was a poor second. Sheikh Mujibur Rahman staked his claim to form the Government and become the Prime Minister of Pakistan. But this was not acceptable to ZA Bhutto. Awami League was declared unconstitutional. Sheikh Mujibur Rahman was arrested on the orders of General Yahya Khan. Martial Law Administrator of East Pakistan unleashed a systemic reign of terror over innocent people of East Pakistan, massacring thousands of them including its intelligentsia-teachers, professors, advocates and doctors. West Pakistani soldiers brutally tortured and raped women of East Pakistan. Exodus from East Pakistan started and about one crore refugees took shelter in the Eastern states of India. Soldiers of East Pakistan revolted and joined the guerilla warfare and created Mukti Bahini. On 26th of March 1971, Bangladesh was declared an independent nation by Mukti Bahini on a Radio station set up by them at a secret place.

The unprecedented influx of refugees resulted in a great economic burden on India. The then Indian political leadership, headed by Smt Indira Gandhi was forced to seek a politico-military solution to overcome this problem. She consulted her political advisers and the Chiefs of the three services. General Sam Manekshaw advised against any precipitate military action without proper preparation. He also told that the action, if necessary, should be taken only after the monsoon season is over. Smt Indira Gandhi's political advisers—Mr PN Haksar and Mr PN Dhar advised that India should first prepare world opinion in favour of any intervention by India. They added that the interim period should be utilized to accomplish this and be ready militarily.

The Politico-military leadership of that time worked in unison to write a golden chapter of Indian history.

The War broke out after the preemptive strike by PAF on eleven Indian Air Force bases on 3rd December 1971. Smt Indira Gandhi addressed the nation on the same night and declared that India was on war with Pakistan. The IAF attacked several PAF bases early in the morning next day.

While the IAF provided excellent air support to the Army in the West, it established complete air superiority in the East which facilitated the advance of Indian ground troops and helped in the famous para-drop over Tangail and Meghna heli-borne operations. The attack on the Governor's residence served as the last nail in the coffin of the Pak armed forces in the East. General AAK Niazi had no option but to surrender to Lt Gen JS Aurora along with 93000 soldiers. This was the biggest surrender after the Second World war. The creation of Bangladesh literally cut Pakistan to size and changed the geo-political situation not only in the Indian Subcontinent but also in the entire South Asia. The prestige of India went up a few notches in the comity of nations.

The IAF pilots covered themselves with glory and a number of them won gallantry awards. The nation is proud of them and is celebrating Swarnim Vijay Varsh this year.

This book is a humble tribute to the bravery and valour of Air Warriors who participated in this war. It carries first hand experiences of some of them. We thank them all for recording an important piece of the IAF history for posterity. Certain changes in the text have been made at a few places to make the article more readable and interesting. However, the originality of the incidents/anecdotes have been retained. The articles have been suitably edited keeping up with the ethos and decorum of the Defence Services. Futher, the articles have been placed in alphabatical order based on the last name of the author. It is hoped that this book will serve as a reference point for future generations, Air Warriors, and researchers of Air Warfare.

Air Marshal Jagjeet Singh PVSM VSM (Retd)

Gp Capt Shailendra Mohan (Retd)

ACKNOWLEDGEMENTS

We wish to express our deep gratitude to the Chief of the Air Staff, Air Chief Marshal VR Chaudhari PVSM AVSM VM ADC for his kind support in publication of this book on the occasion of 'Swarnim Vijay Varsh' and also for the Foreword for it. We are also extremely grateful to Veteran Air Chief Marshal BS Dhanoa PVSM AVSM YSM VM, former President of the Air Force Association, for conceptualising this book which carries first-hand experiences of the Air Warriors who actually participated in the '1971 Indo-Pak War' and also to Veteran Air Chief Marshal RKS Bhadauria PVSM AVSM VM for his encouragement. We are extremely grateful to Veteran Air Marshal Anil Chopra PVSM AVSM VM VSM for his guidance. We are thankful to all the authors who kindly shared their experiences of the historical war. We also wish to thank Veteran Air Vice Marshal SC Luthra AVSM VSM, Veteran Gp Capt Sumesh Saigal VSM and Wg Cdr Arjun Singh for their invaluable contribution in editing this book. Thanks, are also due to Mr Rajan Arya of Pentagon Press and his team for publishing the book within a short period. Sgt Surendra Choudhary, Sgt Madhav Kumar Pathak and Cpl Raj Singh have been very helpful in typing the manuscript.

Air Marshal Jagjeet Singh PVSM VSM (Retd)

Gp Capt Shailendra Mohan (Retd)

List of Abbreviations

Air Force Ranks

MIAF	Marshal of the Indian Air Force
ACM	Air Chief Marshal
Air Mshl	Air Marshal
Air Vice Mshl	Air Vice Marshal
Gp Capt	Group Captain
Wg Cdr	Wing Commander
Sqn Ldr	Squadron Leader
Flt Lt	Flight Lieutenant
Fg Offr	Flying Officer
Plt Offr	Pilot Officer
HFL	Honorary Flight Lieutenant
HFO	Honorary Flying Officer
MWO	Master Warrant Officer
WO	Warrant Officer
JWO	Junior Warrant Officer
Sgt	Sergeant
Cpl	Corporal
LAC	Leading Air Craftsman
AC	Air Craftsman
NC (E)	Non Combatant (Enrolled)

Appointments

CAS	Chief of the Air Staff
COAS	Chief of the Army Staff
CNS	Chief of the Naval Staff
VCAS	Vice Chief of the Air Staff
AOC-in-C	Air Officer Commanding-in-Chief
GOC-in-C	General Officer Commanding-in-Chief
SASO	Senior Air Staff Officer
ACAS	Assistant Chief of the Air Staff

GOC	General Officer Commanding
AOC	Air Officer Commanding
CO	Commanding Officer
COO	Chief Operations Officer
C Adm O	Chief Administrative Officer
CEO	Chief Engineering Officer

Commands

WAC	Western Air Command
EAC	Eastern Air Command
SWAC	South Western Air Command
CAC	Central Air Command
SAC	Southern Air Command
TC	Training Command
MC	Maintenance Command

Awards

PVC	Param Vir Chakra
MVC	Maha Vir Chakra
VrC	Vir Chakra
AC	Ashok Chakra
KC	Kirti Chakra
SC	Shaurya Chakra
PVSM	Param Vishisht Seva Medal
AVSM	Ati Vishisht Seva Medal
VM	Vayu Sena Medal
DFC	Distinguished Flying Cross
VSM	Vishisht Seva Medal
M-in-D	Mention in Despatches

Miscellaneous

AC	Aircraft
ACRR	Air Crew Rest Room
ADC	Air Defence Clearance
ADDC	Air Defence Direction Centre
AEW&C	Airborne Early Warning and Control

AFAC	Air Force Administrative College
AFFC	Air Force Flying College
AGL	Above Ground Level
AOG	Aircraft on Ground
AOP	Air Observation Post
ATC	Air Traffic Control
AWACS	Airborne Warning and Control System
BPI	Bulk Petroleum Installation
C&MU	Care and Maintenance Unit
C&R	Control and Reporting
CAP	Combat Air Patrol
CASEVAC	Casualty Evacuation
CB	Cumulonimbus
CFL	Cease Fire Line
CLMO	Command Logistics Management Officer
COSC	Chiefs of Staff Committee
CTO	Chief Technical Officer
DSS	Daily Servicing Section
DSSC	Defence Services Staff College
ECHS	Ex-Servicemen Contributory Health Scheme
EFS	Elementary Flying School
FAC	Forward Air Controller
FBSU	Forward Base Support Unit
FCL	Fighter Combat Leader
FLOT	Forward Line of Own Troops
GHA	General Hostile Area
GLO	Ground Liaison Officer
HADR	Humanitarian Assistance and Disaster Relief
HAL	Hindustan Aeronautics Limited
IAF	Indian Air Force
IB	International Border
ICRC	International Committee of the Red Cross
IOR	Immediate Operational Requirements
IP	Initial Point
KIA	Killed in Action

LLOP	Low Level Observation Post
LMG	Light Machine Gun
LOC	Line of Control
LZ	Landing Zone
MH	Military Hospital
MT	Mechanical Transport
MES	Military Engineering Service
MOF	Mobile Observation Flight
NDA	National Defence Academy
NM	Nautical Mile
ORP	Operational Readiness Platform
OTU	Operational Training Unit
PAD	Passive Air Defence
PAF	Pakistan Air Force
PI	Practice Interception
POP	Passing Out Parade
PoW	Prisoner of War
PR	Photo Recce
QFI	Qualified Flying Instructor
R&R	Rest and Recuperation
RAF	Royal Air Force
SD	Sector Director
SHBO	Special Heli Borne Operations
STO	Senior Technical Officer
STBY	Stand By
SU	Signal Unit
TAC	Tactical Air Centre
TACDE	Tactics and Combat Development Establishment
T&CD&TS	Tactics and Combat Development and Training School
UNO	United Nations Organisation

List of IAF Gallantry Awards (PVC, MVC and VrC) Winners – 1971 War

Param Vir Chakra

1. Fg Offr Nirmal Jit Singh Sekhon

Maha Vir Chakra

1. Wg Cdr Vidya Bhushan Vasisht
2. Wg Cdr Cecil Vivian Parker
3. Wg Cdr Ramesh Sakhram Benegal
4. Wg Cdr Man Mohan Bir Singh Talwar
5. Wg Cdr Allan Albert D'Costa
6. Wg Cdr Harcharan Singh Manget
7. Sqn Ldr Madhavendra Banerji
8. Sqn Ldr Ravinder Nath Bhardwaj
9. Wg Cdr Swaroop Krishna Kaul
10. Wg Cdr Padmanabha Gautam
11. Gp Capt Chandan Singh

Vir Chakra

1. Flt Lt Manjit Singh Dhillon
2. Flt Lt Manbir Singh
3. Flt Lt Parvez Rustom Jamasji
4. Flt Lt Vijay Kumar Wahi
5. Gp Capt Man Mohan Singh
6. FLt Lt Rajendra Singh Wahi
7. Flt Lt Lawrence Fredric Pereira
8. Flt Lt Syed Shahid Hussain Naqvi
9. Flt Lt Pushp Kumar Vaid
10. Flt Lt Partha Das Gupta
11. Flt Lt Andre Rudolph Da Costa
12. Flt Lt Nitin Gajanan Junnarkar

13. Fg Offr Sudhir Tyagi
14. Flt Lt Dilip Kamalakar Dighe
15. Flt Lt Pradip Vinayak Apte
16. Flt Lt Harbans Perminder Singh
17. Flt Lt Gurdev Singh Rai
18. Flt Lt Aruna Kumar Datta
19. Sqn Ldr Ramesh Kumar Sachdeva
20. Flt Lt Shivinder Singh Bains
21. Sqn Ldr Mohinder Kumar Jain
22. Flt Lt Jagdamba Prasad Saklani
23. Sqn Ldr Jiwa Singh
24. Flt Lt Mohinder Singh Sandhu
25. Flt Lt Ashok Kumar Singh
26. Sqn Ldr Jal Maniksha Mistry
27. Flt Lt Govind Chandra Singh Rajwar
28. Flt Lt Mandepanda Appachu Ganapathy
29. Sqn Ldr Farokh Jehangir Mehta
30. Flt Lt Mahabir Prasad Premi
31. Flt Lt Hemant Sharat Kumar Sardesai
32. Sqn Ldr Arya Bhushan Lamba
33. Sqn Ldr Iqbal Ali Syed
34. Wg Cdr Hersern Singh Gill
35. Flt Lt Somar Bikram Shah
36. Sqn Ldr Ramesh Chander Kohli
37. Flt Lt Ramesh Chander Gosain
38. Flt Lt Bharat Bhushan Soni
39. Wg Cdr Murari Lal Trehon
40. Flt Lt Surinder Singh Malhotra
41. Flt Lt Aspari Raghunath
42. Wg Cdr Ramanathan Sundaresan
43. Sqn Ldr Charanjit Singh
44. Flt Lt Arun Laxman Deoskar
45. Wg Cdr Arun Kanti Mukherjee
46. Sqn Ldr Gursaran Singh Ahluwalia
47. Flt Lt Robindra Kumar Sinha

48. Wg Cdr Ravindar Nath Dogra
49. Sqn Ldr Allan David Alley
50. Wg Cdr Donald Melvyn Conquest
51. Sqn Ldr Krishan Kumar Bakshi
52. Flt Lt Dinesh Chander Nayyar
53. Wg Cdr Narinder Chatrath
54. Sqn Ldr Suresh Damodar Karnik
55. Flt Lt Cherry Hassanand Raney
56. Wg Cdr Krishan Kumar Badhwar
57. Sqn Ldr Ravindra Nath Bali
58. Flt Lt Chidambaram Sarangapani Chandrasekaran
59. Wg Cdr Keshav Chandra Aggarwal
60. Sqn Ldr Jasjit Singh
61. Flt Lt Niraj Kukreja
62. Gp Capt Robert Arnold Weir
63. Sqn Ldr Anil Kumar Bhadra
64. Flt Lt Prem Bhushan Kalra
65. Sqn Ldr Vinod Kumar Bhatia
66. Sqn Ldr Kirpal Singh
67. Fg Offr Kariyadil Cheriyan Kuruvilla
68. Sqn Ldr Dinesh Chandra Bhandary
69. Flt Lt Aditya Vikram Pethia
70. Flt Lt Vinod Kumar Neb
71. Sqn Ldr Sindhaghatta Subbaramu
72. Flt Lt Roy Andrew Massey
73. Wg Cdr Bhupendra Kumar Bishnoi
74. Sqn Ldr Kalyan Kumar Dutta
75. Flt Lt Sukrutaraj Jayandra
76. Fg Offr Satish Chandra Sharma
77. Sqn Ldr Charanjit Singh Sandhu
78. Flt Lt Kuldeep Singh Sahota
79. Fg Offr Sukhdev Singh Dhillon
80. Sqn Ldr Ashok Prataprao Shinde
81. Flt Lt Yogendra Prasad Singh
82. Fg Offr Mohan Dikshit

83. Sqn Ldr Vishnu Narain Johri
84. Flt Lt Winston Rabinder Sanjeeva Rao
85. Fg Offr Harish Masand
86. Fg Offr Jai Singh Gahalawat
87. Sqn Ldr Jagbir Singh
88. Flt Lt Apramjeet Singh
89. Flt Lt Parminder Paul Singh Kawatra
90. Fg Offr Bartan Ramesh
91. Sqn Ldr Sanjay Kumar Choudhury
92. Flt Lt Kukke Sreekantasastry Suresh
93. Fg Offr Sankarnarayanan Balasubramanian
94. Sqn Ldr Ghanshyam Singh Thapa
95. Flt Lt Melvinder Singh Grewal
96. Fg Offr Ballachandra Chengapa Karumbaya
97. Sqn Ldr Dilip Kumar Dass
98. Flt Lt Arun Vasant Sathaye
99. Flt Lt Manjit Singh Sekhon
100. Fg Offr Kishan Lakhimal Malkani
101. Sqn Ldr Preet Pal Singh Gill
102. Flt Lt Chandra Mohan Singla
103. Sqn Ldr Dhirendra Singh Jafa
104. Fg Offr Donald Lazarus
105. Sqn Ldr Iqbal Singh Bindra

The list has been compiled from data obtained from Ministry of Defence, Government of India website for gallantry awards.

Reminiscences of Air Warriors

1 ALL IN A DAY'S WORK—05 DECEMBER 1971

AK Agtey

The account of PAF air activity on 05 December 1971 brings to my mind an incident in which I was directly involved. The ORP at Amritsar was manned at both ends throughout the war and was scrambled numerous times every day.

The 34 Dumbell ORP was manned by 2xMiG-21s from 45 Squadron Detachment (Harry Hardas, Milind Shankar, Tejwant Singh and Biri Singh). The one at 16 Dumbell was manned by us, Gnats of 2 Squadron. There were four aircraft on STBY TWO, two in the covered blast pens and two more in the open blast pens at the edge of the ORP. We did four-hour shifts in the cockpit, 0600-1000, 1000-1400, and 1400-1800.

At around 1400 hrs on 05 December, leader (JW Greene) and I came off ORP. He picked me up in his jeep from my pen and we headed out to the Mess for lunch. We were on the parallel taxiway, a little short of the Mess when we saw two silver specks, at low level, at high speed heading in the direction of 230 SU. The SU ack-ack opened up and we could see the puffs of exploding shells. The two specks turned left and we immediately recognised them as F-104 Starfighters. Then we heard the loud distinctive VROOM roar of the "Vulcan Cannon". They must have been doing about 450-500 knots at no higher than 150-200 feet.

The very first thought that occurred to us was that we should have been in the cockpit and scrambled. These two guys went right over the airfield. As they went past us we saw their engines in afterburner. All of a sudden the afterburner flame of one aircraft went OFF, we saw the pilot eject, the aircraft rolled over and went into the ground just about 800 yards or so from the perimeter fence.

Greene Sir turned the jeep and went up to the fence. On the way, he said, "Go and get the guy before the villagers beat him to death." At the fence, he lowered the barbed wire with one foot and raised the upper strand with his hand and said: "GO". Ahead of me two Army jawans were already sprinting through the fence towards the ejected pilot. I followed in hot pursuit, with wild thoughts going through my head like "I hope the villagers don't think that I am the PAF pilot and beat me to death".

In a couple of minutes, we reached the pilot. The two jawans were, may be 10-15 steps ahead of me. Villagers were running towards us, but they were still not close. The pilot had just about released his parachute and was about to stand up when the first jawan reached him. Without a word or a moment's delay, he hit him in the midriff with his rifle butt. As he was going down, the other jawan slapped him across the face. I got there in time to prevent any further violence. We helped him to get onto his feet and I read his name on the nametag as "Amjad". A jeep from the FBSU reached us and he and his parachute were bundled into it and taken to the FBSU. Not a word was exchanged. I looked around and found his 'wing' lying on the ground. It had been attached by 'tich buttons' and it had fallen off during his ejection. I picked it up and still have it as a memento of the afternoon of 05th December 1971(Please see Picture below). I quickly jogged back and scrambled under the fence for lunch.

That night the TCDTS, (forerunner of TACDE) guys went across for a night strike for the first time. While we were waiting for them to return, we saw a Martin B-57 being hit by ack-ack. We saw it in the air on fire for about 30 seconds or so before it went down.

There was some more excitement on the 5th, but that is another story.

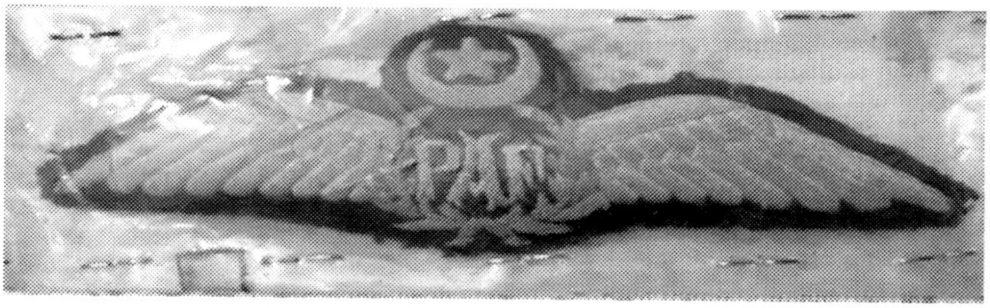

Wing of the PAF Pilot (Amjad)

Return of IAF PoW on the Western Front

Why was the COAS accompanying these two PAF gentlemen back to Pakistan in his Tu-124?

There is a story attached to it and I have been rolling on the floor with laughter the whole day. Finally, I have recovered now, and I have decided to pound the keyboard.

At the cost of digression, I need to give the background, failing which the story will not sound half as good. War ended when the ceasefire was declared at about 1900 hrs on 17 December 1971.

The last Indian Air Force PoW to join the gang in PAF custody did so only two hours before that time. That was Tejwant Singh.

Post 17 December 1971, there was partial de-escalation on our side at Amritsar. The Su-7s of 32 Squadron, went back to Ambala. The 34 dumbbell ORP manned by MiG-21s of 45 Squadron (only 3 of the 4 left now) also went back. The Gnat ORP, of which I was a part, reduced from four to two and we were on STBY 5. This state of affairs continued for months and months.

In the meanwhile, I had got married to Nina in April and done an R&R detachment at Srinagar followed by the Jungle & Snow Survival Course in Srinagar in September and was looking forward to some good dis-similar flying with TCDTS at Ambala.

The Boss (JW Greene) had other plans. He called me and told me, "Ajit take Nina with you and go to Amritsar and Man the ORP. Don't talk of returning till de-induction". He also said, "Fly at least 2 sorties a day and give 230 SU all the PIs they need." I could not have asked for anything more. I put Nina on the pillion of my bike, and I was in Amritsar again. Life could not have been better.

On the evening of 28 November 1972, Zulfikar Ali Bhutto (Pakistani Prime Minister) announced that we would exchange the PoW, taken prisoner on the Western Front, in each other's custody. The following day the date of return was announced as 01 December.

Hence, on 01 December 1972, Nina and I were at the Wagah border at about 1100 hrs, awaiting the return of all my good friends. There was a festive atmosphere prevailing. Lots of people directly or indirectly involved were around. Milind Shankar was there to meet Tejwant. Grace Kuruvilla was there to meet her husband. There were 10 of them. Actually 12 had been taken prisoner (11 pilots and 1 FAC). AV Pethia and Mulla Feroze had been repatriated earlier as sick and wounded.

As the day wore on, noon came and went, early afternoon gave way to late afternoon and there were no signs of these 10 gentlemen. Bill Beddoe was the FBSU Commander, and he found out that the "inner gen" was that the IAF had actually FORGOTTEN that we have two PAF PoW taken prisoner on the Western Front. So, NO exchange. Then some diplomatic wrangling happened, and the Indian side stated that those two pilots were in a place so far away that it would take a little more time to get them across.

It was on this note that our 10 friends walked across. It was great to see Bunny Coehlo, AV Kamat, DS Jafa, MS Grewal, Dilip Parulkar, Tejwant Singh, Harish Sinhji, Brother Bhargava, VS Chati, and KC Kuruvilla. They marched proudly across in jerseys that had PW marked in large letters. Then the celebrations began.

This is the reason that Amjad Hussain and Sardar Wajid, both the PAF pilots, had to go back later. The Army Chief Gen Manekshaw, used to go across to Pakistan for meetings to sort out the border realignment. He went back a few days later and these two gentlemen accompanied him in his Tu-124.

That is the story as far as I know. I do not know, as to what has been actually documented. In the sense, what has been etched on paper on file stating the reason that Amjad and Wajid were not at Wagah on 01 December. I am sure Milind Shankar remembers this occurrence. Nina and I accompanied them back for a reception in Amritsar and later at the 230 SU Mess.

Veteran Gp Capt Ajit Agtey *was commissioned in the Flying Branch on 20 Dec 1969. During the 1971 War he was on ORP duties at Amritsar and flying Gnat MK I. He was an eye witness to a Pakistan Pilot who ejected over the Amritsar airfield. He is a test pilot and was the Project Pilot for a key development programme for improving the operational potential of Jaguar aircraft. He took premature retirement in 1995. He is settled in Bengaluru and can be reached at agteys@gmail.com and 8025393174.*

2 VICTORY BY ILLUSION: BATTLE OF HALWARA, 1971

Sant Vishwanath Anant

Move to Halwara

I was on the posted strength of Air Force Station Hindan. I was a Flt Sgt then, more popularly called as Chiefy. During the 1971 war, we moved to Air Force Station Halwara. I was the SNCO i/c Dett.

05 November 1971: Our detachment moved by AN-12 aircraft to Halwara. We landed there peacefully in the afternoon and were taken to the other end of the runway where we saw the two shining MiGs, which we had seen off earlier from Hindan before our departure, positioned in the open. Our OC personally came to receive us. He then told me, "This will be our operational point". I immediately started work with my team to prepare the MiGs as they would have to be ready for flying the very next day.

06 November 1971: I realised that we have to be in this allotted place and our aircraft should be ready for operational flying within the shortest possible time. With the two shining silver white MiGs in the open, we were sitting ducks for the enemy and a vulnerable target. The station had no other aircraft support and our main task was to protect this day and night. In other words, we had to be on the tarmac ready for flying and to keep the aircraft manned with the pilot at ORP (Operational Readiness Platform) 24x7!

MiGs Parked in the Open

07 November 1971: We reached early for work. After quickly taking stock of the situation, I realised that a few things must be done immediately to safeguard our vulnerability. For this, I needed some help from the i/c Detachment, Station Commander, CTO, and OC Flying. This help was to activate the MES as well as the Equipment

Section for support. Our i/c Detachment arranged a small meeting and I, looking at my list of work needed, said, "Sir, it's too risky to have our two shining MiGs out in the open. Firstly, we need to build temporary pens with three walls with a duct for exhaust and a cover to camouflage our MiGs, along with a bunker and a few trenches. Secondly, I am planning to create AN ILLUSION for the enemy to minimise our vulnerability. For that, I need a few more things." "And how do you intend to create that illusion?" he asked me curiously. "I want to create two dummy MiGs and place them at the opposite end of the runway." "That's a great idea," said the Commander, "Just tell me, Chiefy, what you need and I'll do the best I can to help you." "Sir, I need lots of bamboo sticks and a painted big white cloth with as many working hands as possible from the Station Workshop, so that we can finish this task quickly," I replied.

Building Temporary Pens

09 November 1971: In just two days, two pens with walls and exhaust ducts were ready for aircraft parking. Our team covered them with camouflage nets and dug trenches and a bunker with provision for heaters, blankets, and lights. I was surprised at our speed in creating this. Our next target was to create two dummy aircraft and park them in the open. The same was also achieved in due course of time.

20 November 1971: Night curfew with full blackout was enforced. Thanks to the relentless efforts of our team, we were now geared up and fully prepared for the actual war. Over the past fortnight, we witnessed just one or two sorties flying every 2-3 days. With each passing day, with night curfew and blackout in place, it was evident that we were nearing a war for sure!

Dummy MiGs as Illusion

03 December 1971: It is a full moon night and here are the two dummy MiGs we created as illusions shining brightly parked at one end of the runway, while the real ones could not be detected easily under the camouflage. I was tense but equally happy over the job done by our team.

Our team with pilots was ready at the ORP. At about 5 O'clock in the evening, a news item on the radio began making the rounds that "Pak aircraft have bombed a few of our Air Force Stations." This shook all of us and we were on 'high alert.' With full blackout by around 9 pm, we were physically there on the tarmac anticipating an attack any time. We were ready near our two camouflaged MiGs, with the pilots ready and eagerly waiting to get the 'Scramble' order.

A couple of hours passed and everyone on the tarmac waited anxiously for further orders.

At around 11:30 pm, we heard the sound of aircraft approaching our station. Sirens sounded an alert and everyone ran to the trenches for safety. Except the crew of the aircraft, all others hid in the trenches. Two Sabres of Pakistan appeared and made a low flying pass over our station runway. They passed over without causing any harm as they could not see the target which they would have expected at the end of the runway. Both the planes made a comfortable turn and came back from another direction and located the two dummy MiGs.

As expected, they were fooled into believing that the dummies were the real ones and dropped six bombs in a row along the runway and flew off, thinking that they had destroyed the two MiGs on our Station.

The thundering sound of the bursting of six bombs was accompanied by huge flames towering just around the runway. We were horrified and looked at each other with an unknown fear. The bombing had tossed up a large quantity of sand, mud, and debris onto our runway. Luckily, it was not damaged. Our two pilots were already in the cockpit ready for take-off but did not get the 'scramble' order, because with the enemy just overhead, 'take-off' was impossible.

As the noise of the enemy aircraft engines faded away, an 'All Clear' siren was sounded. The Station Commander, Admin Commander, and station authorities rushed to our ORP on the runway. After finding all of us safe and sound and, more importantly, seeing the safe condition of our MiGs, we congratulated each other.

Within next four to five hours during the night itself, the entire runway was cleared for use by other aircraft before sunrise.

04 December 1971: We heard a radio broadcast at 12:01am in which our Hon'ble Prime Minister, Smt Indira Gandhi, officially declared war on Pakistan. By that time, the enemy had already attacked Halwara Air Force Station and thought that they had damaged the target. They were right, but just partially! **They had damaged the target, but it was not the real one. They had bombed and damaged the 'illusion' that we had created—the dummy aircraft.**

In the morning, we learnt that the two enemy aircraft that had attacked us were ultimately tracked by Indian Army Ack-Ack guns and that they had downed one of them.

Heavy Landing and the Subsequent Repairs

Our first attack with Hunters and Vampires started in batches of four aircraft with both our MiGs escorting them. I was SNCO I/C with the added responsibility of Airframe trade. Under full blackout, the guide-lamps along the runway had to be switched off. Pilots had to judge the runway with the help of goose neck lamps held by certain personnel especially positioned for this job when Flying Control gave the signal to take off and land. During an operative scramble to chase out a Pak aircraft at night, one of our MiGs had an accident and the pilot had a heavy landing resulting in tyre burst.

This was a serious matter. The operational activities of the station were completely dependent on our two escorting MiGs. All the authorities were worried as to how to overcome this situation. I voluntarily shouldered the responsibility to service the aircraft in the night and try to make it ready for flying by the morning. We had hardly four to five hours of the night to complete the work.

As my fear was not as strong as my confidence, I defied myself to accept this challenge. My 22 years of service experience had embossed the significance of preparedness to face unexpected situations in me.

I had one ready wheel assembly with brakes along with all the other fittings in my spares. I inspected the undercarriage of the aircraft for damage and realised that I had to replace the burst tyre wheel assembly. Our spare wheel assembly was the solution to make the aircraft serviceable. My entire team joined hands and within two hours, we finished the task. However, the real problem lay ahead. To make sure that the job was executed with 100 per cent correctness, I needed to check the wheel rotation and brake operation with all the fittings and other safety precautions including the retraction test. Against all odds, we completed this job around 5 am and I lowered the aircraft on the ground by removing the jack. Being sure of the job done, I assured the authorities that the aircraft was perfectly okay from my side, except for the retraction test. This was an extremely critical requirement; to confirm the functional veracity of the job done, the aircraft needed to successfully clear a 'Retraction Test', before being declared 'fully serviceable'. This could be done only at our Hindan base. To carry out this retraction test, the aircraft must fly from Halwara to Hindan. I informed the CTO, "For this, I am ready to certify the aircraft fit for flying under one condition, that is, the pilot will not retract the undercarriage while flying to Hindan. He must fly the aircraft with wheels down." The CTO happily granted my request. The aircraft flew with wheels down and landed at Hindan. After the 'Retraction Test', it was certified 'Okay'. Waiting anxiously at Halwara, it was 7:30 am when the aircraft returned and touched down. The entire Air Force Station was extremely happy. Everyone was thrilled and filled with joy because without wasting even a split second, in full blackout, we had successfully completed our job! The operational sorties as programmed resumed with both our MiGs escorting each batch of bombers and fighters as if there was no hindrance at all. I was greeted by everyone for achieving this.

Award for Me

War over, to my surprise, I was recommended for a Gallantry Award—'Mention-in-Despatches', which was declared and awarded on 31 December 1971. Humbly, I gifted this award to my father as a 'New Year Gift', a proud moment for me in my life. Last, but not the least, I cannot end this story without thanking the Station Authorities, who were always ready to help me in carrying out my duties during this short war.

Station Commander: GP Capt Gole

Officer i/c Flying: Wg Cdr Sen

Chief Technical Officer: Sqn Ldr Y Singh

Our Detachment Officer Commander: Sqn Ldr Bharat Kumar

Today, as I look back, I realise that on 03 December 1971, the enemy did achieve some destruction of the runway, but ultimately, it was our Victory. The Battle of Halwara was won by the illusion we created. Jai Bharat!

Veteran Honorary Flt Lt Sant Vishwanath Anant *was enrolled in the Indian Air Force on 13 May 1948. He had the fortune of working on a variety of aircraft during his years with the Air Force. He was in-charge of the DSS at almost all the Squadrons that he worked in. He did a commendable job during the 1971 operations and was awarded "Mention in Despatches". He served for 35 years and retired in 1983. He is settled at Pune and can be reached at vishwanathsant31@gmail.com and 9767024074.*

3 ATTACK ON KARACHI

KK Badhwar

The Beginning

During the 1971 Indo-Pak War, code-named "**CACTUS LILY**", I was in command of 35 Squadron AF equipped with Canberra aircraft and based at 2 Wing Pune. After the first mission on 03rd Dec 1971 to attack the PAF at Musroor, Karachi, with four aircraft, I spotted a large oil installation, located about 15 NM South on our escape route. The storage tanks of aluminium metal were shining brightly in the full moonlit night. When filing the mission completion report later after landing at base, I mentioned this observation and asked for permission to attack "Karachi Oil" which was a very lucrative and vital target. However, for the next two nights, I was repeatedly tasked to attack PAF Musroor and each time whenever I filed the mission completion report, I requested permission to attack 'K Oil'. HQ CAC, the controlling Command, did not accede to my request, for the reasons best known to the higher ups.

Suggestion to Attack Karachi Oil

On the intervening night of 8-9 Dec 1971, I was tasked to attack PAF Drigh Road, Karachi, with four aircraft. PAF Drigh Road was near the 'Karachi 'Oil' installation and I thought it was an opportunity to fulfil my dream to make it a target as it was the country's "Bulk Petroleum Installation," BPI. I, therefore, requested HQ CAC again to let me attack PAF Drigh Road with eight aircraft. My request was reluctantly granted on the condition that I must not land the additional four aircraft enroute at AF Jamnagar for refuelling. I readily accepted the condition.

The Actual Attack and the Follow up Reaction

Therefore, now we were required to launch two different attacks with four aircraft each, four for Drigh Road to be refuelled at Jamnagar and four for the Karachi oil installation (to carry wing drop tank). I ordered four aircraft to be fitted with wing-tip tanks for the extra fuel required. Handing over the lead of four aircraft to my Flight Commander to route out via Jamnagar for refuelling, I led the other four aircraft with wing-tip fuel tanks. The attack on 'Karachi Oil' was carried out following a suitable Hi-Lo-Hi profile with Flt Lt YP Singh as my Navigator. After successfully carrying out the attack, while filing the mission completion report, my AOC, then Air Cmde Dilbagh Singh, advised me not to mention the attack on 'Karachi Oil' as there was no permission to target it. He also warned me that the consequences could be serious for attacking a target without permission. I was not feeling comfortable to hide the truth and submitted a true report. This annoyed the AOC-in-C who recommended drastic action against me by Air HQ. However, to my good luck, at Air HQ, Air Marshal Chatterjee who was Head of the Operations Branch, turned the episode in my favour and I escaped punishment. In due course, the matter came to the notice of the CAS, Air Chief Marshal PC Lal. After the cease-fire, he visited AF Station Pune on 20 Dec 71 to personally ascertain the facts. On hearing the truth, he told AOC Dilbagh Singh to put up my name again for a suitable award. This was done by my AOC the next day and about a month later I was awarded an AVSM in addition to a Vir Chakra awarded to me earlier in Dec 1971. Thus, I received my "MVC" in two instalments. The AOC, Air Cmde Dilbagh Singh, wrote a very nice letter of appreciation on 19 Jan 1972 as a tribute to my achievements during the war.

Appreciation on my Role

The initiative on my part and the impact of the attack on the oil installation is amply covered in Air Chief Marshal PC Lal's book, *"My Years with the IAF"*. He has devoted five pages, 294 to 298, to cover the episode in great detail. I reproduce his concluding paragraph from page 298 of his book.

> ***"The loss of probably millions of litres of oil was undoubtedly a major factor in the growing realisation amongst military commanders in West Pakistan that they could not fight a war of any duration against India. It gave them justification for ending the war when that opportunity was offered by the Indian Unilateral Declaration of a Ceasefire on 17th December 1971."***

Awards

The Squadron was honoured with five Vir Chakras, one AVSM, one VM for Gallantry, six VSMs and three Mention-in-Despatches. It flew a total of 92 missions dropping 630,000 pounds of bombs over enemy targets. To inspire and encourage morale of the Squadron personnel, I led all the missions entrusted to the Squadron. The morale of the Squadron was sky high. The entire lot of highly motivated men, living-in/living-out worked day and night in the Squadron hangar. Aircraft serviceability state kept rising during the war and it was 100 per cent when the cease-fire was announced. The Squadron's sick report register did not have a single entry. Station Armament Officer Sqn Ldr Sesha Chari and the CTO, Wg Cdr Gursharan Singh, gave their full support to the Squadron. Station Logistics Officer Wg Cdr Lala Dey told me to concentrate on fighting and that he would take care of all our logistics requirements. The Squadron was allowed by Lala Dey to draw rations as per Squadron's actual need and not as per the ration strength.

Memories and the Good Feelings

In 1983, when I was attending the National Defence College Course, we called on the CAS Air Chief Marshal Dilbagh Singh, when he mentioned that my role and achievements as a Squadron Commander during the 1971 Indo-Pak War had been recorded in the history of the IAF written at the time of the IAF's Golden Jubilee in 1982 and was kept in a copper capsule, which was ceremonially sealed as part of the Golden Jubilee Celebrations. The capsule will be opened when the IAF celebrates its 100th anniversary. I am looking forward to see that ceremony if I am around. I was born in 1932 and would be 100 years old along with the IAF, with God's blessings.

The Squadron was christened "RAPIERS" with the motto "DRUT PRAHARNA YUDHA" which roughly translates to "ARMED TO STRIKE FAST". Its emblem is an erect RAPIER—a double-edged sword. The Rapiers lived up to their motto during the war which was announced over AIR at 1800 hrs on 3rd Dec 1971 and the Squadron's first mission led by me and Sqn Ldr Thapa as the lead navigator was on its way by 2200 hrs. This was one of the first counter attack missions of the IAF.

It is a matter of professional pride and satisfaction for me to derive from the fact that I made optimum use of the operational potential at my disposal as a Squadron Commander and I was thus able to contribute to the glory of my country and the service to which I belonged.

Healthy Feedback from Ex PAF Chief

About a year after the war, the then CAS, Air Chief Marshal P C Lal, happened to meet Retd PAF Chief, Air Marshal Noor Khan who lived near PAF Drigh Road. Air Marshal Noor Khan greeted Air Chief Marshal PC Lal, "Pratap, this time you bombed the daylights out of us". He was referring to the pall of smoke over Karachi due to the oil on fire.

Conclusion

The squadron's Mascot Rapier was kept in a decorated case next to the Honours Board at Squadron HQ. I had added a plaque that read:

> *FIX YOUR EYES ON THE GREATNESS OF RAPIER, THE SQUADRON MASCOT. AS YOU HAVE IT BEFORE YOU, DAY BY DAY, FALL IN LOVE WITH IT AND WHEN YOU FEEL GREAT, REMEMBER, THIS WAS WON BY MEN WITH COURAGE, DEVOTION TO THEIR DUTY AND SENSE OF HONOUR IN ACTION.*

It is matter of special honour to know that Air Chief Marshal Dilbagh Singh in his memoirs *"On the Wings of Destiny"* has included a chapter to cover my story of the 1971 War.

***Veteran Air Commodore Krishan Kumar Badhwar** was commissioned in the Flying Branch in January 1954. Initially, he served in fighter and fighter bomber squadrons, and then, after successfully completing a course at the Flying Instructors School, he served as a flying instructor at the erstwhile Air Force Flying College. In 1964, he converted on to jet bombers, and thereafter served in a Canberra bomber squadron. During the operations against Pakistan in 1971, the bombers of his squadron carried out devastating raids against the enemy's war potential. He took part in each one of the operational missions entrusted to his squadron. He was awarded two medals in the 1971 War, an AVSM and the Coveted Vir Chakra. He retired on 31 Aug 1986. He is a resident of the Air Force Association Senior Citizens' Home at Tughlakabad New Delhi and can be reached at afasch_afaindia@yahoo.in and 9958409513 or 7042706251.*

4 'BATTLE OF CHHAMB '71: AS I SAW IT!'

HK Bajaj

'Permanently etched Personal Video Tapes' of the war experiences of all veterans are very unique! These start to auto play at any small trigger & could display even very minute details; and 1971 Indo-Pak War cassette is just half a century old (pun intended)!

In this short, abridged article, I wish to narrate, my induction (first day's experience) as a young air force pilot (Forward Air Controller) into '71 War and the Bloody Nose that the Indian Army & Air Force jointly gave to the attacking Pak forces on 10th Dec 71.

Prelude to the War

In 1971, when the war clouds were building up, ours was the fortunate Pilots' Course (106th PC), with not even six months of service, which was available to perform the crucial role of Forward Air Controller (FAC); & some of us were further lucky to be positioned along with our frontline troops & participate in the ground battle! We were extensively trained in this role by the then Wing Commander MS (Minhi) Bawa (later Air Marshal & C in C) at OTU Jamnagar. The excitement peaked in Sep '71 when our Course was attached to Air Headquarters (Air Hqs) for two months. With final destination not known, I with a suitcase full of 'suits-boots & ties' and a bed-holder, landed up in Delhi. But, the next day, we were issued a revolver & 24 live rounds each; and some of us were flown to Udhampur, 4 TAC AF, commanded by then, Gp Capt (later Air Mshl, C in C) KIS Chhabra. After extensive ground training and air exercises, on 25 Sep, I landed up in a bunker with 5 Sikh Regiment (regt) of 191 Infantry Brigade (Inf Bde) of 10 Div / 15 Corps at Chhamb. I was subsequently attached to 68 (I) Inf Bde, the Corps reserve, meant for the offensive & located at Akhnur.

First Taste of the Battlefield!

On 03 Dec 71, Pak army launched a major offensive in Chhamb with four infantry brigades, three armoured (armd) and eight artillery regiments (arty regts). The attack in 191 Bde defended sector came through the intentional gaps left in defensive minefields through which 68 (I) Inf Bde group was to have launched their offensive. Yes, in Chhamb area, Pakistan had achieved surprise both at tactical and strategic levels. All forward posts were subjected to intense arty fire & a few of our Border Observation Posts (BOPs) were overrun. Looking at the buildup, on 03rd night itself, 7 Kumaon Regt was ordered to move up and occupy positions at Kachrial heights (hts). However, they were surprised by the infiltrators who had already dug in there. They suffered major casualties, with their Commanding Officer (CO) and three other officers (offrs) being wounded; and three tanks of 72 Armd Regt (under Command of 68 Inf Bde) also damaged.

On 04th Dec morning, our four Hunters, on a strike mission (stk msn), over flew Akhnur bridge at tree top hts. Although the Air Force markings were clearly visible, not only our L-60 guns opened up but also the small arms started firing; and a revolver round fell right in

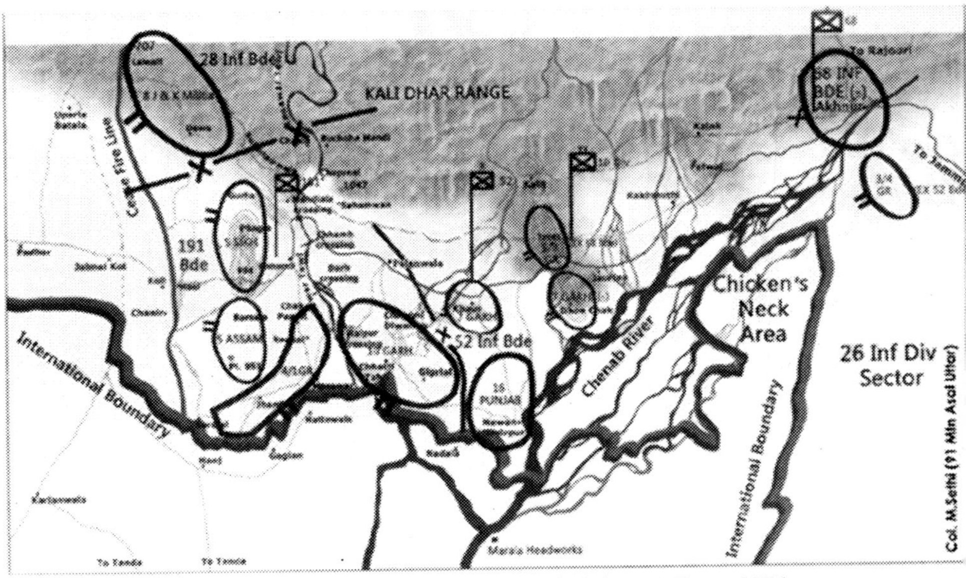

Deployment of 10 Infantry Division, 3 Dec. 1971

front of Brig Tom Morlin, Commander, 68 (I) Bde, having breakfast under a tree!

Later, the Commander (Cdr) along with his G3 (Capt Chatterjee) & self (on request & insistence) with my tentacle vehicle moved to 10 Inf Div Advance (Adv) Hqs at Palanwala. En-route, we saw waves of villagers, including men, women and children moving back from villages close to the border with their life's precious belongings! One could well imagine the pain, agony and trauma the people would have gone through at the time of partition! It was indeed a very painful sight!

At the Div Hqs, Commander took reinforcement of one squadron (Sqn) of armour and a Company (Coy) of 9 Jat Regt. As we moved further towards the second line of defense on eastern bank of Manawar Tawi, it was a pleasure to interact with Maj Guleria, Coy Cdr, 9 Jat who was bubbling with enthusiasm and that killer spirit. I also, for the first time, saw a very seriously wounded battle casualty being taken on an open jeep; and the reality of war was slowly sinking in!

Next, we first came across around 30-40 troops of 7 Kumaon falling back, followed by 3-4 tanks retreating. It was all very disturbing. We gathered the men and the Cdr motivated the troops to move back to their defenses; and thus restored the situation. We had an admin halt along with a Troop (Tp) of (three) tanks. Bde Cdr then decided to take a tank and visit 7 Kumaon and also look up the armd regt at Kachrial hts. The general area being close to our likely area of deployment, I managed to argue my case & was permitted to follow them in another tank. Half way through our move, the Cdr summoned me to his tank. I jumped over and sat on the turret while the Cdr and Troop Commander stood in the two copulas. Soon, our tank was stopped by a Lieutenant (Lt) who informed that there were infiltrators just 50 mtrs on our left and were firing with automatic weapons. As soon as the officer & his team of ten men started firing at the hut in a cluster of trees, the bursts of fire started coming from the other side! As the bullets started whizzing past, the two copulas closed; & I found myself prominently sitting alone on top of the tank in my blue flying overall and of course with **NO WEAPON** (I had deposited my revolver with our Bde armory! Yes; it was a case of NO HOLSTER! I had not brought my webbing from Jamnagar; and from the Bde, I could not get a spare holster!!)! The quick reaction was to jump down and run along the tank taking shelter from its hull. Then, the tank stopped, the turret moved and a tank shell was fired. The hut went up and came down; and there was all quiet thereafter!

The young, inquisitive Plt Offr also followed the Cdr to see what was inside the hut! As I was moving through the shrubs, I noticed two bodies (dressed in turbans; – yes, they were the infiltrators in disguise) lying in the approach path. I was about to cross over them, when I was stopped by a jawan following me stating, 'it's not respectful to cross over the dead'! Yes, that was the second reality of war that I had seen on my first day of induction! In the meanwhile, the Cdr walked out with a walking stick in his hand (found in the hut) and gestured, *'How do you like this as a souvenir of war?'* In the situation, my only response was, *'as long as we last the war, Sir!'* ***In the cache, we found, two LMG, 6-7 semi-automatic rifles & a Chinese communication set!*** This communication set, for rest of the duration of war, became a source of entertainment (with a crosstalk with Paki's on their network) at our offrs' field mess! Commander offered me to pick-up any weapon for my self-defence which I politely declined!

- It now occurs to me that had we (Cdr & Self) preferred to travel in our own light Vehicles (vehs) on this route, we all would have been easy targets (tgts) for the infiltrators; and 'our war' might have been over then and there; or at least, very different from then on!
- Secondly, had this enemy position (ambush) not been neutralised (with a tank shell) then, these infiltrators could have caused extensive damage to the subsequent build up of our forces on this axis!

Once at base of the hill (Kachrial hts), still appx 7-8 kms from the Cease Fire Line & less than a km from eastern bank of the Tawi, we parked along with another 10-12 tanks under a large cluster of trees. It was these tanks which had been attacked by the infiltrators on 03rd Dec night. The Cdr found that though no tank had been destroyed, the three tanks had been externally damaged by the infiltrators. ***It was the surprise, shock effect & the casualties among the key personnel which demoralised the men; and subsequently led to moving back of some of the tanks & troops of 7 Kumaon.***

These tanks presented an ideal target for an air strike! The Bde Cdr ordered a quick dispersion of all the tanks. However, the process had yet not started, when we heard Sabres (F-86) overhead and saw the first ac already in a dive attack on us! In a quick move from top of the tank, the Bde Cdr went into a nearby, already overflowing trench; and I laid down in the open. The first aircraft (ac) released its bombs and it appeared as if they were coming only for us! The bombs overshot our position by just about 10 mtrs and exploded. I was literally lifted off the ground. I looked around and found, all our tank crew were engaging the ac with their ack-ack guns. There were total of five ac and they were rolling in from different directions!

Realising that the tgts for all five Sabres were just the tanks, I ran 50 odd yards away from this area and lay in the open. Subsequently, they strafed us with their six 20 mm guns (each). I, along with another army officer, who also did not find any shelter, kept count of all five ac and laid clear of their strafing path every time! Yes, they had a free hand & attacked us for 20 mins! Fortunately, there was no damage to any of our tanks or personnel! Just the outside slung beddings of two tanks caught fire, which were soon brought under control. I went back to my own tank for the return. But to my surprise, that tank moved to another position & stopped. I ran to board the Bde Cdr's tank which had already left. At this point I realised that I had lost my watch (a gift from my father on my commissioning!) during the 'circus'; which I found lying at the same place on 18th Dec!

Yes, it was a 'jolting, lifetime experience' to be in the 'gun sights' of five fighter ac and yet get away! By sunset of 04th Dec, then, Plt Offr HK Bajaj had got his first taste of the war; and was well inducted! From then on, ***my belief in the 'Destined Life-Lines' had been further reinforced***!!

Buildup to 10th Dec

191 Brigade Group with active Close Air Support (CAS) from 101

Squadron Air Force (Falcons of Chhamb – as christened later), under control of then, Flight Lieutenant (Flt Lt) VG Kumar (FAC 191 Bde), fought valiantly, initially held its ground stoutly and also repulsed their attempts to establish a bridgehead across Manawar Tawi! However, on 05th / 06th Dec night, when holding west of Tawi became untenable against the fast advancing enemy, 191 Bde group withdrew east of Manawar Tawi; and 68 (I) Inf Bde with 5/8 Gorkha Regt (GR) deployed astride Chhamb bridge, 7 Kumaon covering from Mandiala crossing to Buchohe Mandi in the North & 9 Jat securing the eastern bank at both Dhar & Raipur crossings, came in contact with the enemy. 10 Garhwal Rifle (Garh Rif) was also deployed at Raipur Crossing; while, the Southern half of the Tawi was defended by 52 Inf Bde. Pakis did try to cross over on 08th / 09th Dec night as well but their attack was repulsed by the holding battalion; and the enemy suffered very heavy casualties and we also got a few PoWs.

The Knockout, Two Dimensional, Punch!

Let me recall the events as they unfolded from break of dawn on 10th Dec 71!

"I, as the FAC, was at my 'operations (Op) site' (a trench) with D Company (Coy) of 5/8 GR, Commanded by then, Lt Col (later, Lt Gen & Army Cdr) AS Kalkat and was located appx 700 mtrs from the destroyed Chhamb bridge. The distance between the two opposing forces was about 60-70 mtrs. From early hrs, the arty fire was just nonstop. ***In the morning, I had two 'pre-planned' CAS missions. The first formation attacked enemy gun positions south of Chhamb; while, the second was a Search & Strike msn of two Hunters lead by then, Sqn Ldr (later, Air Marshal & C in C) RN (Mummy) Bhardwaj (No. 1) & then, Fg Offr BC (Lofty) Karambaya as his No. 2. The targets (tgts) for them were troops and tanks concentrations. As the formation set up an orbit over the area and was looking for the tgts, I reported,*** *'two bogeys (2 Sabres), right one O'clock* ***to the formation. However, the No. 2 had already picked up the enemy aircraft (ac). In the ensuing air battle, the No. 2 called out,*** *'I am hit'*; ***and a little later, Mummy Sir said,*** *'I got one'!* ***I remember last seeing No. 2 flying very low over the hills, streaming fuel (white smoke) and both ac pulled away to the East. The***

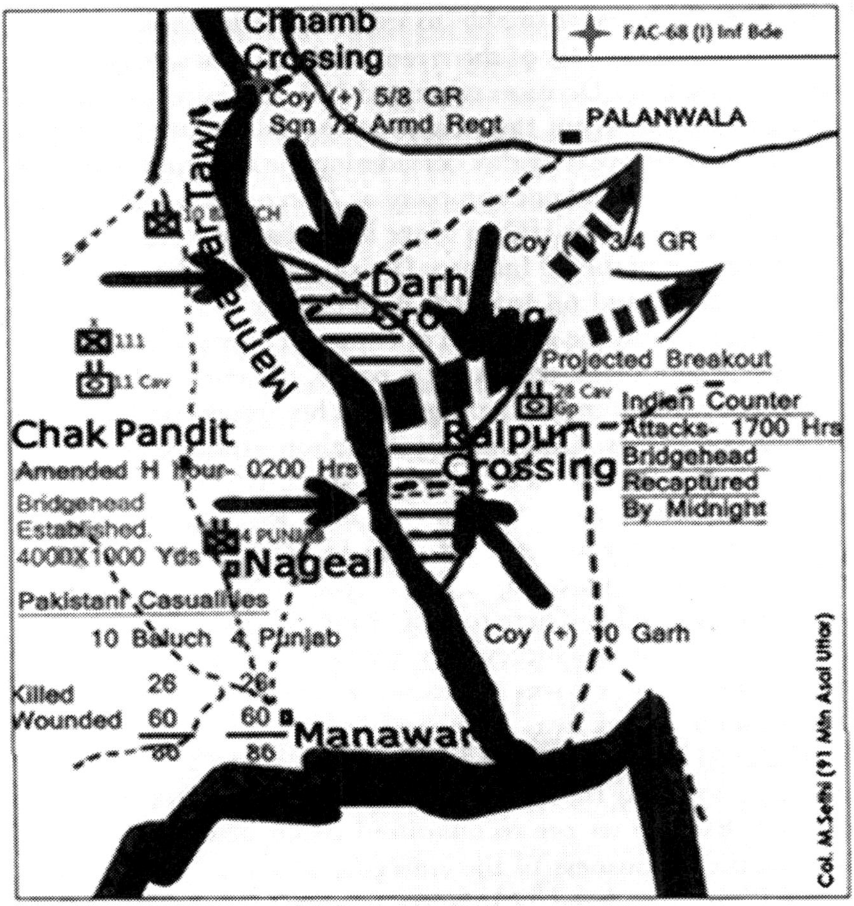

111 Infantry Brigade Attack and Indian Counter Attacks, 10 Dec 1971

Note: Casualty figures taken from the book Battle of Chhamb (1971) by Lt Col Ahmad Saeed.

formation returned to base safely. The news of shooting down of one Sabre also had the troops dancing with joy! Yes, it was a proud moment for us all!

Subsequently, we three comrades, the trench neighbours (self, Sec Cdr 5/8 GR (a Capt) & Troop Cdr (2nd Lieutenant Prashant Gupta) 12 Guards (Anti Tank Guided Missile), came to know that ***Pakis had launched a major offensive, with one infantry brigade supported by a regiment of armour, across Dhar and Raipur crossings.*** I had **no GLO.**

I had the 'Immediate Demands' raised for CAS. In this operation, 52 Inf Bde, 72 Armd Regt and Deccan Horse were also directly involved. ***I had a total of five CAS msns over the day against tanks, guns, vehs and troops concentrations in this area;*** while, in addition to the air effort directly allotted to the above mentioned two formations, as per the records from my Pocket Diary of 1971 War (which I still have), another two msns of four S-22 ac each & one msn of two Hunters were also controlled by the FAC of 52 Bde / 72 Armd Regt (Plt Offr Y (Yuri) Suri, a Course mate); and struck enemy forces in this crucial land battle. ***With a well defined Forward Line of Own Troops (FLOT) along the Tawi and good reference of Dhar & Raipur Crossings (two & four kms south of destroyed Chhamb Bridge, respectively), the large concentration of enemy tanks and troops west of Tawi presented good tgts for strike ac the whole day; and Indian Air Force with Sukhois from Falcon (101) Sqn and Hunters from Lightening (20) Sqn, loaded with 500 kg/1000 pounder bombs, 64x57 mm Rockets/68mm SNEB Rocket Pods with 19 rockets in each pod & 30mm guns caused massive destruction and thus played a decisive role in blunting the thrust and forced the enemy to retreat from east of Manawar Tawi.***

The defending 9 Jat fought valiantly at both the crossings and repulsed the initial offensives but were overrun in the subsequent attacks. ***Maj Gularia, Coy Cdr (whom I had met on 04 Dec) & his Coy Subedar, at Dhar crossing, were captured, inhumanly tortured and brutally killed. RIP Brave Hearts. The enemy managed to ingress and establish a bridgehead of appoximate 3000 × 900 mtrs but their tanks got bogged down in marshy land opposite the crossing.*** With a counter attack with tanks and infantry, the enemy's advance was stalled and the bridgehead contained. ***At both Dhar and Raipur Crossings, the quickly reinforced troops and the repeated air strikes on the western bank, caused heavy casualties and destruction on Pak's subsequent build up & stopped their momentum. Thus, before the last light, Pak troops were completely shaken, disorganised and were forced to pull back from east of Manawar Tawi. Though, it was claimed to be a 'miss reporting' by Major Nazar Hussain, Brigade Major (BM) of Pak 111 Bde; but if he was to be believed, 'by mid afternoon, the attacking 28 Cavalry was down to FOUR tanks; & at 1400 hours, the new GOC 23***

Pakistani Division ordered withdrawal of 111 Bde from east of Manawar Tawi'.

Finally a two-pronged counter attack by 5/8 GR, 7 Kumaon, 3/4 GR and 10 Garh Rif supported by armour was launched from North and South, along the eastern bank of the Tawi. It was only by mid night that Pak forces were completely pushed back to west of the Tawi. In this attack, Pakis suffered very heavy casualties. The next morning, the whole area (east of Tawi) was found littered with bodies, indicating intensity of the battle. Six of their tanks were destroyed east of Manawar Tawi by our grd forces and one serviceable tank was also found abandoned.

Back at 5/8 GR location, during a short lull in the air activity, while we were having packed lunch, one mortar shell hit the bundh, just outside our trench and the tail unit fell inside. Yes, it was 'close'; my fourth in the week; but sure, our number was not up! Once, the firing stopped, we found that the jawan who had delivered us the lunch had been martyred; while another three were wounded. ***My FAC jeep also got a direct hit from an arty shell, split into two & was on fire! My R/T operator and the driver too were lucky to be saved! From the burning vehicle, we could only retrieve one wheel which I had borrowed from my friend, Yuri's jeep!"***

Yes, the memories are still very fresh, vivid & lingering!!

Veteran Gp Capt HK Bajaj *was commissioned in the Flying Branch in June 1971. He had barely six months service when the 1971 war broke out. He actively participated in the war. Later, he rose to become an A2 QFI and has 3000 hours accident free flying on single engine aircraft. During his 32 years long service he commanded an OSA-AK missile Sqn. He also commanded Air Force Station Rajokri. He superannuated in 2003 from DSSC, Wellington. He is now settled at Greater Noida. He can be reached at hkb2003@rediffmail.com and 9891446039.*

5 Operations at Srinagar

A Balachandran

As a young 30 years old Flt Lt, I was the STO of 18 Squadron, also known as the Flying Bullets. I was part of this Squadron from 1969-72 and was responsible for servicing/maintenance of the famous Gnat aircraft. The Squadron was stationed at Ambala.

On 3rd Dec 1971 at around 6 PM, I was in the Officers' Mess Ambala along with my wife. Suddenly, we heard a loud Air Raid warning signal and we could see and hear the Pakistan Air Force Jets dropping bombs around the Airfield and officers' quarters. There was an intelligence report that Pakistan might make a pre-emptive attack in retaliation to our operations in the East Pakistan-now Bangladesh.

On hearing the Air Raid warning we rushed to the freshly dugout trenches. Luckily, there was no damage.

The very next day, our Squadron moved to Srinagar. I along with the technicians and required ground equipment were airlifted to Srinagar.

As per the existing UN Peace Force Resolution, no fighter Squadron was allowed to operate in Srinagar. The required facilities to operate and service the aircraft were not adequate. Therefore, immediately on landing there, we started with establishing adequate servicing facilities so that the aircraft could be made ready for operations.

The weather was not very good with the temperature dropping to sub-zero range. We were operating from make shift facilities, carrying out night servicing with the help of torches due to the blackout conditions. In any case, none of us was concerned about food and personal comfort as the aim was to defend our country.

Pakis flew lots of sorties to cause damage to the Srinagar town and the defence establishments. But the sorties flown by our Gnats and the

Vampires of the other Squadron based at Srinagar acted a big deterrent and the Pakis could not achieve much.

In one of the sorties, Fg Offr Nirmal Jit Singh Sekhon, in quick response to the Pakistani air attack over Srinagar shot down their Sabre jets. But unfortunately, his aircraft was also shot down. We lost him. It was a very tragic moment for all of us. But there was no time for emotions as the show was to go on to defend our motherland. He was posthumously awarded the highest gallantry award, the Param Vir Chakra.

Our Squadron did not lose any other aircraft thereafter and no damage was done to Srinagar airfield. We continued staying there in Srinagar even after the peace treaty was signed and we returned to our parent base Ambala in Mar 1972.

I am 80 years now. The memories of Indo-Pak war are fresh in my mind even to this day. I can never forget this as that was the greatest experience in my life. I can vividly recollect the names of some of the officers of the Squadron who took part in the war namely Bopaiah, Ghuman, Pathania, Satur, David, KS Rao, George, and Manchi Captain (Sorry, I would not be able to recollect their rank). I do not know as to how many of the Squadron personnel, who participated in the War, are alive as of today. RIP to all those air veterans who are not there with us.

I salute all of them for their contributions to the War fought by India for a good cause.

Best wishes and Jai Hind.

Veteran Sqn Ldr A Balachandran *was commissioned in the Aeronautical Engineering Branch on 01 Feb 1963. During the 1971 war he was the STO of 18 Sqn which was based at Ambala but moved to Srinagar during the operations. The Veteran officer was actively involved in the Gnat operations at Srinagar during the war. He took premature retirement in Mar 1983. He is settled at Bengaluru and can be reached at balas_kb@yahoo.co.in and 9880865780.*

6 VIGNETTES OF 1971 WAR

S Balasubramanian

Prelude

The story of the 1971 war is now fifty years old! Yet, every event and every little detail of those glorious days was so well ingrained in me that passage of time has not been able to wipe away even the minutest of them. Volumes can be written of that golden chapter - from the preparation to the grand finale. The stories below have been pieced together to provide a glimpse of the action spread across different facets of those wonderful days.

Our unit, 20 Squadron Air Force, The Lightnings, was commanded by Air Vice Mshl CV Parker MVC VM (then a Wing Commander). The Squadron, honoured with two MVCs, five VrCs, one VSM, two Mentioned-in-Dispatches and ten commendations by the CAS/AOC was perhaps the most decorated one in the war. The credit, without doubt, goes to the excellent leadership by the CO and our Flight Commanders.

To Sweat in Peace

We were equipped with the Hunter - God's own aircraft. I am sure that those who have flown it would readily agree! Our Mk 56As had a longer reach and having been based at Pathankot they could strike right up to Peshawar which was hitherto possible only with Canberra bombers.

Live trials were carried out to assess and re-evaluate the range of these aircraft. They were flown with different configurations and profiles like low, high or mixed. The aircraft had been inducted into the IAF for air defence but with the induction of Ajeets/ Gnats and later the MiG 21s their role was changed to ground attack. Long navigation routes required good time keeping but the aircraft did not have any stop clocks! Quick search helped in locating some clocks in the junked Mysteres in the Station. Being available in limited numbers, clamps were designed in the local workshop for temporary installation. Yes, at times the 'jugad' clamp slipped and the clock would disappear for rest of the flight!

Maps were prepared for the likely targets. Pencil lines on the paper maps helped us perfect the TPS (Thumb Positioning System - in the absence of GPS!). The thumb would be placed on a position flown over and confirmed by visual sightings. Thumb would then be moved forward as the flight progressed. Armed with the maps, briefings were done over and over again. Long discussions followed these briefings to ensure that all the doubts were cleared. There was total clarity and this also helped in maintaining near total R/T silence throughout the flight during the actual operations.

All pilots, technical and administrative personnel were trained well and knew exactly what had to be done. The Lightning tribe, brimming with confidence and sure of their invincibility, was ready to hit and hit hard.

Mother's Love

I met Mrs Malati in Delhi sometime in mid '71. There was something about this tall and graceful lady that did not fit in. She looked upset. She was upset that her only son, Fg Offr Muralidharan would not be able to take part in the war!

Murali, my room mate, had joined the forces against heavy odds. His family was against it. In his first attempt he had failed the selection for being grossly underweight. Yet, he subsequently made his dream come true. The ace flyer with his cheerful disposition was an asset. Unfortunately, he had been temporarily grounded by IAM Bengaluru on medical grounds.

His mother was fully aware of the risks involved but yet wished her son could fly. She knew that it would break his heart if he did not. It was a strange miracle then that he was back in the air just a few months before the war.

Unfortunately, Murali went down fighting in his very first mission.

I understand that he was outnumbered by the adversary. Murali lived his life on his own terms. His determination always got him what he wanted. Muralis are rare to come across. Also, there are hardly any parallels to Mrs Malati who prayed for her son's return to fight a war for his motherland.

Jumping Runway Lights

The war clouds had been building up. In order to thwart losses due to any pre-emptive strike by enemy the Squadron pulled back its aircraft to safer havens from time to time. In one such move we had moved over to Ambala. Under heightened tension, it was decided to pull back further to Hindon. It was late in the evening and my aircraft refused to start. Men worked hard but it was dark by the time we got it going. I was given taxi clearance but the ATC refused to switch on the runway lights for take-off due to perceived air threat. It took another 10 minutes of requests before they agreed and gave me right side edge lights for take-off. By the time I was getting my nose wheel off the ground these too were switched off! A few seconds later the edge lights of the left side came on! It was like my aircraft jumping over to the other side of the lights! Was this done to confuse any lurking PAF aircraft? Whether that did happen or not, it surely did for me and that too at a crucial time!

Friendly Fire

PAF attacked our forward bases on the evening of 3rd Dec 71. It was around 3 AM on the 4th that about twelve of our planes took off from Hindon for Pathankot. There was a total black out as we proceeded. As we reached overhead our base, suddenly, all hell broke. The whole sky was filled up with red streaks of lights! It took us a few seconds to realise that it was our own friendly anti-aircraft guns that had opened up on us and we were actually noticing the beauty of tracers! The firing may have been due to the limited communication systems available at that time but the sight was beautiful – our first real encounter with anti-aircraft fire!

As an urgent safety measure the aircraft peeled off in all directions. It was only after the exchange of some expletives over R/T that the guns were lowered. Fortunately, there was no loss and all of us landed safely.

The Yellow Building

The war had started! Having ferried in our aircraft from Hindon we trooped into our squadron crew room in the early hours of 4th Dec. The atmosphere was calm! It was as if nothing serious was on! Breakfast, hot tea and jokes - it was all there like any other day.

Our Flight Commander walked in and announced the next mission - and lo, it was then that all hell broke! Shouting and screaming, our pilots fought with each other to be included in the mission! The scene was repetitive – it occurred every time a new mission came in! I wish we had cell phones to record the video. Everyone in the pack wanted a piece of the cake. Such was the morale! What was it that drove us to this spirit?

I was lucky to be included as number two on a four aircraft strike on a PAF airfield that afternoon. As I was strapping in, our airmen, the men behind the scene that kept these wonderful machines flying, were very excited. Along with multitudes of good wishes came a strange request. "Sir, after your attack, if you still have some ammo and spare fuel please destroy the yellow building just north of the airfield" he said in firm words. Noticing the question mark on my face he continued in a toned down voice "I do not want any Pakis living in a house that belonged to my grandfather"! The picture was complete.

It was an experience of a lifetime. Confidently entering another country without a passport and firing short bursts of your guns to check their operation gave me a sense of power. Closing in on to the target zone, I pulled up. Ignoring the grey puffs created by heavy anti-aircraft fire, I looked for a suitable target. Soon I spotted the pointed nose of a fighter plane just about visible in its protective pen. Rolling into a dive I eased my pipper on to the target. It only took a short burst from my 30 mm Guns. Watching an enemy aircraft explode in a ball of fire shall remain permanently etched in my memory.

Back in my pen, our men were overjoyed by my 'kill' and literally carried me to the waiting Jeep. However, I could not realise the dream of my young friend, the yellow building remained intact ...

Sleeping Tablet

The proximity of Pathankot to the border made it an attractive target for the enemy. While they dared a few attacks by day, their bombers were overhead to drop their load every night without fail! When one finished - the next one would appear. It was not their bombs but the relentless firing by our own anti- aircraft guns which soon became a big nuisance and kept us away from getting a good sleep. So, a hotel, well away from the airfield, was booked for the aircrew to get a sleep they deserved. Unfortunately, the bus departure depended upon the bar closure time. Discussions over dinner added to the delay!

I was a non-drinking type. However, I decided to take a barman's suggestion seriously - that I down two large rums as soon as the bar opened! It was difficult but I tried the trick and followed it up with a quick dinner. The magic worked and it knocked me off for a better part of the night. I repeated it night after night! The ack-ack guns and exploding bombs failed to disturb my sleep thereafter. I had not really known what a sound sleep was till then!

A Bomb Explodes

While eagerly waiting for another mission one fine morning I got a message that a bomb had exploded near my room. It was important to check the damage. Soon, joined by a few others of the adjoining rooms, we departed in a jeep. As we reached about half way across the airfield air raid warning got us jumping out and hiding in a trench. We looked up to see 5 PAF Mirages pulling up, one behind the other. It was a magnificent sight to see them rolling-in to attack! Unmindful of the threat, we all stood up watching. Their bombs fell all over the airfield. I remember the one that did not follow normal trajectory but looked more like a tumbling drum that passed over our heads to explode well behind!

The damage to my room was extensive. The door and windows had been blown away. My sparse belongings were strewn all over. I had lost a lot of valuable photographs. It was a sad scene but what shook me was that the spread included belongings of my roommate, Late Fg Offr Muralidharan, whom we had lost a few days ago on a mission. As suggested by my seniors, I put in a claim for war damages and in time received a payment of Rs 317/-.

The Vertical Attack

I was detailed to lead a two aircraft Close Air Support mission in Poonch sector - the first in the area for me. My wingman was a course mate and an ace pilot, Fg Offr R DeMonte. We were briefed in detail about the enemy Brigade HQ, our main target, by the GLO (Ground Liaison Officer, from the army) of the station. Keeping the ground situation in mind we had planned a route through the valleys. A careful navigation route is needed to avoid getting into a blind valley that leads to nowhere and threatens the plane.

Soon our planes were winging their way in a north westerly direction towards the border. We were keeping low and flew behind the curtain of mountain ridges. Flying at these levels, navigation in the valleys, is not an easy task. We had to keep a good look out for enemy aircraft too. In time we were closing in on our IP (Initial Point - located in own territory from where the FAC provides the strike force with visual guidance to the target). In this case the FACs (Forward Air Controller, an Air Force pilot, moving with the army and hence knowledgeable of the exact forward line of own troops), Plt Offrs Talwar and Thapar, were from our own squadron. I started calling the FAC on our discreet radio channel and it was some time before I heard them. Their transmission was garbled. It so happened that they were actually fighting with each other for the right to control our attack and while trying to snatch the microphone from each other, it's transmit button had been on!

The FAC made visual contact with our two aircraft over the IP and gave us a short description of the target and direction to fly. Keeping an eye on the airspace above we headed that way. Only when we were over the actual target that the complexity of our task dawned on us! The enemy had smartly located the HQ on a steep hill side that faced away from the border. To add to our difficulties, there were steep hill features all around that rendered it impossible to acquire the required dive angle for firing the rocket pods that we were carrying. The gunsight was incapable of allowing for correct gravity drop for the higher dive angles now needed. Time was of essence. I quickly revised the attack pattern and decided to launch the rockets in a vertical dive and thus reduce the error to minimum. I briefed my wingman even as I started my pull up with him providing suitable air cover since we were highly exposed and at low speed! At about eight to ten thousand feet above the ground (I guess!) I rolled in and got into a near vertical dive. I fired my salvo from a longer range and it was exhilarating to see them find their mark. I did not have much time to enjoy the sight as my speed was building up and the mountains were rising fast. I pulled out of the dive and kept my eyes open even as DeMonte carried out his attack with equal precision!

The return flight was uneventful. After landing we headed to the operations room for filing our debrief. The broad smile on the face of our GLO was reassuring indeed - ground report had already reached him. The Brigade Headquarters had been badly hit and destroyed! I owed a drink to our two FACs...

Mistaken Identity

We had a very successful attack on Chaklala airfield in the wee hours on 8th Dec. I was the wing man of our CO. It was still some time for sunrise as we headed home in a broad front formation. We had extended our speed brakes and were using higher power to maintain speed and thus burn up excess fuel. My eyes searched for any suspicious enemy air activity around us and the reward came soon. In a distance, to my right and slightly high I saw a pair of aircraft. Even as I was focusing my eyes to identify the type, I saw the two break the circular orbit and turn towards us! "Bandits, 2 aircraft, 4:30, slightly high turning in towards us" I cautioned my leader. A few seconds later I heard my leader's call "contact, they are our boys" in a cool voice. Reassuring - yes, but I kept my eyes on them as I noticed one of them getting behind me. Retracting my speed brakes I again called out "one getting behind me" and was getting ready for a break even as my neck had reached its maximum twist limit! It was going to happen anytime now! Suddenly, I saw the aircraft pull up and the pair disappeared. I recognised the familiar Hunter aircraft and cursed myself for the unnecessary pumping of adrenaline!

Later in the day I met Fg Offr JS Gahlawat, of a sister squadron, flying the same machines as us. His face ashen and clearly indicated that something was amiss. "Sorry, so sorry" he blurted, "my finger was on the trigger, I almost shot you down this morning". He continued "I was in firing position but the rising Sun made me bend and brighten the gunsight - and at the closer range I suddenly recognised that it was a Hunter aircraft"! Clearly the Sun God had turned my saviour that morning.

As mentioned earlier in this article, the memories of those 13 days of war are as fresh as if it had happened yesterday only. I cherish the memories and those feelings are going to continue to live with me.

Veteran Wg Cdr S Balasubramanian *was commissioned in Flying branch on 04 Jun 1967. He actively participated in 1971 War as part of air strike missions over West Pakistan. He was awarded VrC for his exceptional performance. He is an alumni of DSSC. As a qualified Instructor he served at AFA, Bidar, FIS and in Iraq. He retired in 1985 and joined Air India. He became Airbus Examiner and Simulator Instructor on Boeing 787. He is presently trustee of an NGO and settled at Mumbai. He can be reached at bala1hm@hotmail.com and 9820420848.*

7 Looking Back at 71 War

RK Batha

I was a young Flight Lieutenant, a bachelor, posted to 101 Sqn (SU-7 BMK) at Adampur in early 1971. Reflecting back, this posting was one of the most cherished of my early days in the Air Force, with friends (officers and airmen) all around me, affectionate and helping seniors and my utmost admiration for those rearing to go, young pilots and the commanders of squadrons and wing sections. It was a great feeling of a family preparing and going to war.

Being a member of the Technical team at Adampur, there were so many happy and a few not so happy instances/episodes, that each of these would itself be a story to recount.

It was a 'symphony orchestra' being played out at our Base with the conductor being none other than AOC Air Cmde Randhir Singh. He was all over, with infinite energy and a cherubic smile, motivating all in uniform, civilians and the villagers around, ensuring the safety of the Base, its personnel, its assets etc. The cohesiveness of work at Base and the AOC's astute counter-intelligence resulted in the Pakis not being interested in their pre-emptive strike on Adampur on 03rd Dec 1971, the beginning of the formal war.

At the Base and in the squadrons, the young fighter pilots, COs, Flt Cdrs, Sec Cdrs and the rest of the personnel were in high spirits as soon as the balloon went up on 03rd December 1971. I can still picture our C Eng O, Gp Capt Anadi Sarkar, driving in his Willys jeep to our billets to announce, and to pick us up for what we had been eagerly waiting for, and from then on, we, technical officers and airmen, were mostly at the work site to take/give orders and execute them post haste, for aircraft servicing/repairs, arming, turnaround, etc. The Russian team at Base was of great help for aircraft battle damage repairs and their miracle "Grimmechik" compound, in bullet-hit repairs to the fuel tanks. These activities were rightly a part of the Base's symphony orchestra.

On the 14th day of the war, strike achievements of 101 Sqn were phenomenal. The soft spoken, gentle and humane, KC (CO-

Wg Cdr KC Khanna), Flt Cdrs, Sqn Ldr Madhav Banerjee (Banjo) and Sqn Ldr Ashok Shinde led the young fighter pilots from the front to demolish the Pak tank attack in Chhamb Sector, rightly to be christened, as "Falcons of Chhamb" and the pilots were decorated handsomely for their valour. Bhattu walked back from the enemy territory after his aircraft had been shot down, which was a great morale booster and that spread happiness among all the sqn personnel. Sadly, two young pilots were martyred—Flt Lt Vijay Wahi and my unassuming roommate, Flt Lt Jayant Rishi.

Overall, the pre-war visits to Base and talks by VIPs i.e. Ministers, Chief, C-in-C etc, added to the high morale of the personnel. One such visit was by the Honourable Defence Minister, Babu Jagjivan Ram. His talk to us at the Base was awesome and he assured us that this time whatever we would win, would not be given back, unlike in the 1965 victory.

India's national and political aim of breaking Pakistan and forming a new country Bangladesh, was achieved on 16th December 1971. However, the truncated West Pakistan got back all our war gains, including the over 93,000 Pak soldiers who had surrendered and were returned by India. This is a big story by itself, and there will be many who would have been privy to it, to recount it.

Lastly, having retired with access to news/media only, I most sincerely as a fauji, congratulate our Defence Forces in standing up to the mischievous Chinese aggression on our borders since last year, and especially to the IAF in the rapid mobilisation of troops and armour against the Chinese, which must have shocked the Chinks. To an extent, the Defence Forces have redeemed the debacle of 1962, but we have to be always wary of China and its mischievous intentions against India.

Jai Hind.

Veteran AVM RK Batha *was commissioned in the Tech Signals (Now AE (L)) Branch on 04 Oct 1965. He is a highly qualified Engineering officer with vast experience. During the 1971 war, he was posted at Adampur and was actively involved in the operations. He has been an instructor at Air Force Technical College. He also commanded the prestigious Software Development Institute at Bengaluru. He is presently settled at Bengaluru and can be reached at ramyarbatha@gmail.com and 9886026344.*

8 Campaign of Longewala

MS Bawa

Upgradation of Jaisalmer

Things had been hotting up on our Western border for quite some time. By the middle of Jun 71, rumours had started doing a round about an imminent war with our neighbours on the Western front.

The IAF units in the North and those along the Western borders had started preparing themselves for taking part in the operations; should a need so arise.

One such unit along the Western border was 14 Care and Maintenance Unit based at Jaisalmer. Both Jaisalmer and Uttarlai were meant to be forward airfields, to be supported from Jodhpur in the event of war. The unit was commanded by Flt Lt NK Sharma. Going by the importance of the place, there was an immediate change and I was posted there wef 10 Sep 71 to assume command of that small C & MU which later on became an FBSU and is now a full-fledged Wing.

During the war itself the unit was to act as a Mini Wing. The day I assumed command of the unit, it had still many installations under construction. The existing offices and sections were deployed on peace time basis.

The Challenge

My immediate task was to make a quick assessment of the available resources and to work out the requirements for the unit to operate as a mini Wing. The task was not too easy as some of the sections had no Section Commanders.

The first and foremost task was to gear up the unit to the maximum required degree of operational preparedness. The most vital of all these were (a) Ground Defence (b) Air Defence (c) Communication (d) Rad and Nav Aids (e) MT (f) Accommodation.

The details were worked out and we started moving forward. Soon the Station was humming with activity. Everyone was busy with something or the other. We had no time to waste. As the strength of officers was negligible, I was virtually present everywhere. That was the need of the hour.

The original strength of personnel was grossly inadequate to accomplish the perceived task.

The men were to be replaced fortnightly to recoup from the fatigue of this drab and dry town, which had little to offer other than abundance of sand and hot burning air. Faster than men were the stores to arrive. The wagons arrived in large numbers, but there were very few vehicles and personnel to unload them. It was a challenge which had to be met irrespective of the time involved. These essential stores added additional risk, as such had to be dispersed in a planned manner. The vital and vulnerable technical equipment had to be moved to underground complexes with the help of Collector's manpower. Base Operations room, which had never functioned at this base had to be started from scratch. The administrative set up and its allied sections had to be moved under tentage. The concealment of these posed a major problem as the terrain offered scant shrubbery. Regular programme of camouflaging the stores, equipment and tentage was initiated and every morning one hour was devoted to camouflaging, till satisfactory standards were reached.

While the Radio and Navigational Aids were made operational and rose to the occasion, however, the telephone communication with the rear base lagged far behind and remained unreliable for a very long time. The phone call through civil could mature in a minute, while the service line did not respond for hours and days together.

Motivational Address

In one of the Station gatherings, in order to motivate the men, I gave a fiery and belligerent speech, outlining the purpose of their gathering at this Mini Wing. During the speech, I clearly stated, "Gentlemen, we are here to restore those Ten Million people back to their homes, who have been rendered homeless, who have been deprived of their self-respect, honour, wives, children, the near and the dear ones. If we do not react now, then coming generations will hang their heads in shame for lack of action on our part. We have come here to achieve this aim and whatever be the cost, we shall not return without it. I ask you all this but offer you nothing in return. I am more aware of your needs and the sub-standard facilities, but I assure you that I shall make every endeavor to provide you what I can. What I cannot, I shall not hesitate to project the same to higher authorities." To infuse the spirit of dedication I summed it up by giving a slogan:

> ***Sar Faroshi Ki Tamanna Ab Hamare Dil Mein Hai,***
> ***Dekhana Hai Zor Kitna Bazue Qaatil Mein Hai***

With this in the minds of every-one, there was no requirement for anyone to be told as to what was to be done. People worked with a smile from morning to night without complaint.

Continuous Improvement and the VIP Visits

The Chief of Air Staff Air Chief Marshal PC Lal visited the base within four days of my assuming the Command. He had little to say in so far as the work being done was concerned. He went back happy.

The biggest problem for me at hand was the fortnightly rotation of mainly ground defence manpower as I had to infuse the same spirit in the new arrivals.

I would carry out a periodic review and by and large at the end of the day I would be a more satisfied man as the personnel were coping up with the requirements.

On 15 Oct 71, the long awaited detachment of 122 Sqn arrived with two Hunters from AF Station Jamnagar. Within one week of that, we had 105 GL Section Type 'B' moving from Armament Training Wing (ATW) Jamnagar, 12 AOP added to us, a troop of 152 AD Regt (L/60 guns) moved in to take complete control of Air Defence at the Base. P-30 radar was added to the C & MU family to act as the eyes and ears of the base. This radar came from 15 Wing. It took some time for these units to become operational and be fully available to us. The radar became fully operational on 31 Oct 71.

In between, we had a visit each by the Chief Minister of Rajasthan, and General SHFJ Manekshaw, Chief of the Army Staff.

On 3rd Nov 71 the ADDC at Jodhpur ordered its first scramble after sundown at 1804 hrs. The mission was subsequently abandoned. The aircraft had to be recovered under emergency conditions by our base.

We were now making steady progress. On 8th Nov 71, Sh. Jagjivan Ram, Defence Minister visited us. He was accompanied by Mr Barkatulla Khan, the Chief Minister of Rajasthan. The Defence Minister addressed all the Station personnel apprising them of the latest border situation and the operational commitment of the IAF in the area. He informed the gathering that this time the battle will be fought on the enemy's soil. In between we had two joint Army Cooperation exercises named "Non Plus" and "Sky Hawk". Both the exercises were very useful, and these were conducted successfully.

On 28 Nov 71, the Prime Minister of India Smt Indira Gandhi visited the area. I had the proud privilege of meeting her. Soon thereafter, we had a visit by the Chief of Air Staff who addressed all the ranks of the Station and apprised them of the situation. He urged them to maintain a high degree of preparedness as the enemy was likely to make a pre-emptive strike.

The War Begins and our Participation

Sure enough Pakistan did make the first pre-emptive strike on 3rd Dec 71. We were prepared for this and were waiting for further instructions. Complete black out orders were already in force. On 4th Dec, the station launched five missions comprising of two aircraft each as per the task given by the Command.

There were two targets Jacobabad airfield, Rahimyar Khan airfield and the SU. In addition, four close support sorties were also carried out in the area where 12 Inf Div was supposed to launch an offensive enabling them to capture Sakhirewala Khu and Islamgarh. When 12 Inf Div was concentrating on their area of advance to Rehimyar Khan, the enemy sneaked in with sufficient strength towards Longewala. They bypassed Longewala and were seen advancing towards Ramgarh, past midnight. Fortunately for India, the front column of tanks turned back as they found that the rear was not catching up. This was a very big mistake committed by the Pak Army. Had these tanks continued on their course, they would have easily over run Ramgarh.

The situation was becoming worrisome. The GOC 12 Inf Div tried to get in touch with me but to his bad luck the telephone lines had been cut by the enemy. Finally we were able to speak to each other in the early hours of 4th Dec 71 when a radio link was established. I immediately ordered the missions to be on standby. There were repeated calls from Div HQ on 4th morning. I immediately ordered a hunter mission which was on site scanning the road between Ramgarh and Longewala. The mission reported presence of T-59 tanks which was confirmed by the choppers of AOP also. The mission lost no time and engaged the tanks which were advancing towards Longewala. Missions were launched one behind the other in quick succession to destroy the enemy's armoured thrust. It was a one Vs one fight between the IAF and the Pakistan Armour. We had total four hunters and we launched 17 Missions thereby destroying 15 tanks, one armour recce vehicle and damaging 23 tanks. I reproduce a part of army intercept by our Air Force:

> ***"Dushman Ki Hawai Fauj Ne Nak Me Dam Kar Diya Hai Ek Hawai Jahaz Jata Hai Aur Doosra Atta Hai Aur Bees Minute Ooper Nachta Hai Chalis Fisadi Fauj Aur Samaan Hallak Aur Tabah Ho Chuka Hai Aghe Jana To Kya Peeche Murrna Bhi Mushkal Ho Gaya Hai Jaldi Hawai Fauj Madad Ke Liye Bhejo Warna Vapas Murrna Na Mumkin Hai"***

The GOC 12 Inf Div acknowledged our excellent support through a message.

On 5th Dec 71, early morning at around 0440 hrs, a bomber raid was reported heading towards Jaisalmer. We had prior warning about such an attack as the Div Cdr had spoken to me at around 0130 hrs. Anticipating this, we had put our guns on high alert. On hearing the noise of the approaching aircraft, the guns were ordered to open fire.

The aircraft made a hasty retreat by putting on a sharp bank and off-loading all the weapon load of bombs just outside the perimeter. One of the bombs hit the under-ground power cables which disrupted the electricity supply and communications for the next six hours. We continued with our missions on all routes leading to Jaisalmer and continued destroying the tanks one after another. By the evening nearly 37 tanks lay burning/damaged and scattered in the Thar Desert. Due to timely action by the Air Force, Pakistan met its waterloo.

Pakistan was however at it again on 7th Dec early morning when a low level bomber raid was reported at 0420 hrs. We did try to engage the aircraft but the aircraft managed to slip through the barrage of fire at very low height flying along the taxi track. The taxi track was damaged a bit which was repaired on top priority. We launched 20 missions that day. In one of the missions, the CO of 122 Sqn, Wg Cdr Conquest got injured as while engaging an enemy tank he sustained a bullet injury in his foot from one of the small arms fired by the enemy. He safely brought the aircraft to base. He was immediately evacuated to MH and the injury was declared a minor injury.

On 8th Dec 71 we launched 14 sorties and continued damaging the Pakistan army resources. A flash message was received that day from the Chief of Air Staff conveying appreciation by the Defence Minister and Army Chief for the excellent performance by the Station and 122 Sqn. This was a big morale booster for the Station personnel.

More aircraft moved in taking our strength to 14 on the 9th evening as planned. I felt that now we were underutilised. I conveyed the same to TAC Commander.

We continued with our efforts and on 9th Dec, the Station launched 22 hunter sorties. In addition there were casualty-evacuation sorties by the Helicopters. AOC-in-C, WAC complimented the Station for its contribution to the on-going war and conveyed the appreciations on behalf of the Army Commanders who were highly appreciative of the contribution made by the IAF pilots in the Rajasthan Sector. This was a further morale booster for the personnel.

The Mujahids were time and again attempting to neutralise the targets at the Station but every time they were given a hot reception by the bullets.

On 10th Dec and 11th Dec, a total of 24 sorties were launched causing further damage to the resources of Pakistan.

Early in the morning of **12th Dec at 0230 hrs, the enemy bomber again** made an attempt but without much joy. We continued with our sorties in support of 11 Inf Div and 12 Inf Dev. But there were not enough targets left.

On 14th Dec 71, I proposed to the GOC 12 Inf Div that I can arrange for him to have an aerial view of the damage done and that we can move further to stake our claim on enemy territory. The response was not encouraging for the reasons best known to them.

Similar offer as earlier was made again on 15th Dec 71 to capture maximum territory in view of imminent fall of Dacca but to no avail. We continued with our contribution, launched a total of 21 sorties, destroyed a few tanks, some goods trains and ammunition.

It happens to be my birthday on 16th Dec, and of-course, the same day in 1971, a new nation BANGLADESH was born. While thanking the God Almighty, I thanked all station personnel for showing grim determination to repel the enemy from our soil.

War Ends

Finally orders came that unilateral ceasefire was to be observed from 2000 hrs on 17 Dec 71. We were asked to cease all offensive action after 2000 hrs on 17 Dec 71 but were permitted to take retaliatory action in self-defence if required.

The ceasefire was accepted by Pakistan after this short, crisp and decisive encounter with India.

Rich Dividends

In all, it was a very satisfying experience where the Station launched

222 sorties with NIL loss and lots of damage to the enemy resources. I forwarded my recommendation on the lessons learnt to the higher ups.

The Station was richly awarded wherein we received 2 AVSMs, 10 VrCs, one Sena Medal, 10 M-in-Ds. I was awarded an AVSM.

Veteran Air Marshal Mohinder Singh Bawa *was commissioned in the Flying Branch in April 1953. He has served in a number of fighter and fighter bomber squadrons and has commanded one of them. During the 1971 War with Pakistan, Wing Commander Mohinder Singh Bawa was in command of an airfield. He transformed the airfield into a major base, capable of sustaining intensive operations by a number of aircraft. Aircraft operating from this base mounted large scale operations in close support of the Army, knocking many enemy tanks and vehicles. He is fondly remembered by all because of the "Battle of Longewala." He is settled down at New Delhi and can be reached at minhibawa@hotmail.com and 8826747082.*

9 Down the Memory Lane

JS Bhalla

The Background

I was posted to Air force Station Bagdogra in 1970. There was general shortage of married accommodation. However on arrival we were given a Basha with an area of 25′x15′ with thatched roof which accommodated my wife, me and my one year old son. It provided us with the basic amenities which we required for our day to day living. There was a small living room and a kitchen where we prepared our meals using kerosene oil. Cooking on gas was unheard of in those days. A western style bathroom and a bedroom with folding cots was all that we had. During the rainy season umbrellas would protect us from the rain water dripping from the thatched roof and during winters icy cold winds would penetrate the bedroom through the tiny holes of the thatched roof. However we took life in our stride and even with these bare minimum facilities happiness was galore, at least we were together.

Much before the commencement of the hostilities in Dec 1971 Wg Cdr Shah, Chief Operations Officer took me to VIP room at Bagdogra airport where we met Sheikh Mujibur Rahman not realising that we were interacting with the future Prime minister of a Nation. He was on his way to Delhi. An unassuming personality, he was very simple and soft spoken. He frequently visited Bagdogra interacting with Army Commanders.

Preparing for the War

Hunters and the Sabre killer Gnats were based at Air Force Station Bagdogra. Much before the commencement of war we had moved to our ops location. A watch tower adjacent to the DGCA complex surrounded by jackfruit trees was activated as an alternative site for providing Air Traffic Services during the war. The makeshift Air Traffic Control tower could accommodate only one person due to paucity of space. Trenches were dug to protect the working manpower from any air raid .

During the months preceding the war, we could clearly hear the sound of firing across the border, as we were not far-off from the border. This sound used to be more clear at night. As the days passed the intensity of firing increased and the sound became louder making us realise that some tension was brewing up across the border. This was followed by the black-out in the camp creating a feeling of uneasiness amongst the family members. One fine evening, the families were told to vacate the accommodation and move to a safer place as the war was imminent.

The War broke out

On 3rd Dec, Pak Air Force carried out pre-emptive strikes on 11 Indian Air Force bases in the western sector. At 1740 hrs Pathankot was attacked and little later Amritsar runway was damaged and by 1800 hrs Agra , Halwara, Srinagar, and Ambala were in the line of fire. In the night Prime Minister Smt Indira Gandhi addressed the Nation saying "the war has been enforced on us" India responded with retaliation strikes the same evening.

As the tension was building up, all of us usually used to assemble in the Officers' Mess in the evening. When the news of pre-emptive strike came we were in the mess. Our josh was at its peak. As we used to follow black out in the evening, someone shouted "The Balloon has gone up. Let us teach them a lesson". I asked my number 2 Flt Lt Tomar to wind up being on early morning duty next day. Little later, I received a message that Flt Lt Tomer had met with a road accident while crossing the road in front of the Officers' Mess. He had hit a cyclist with his Royalenfield—the outcome of black out.

Sorry, I lost my Neighbour

On 4th morning after the normal ritual of the morning briefing at 5 am, I took over the controls in the ATC tower. A Hunter formation with Sqn Ldr Gupta as No 1 and Flt Lt D'Costa as No 2 taxied out for a counter offensive mission. Flt Lt D Costa was our next door neighbour in the DGCA colony. The formation was tasked to destroy Lal Munir Hat control tower in the eastern sector. This was in response to Pak attack on 03 Dec 71 in Western sector. He carried out his task accurately destroying the enemy positions as briefed. His leader commented 'good burst'. After successfully strafing enemy targets D' Costa turned to attack a goods train south of Lal Munir Hat possibly carrying war material. The train was well guarded by the military personnel. Unfortunately, his aircraft was hit. He tried to bring back the aircraft but it crashed. I lost my neighbour. He was awarded Vir Chakra Posthumously for his bravery and devotion to duty during the operations.

In the evening again in the Officers' Mess the aviators were discussing threadbare the day's operations. We all used to listen to the transistor to get an update on the War. It was quite funny to listen to the Pakistan radio claiming that the Pakistani forces have reached Siliguri. We really had a hearty laugh. Life carried on as usual. The IAF continued with mounting its strike missions.

Next morning as usual the majestic Hunters with Squadron Commander Wg Cdr Coelho in the lead roared with gusto to destroy enemy targets in the Eastern sector.

It was a short War of just 14 days. We did lose some precious lives but then there was pride as we were instrumental in creating a new nation "Bangladesh". The memories of those days are still very fresh.

Veteran Wing Commander JS Bhalla *was commissioned in the Administrative Branch of Indian Air Force on 27 May 61. He participated in all the three wars of 1962, 1965 and 1971. While being posted at Air Force Station Bagdogra as SATCO, he actively participated in the 1971 War. He superannuated on 31 Aug 1989. Presently he is settled at Chandigarh and can be reached at rajjaswant@yahoo.co.in and 9815643169.*

10 Participation in 1971 War

Hironmoy Biswas

During the period 1970 to 1975, I was on the posted strength of 43 Sqn, AF. I was a Flight Lieutenant and was an Air Signaler. On 04 May 1971, I was at Mohanbari as a part of an air-dropping mission in Monigong, erstwhile NEFA Valley. We were called and told to return to base at Jorhat. I, along with Fg Offr C Rajan, Fg Offr Karandhikar and Flt Lt PL Chopra went to Station Commander Gp Capt Chandan Singh for a briefing led by our Commanding Officer Wg Cdr KC Sharma. We were told to proceed to Barrackpore and report to Major General Jacob, Chief of Staff Eastern Command, for further instructions and remain there. On 05th May 1971, we were asked to proceed to Balurghat—then to Cooch Behar—via Bagdogra-Gauhati to Kumbhigram and finally to Agartala. The aircraft carried two Brigadiers and 18 Commando School Instructors. We dropped some of them at various places and the two Brigadiers along with the remaining Instructors went into erstwhile East Pakistan to train the Mukti Bahini. Like this, we did number of sorties from 08th May to 18th May 71 and we returned to our unit on 19th May 71.

We were also sent for paratrooper training to Agra so as to get fully prepared for any eventuality. We successfully completed this training in mid Nov 71. From Agra, we went to Bombay-Pune-Gauhati-Jorhat on a cross-country flight. Fg Officer J D'Souza was the captain and enroute we landed at Agartala on 17th Nov 71, from where we were to go to our base at Jorhat via Gauhati. There we met General JS Aurora, who asked us as to where were we going? The Captain informed him that we were going to Gauhati first and then return to Jorhat. He said that he and a few other officers were stranded since the IAC flight had been cancelled and he was urgently required at Calcutta. He requested us to take him and the other Army officers to Gauhati. We did so. When we were airborne, he came into the cockpit and asked me to pass a message to EAC, IAF, to arrange for his onward flight to Calcutta. The answer came promptly asking our endurance. The captain informed that he can fly for another six and a half hours. The next order came for us to proceed to Calcutta. We complied with the same. On landing at Calcutta, we were tired and received instructions to stay for the night and fly back the next morning. The above was during pre-war preparation.

During the War, on 06 Dec 71 we were asked to proceed to Bihta, where we were told to stay in a damaged house with no bathrooms or even water. Water was available for only half an hour in the evenings. On 11th Dec 71 we took off for Kalaikunda. We were given many briefings. About 56 Dakotas took off with paratroopers to drop them in Tangail, erstwhile East Pakistan, in the night. For identification Gooseneck lights were lit by an Army advance party. It was two hrs day flying and two hrs night flying.

On 13 Dec 71, our CO Wg Cdr KC Sharma captained a flight to Gauhati. The next day Air Cmde Ram, Air 1, EAC arrived and told us to fly over Dacca airport; we were under radar cover. We went over Dacca airfield and were told to descend to 2000 feet AGL and encircle the airfield. From there we were asked to proceed to Jessore and fly over it and perform a trial landing. We did so. The CO of a Hunter Squadron was also with us.

We returned to Gauhati to drop the Air Cmde. Later, we made a couple of sorties to position Hunters in Jessore from Hashimara. From that day onwards, the Hunter Sqn was operational.

Veteran Wg Cdr Hironmoy Biswas *was commissioned in the Aeronautical Engineering Branch on 18 October 1965. Subsequently, he got trained as an aircrew and was a Flight Signaller with Dakotas and Avros. He took active part in the 1971 war and was a part of the crew which flew paradropping sorties over East Pakistan. Even after the surrender ceremony, he landed at Jessore a few times in support of the Hunter Sqn movement. He retired from the Air Force in 1993. Thereafter, he served in the Hindustan Cables Ltd as DGM. He is now leading a retired life and is settled at Kolkatta. He can be reached at hironmoy66@gmail.com and 91238 32994.*

11 INDO-PAK WAR - 1971
(As witnessed at a frontline Air Defence Unit)

ML Bountra

This is a personal narrative of happenings before and during the war of the day-to-day activities. It is possible that there could be a mix up of dates in respect of one odd incident.

Introduction

I was posted to 230 SU in May 1970. The unit operated P-30M radar and functioned as Limited Air Defence Direction Center (ADDC) under 501 SU. It could initiate tactical action and order scrambles in its area of responsibility from Pathankot, Adampur and Amritsar air bases.

In March 1971, I took over as S Ops Offr (re-designated as COO). From April onwards, situation in East Pakistan (now Bangladesh) started deteriorating. Though it did not affect us much at that time but a sense of urgency did creep in, as some emergency works like ballast walls and bunkers etc. were initiated and dispersal of sensitive equipment was planned. From mid-October onwards we were put on 24 hours watch and additional AD deployment too commenced. Interaction with a young and enthusiastic officer from a surveillance unit gave us useful information on enemy air to air combat and tactics. He was also instrumental in providing us a limited monitoring facility in our ops room at a later date.

Imminence of Hostilities

One day, during the first week of Nov 71, Air I WAC, came to the Ops Room and queried me about the current situation, intensity and pattern of air activity in GHA (General Hostile Area). He asked me to personally monitor the console and look for any abnormal activity in a specific area of GHA. He sat with me watching the air situation on the console for about an hour and then went back to Delhi. Later on we came to know that one of our aircraft had gone for a PR (Photo Recce) mission and he had come to personally supervise the mission. Thereafter, he would often visit the unit and we would go through the same drill. All these PR sorties were carried out at low levels (100-200 mtrs) with very little radar and RT assistance. On 30th Nov, he again visited the ops room and asked me to use code word 'XXXXX' in case of any unusual activity. This time we picked up a big formation of seven to eight aircraft flying abreast in Pak Pasrur bulge at a height of about 2.5 kms heading south towards Indian border. The SD (Sector Director) on duty scrambled ORP missions and I also transmitted the code word. Immediately, five sections of interceptors popped up close to international border asking for instructions.

It took me a while to identify each section and started guiding ORP mission and another section close to the incoming unknown formation and instructed others to hold position. The unknown formation was intercepted and identified as Indian Su-7s. At this stage, the Air I instructed me to break off and appreciated our response. We at the unit felt bitter that we were not taken into confidence and told him so, but he passed it off lightly and complimented us on our handling of the situation. Next day one Pak F-104 flew over our unit for a photo recee in the afternoon and went back before anyone could react. This aircraft was not picked up on radar but visually seen overflying the unit.

Reporting of Low Flying Aircraft

MOFs (Mobile Observation Flights) were still in formation and being operationalised. Therefore, it was decided to integrate the network of railway stations along the border. Railway Divisional Hqs at Amritsar had a string of stations along the border communicating directly to it. It was decided to train the staff at these stations for reporting low flying activity. Two teams of one Controller and one ADSO each were formed to visit these stations and train the railway staff about the procedures and sequence of reporting. Compass circles were drawn at each location for ease and accurate direction reporting. A cell was created at the communication centre of Railway Div Hqs to pass the info to the Ops room. This network proved very useful especially at nights. Due to effective Op contribution and on our specific recommendations, the

ASM (Assistant Station Master) at Gurdaspur was given a commendation.

Commencement of Hostilities

03rd Dec 71: In the evening I was waiting for my turn at a barber shop when I heard the sound of an aircraft flying overhead. We used to have a CAP of Gnat aircraft at dusk time but the sound did not appear to be that of Gnat. I came out and saw a PAF F-104 heading towards our unit and also heard the sound of firing. Initially, I thought that our AD guns had opened up but then I realised it was the aircraft which was carrying out an attack indicating that war had commenced. Immediately, I rushed home, changed into uniform and drove to the unit in quick time. Most of us were staying in civil areas as AF accommodation was yet to be built.

After reaching the Ops room, I along with CO took a round of the technical area to assess the damage. Luckily, except for a small hole in the top portion of slant aerial of radar, there was no other major damage and we continued to function normally. Watch hours and manning was rearranged. Aerial tilt was adjusted for better pick up on low flying aircraft. We rigged up four speakers in our Ops Room to monitor surveillance inputs. More flying units moved into the sector. Around midnight, war was officially declared by the Prime Minister and IAF was given clearance to strike back with full force. CO briefed me on the top secret Op matters and the role of own strike missions attacking deep inside enemy territory especially during the night. We were to plan and provide advanced warning about availability of recovery bases to these returning strike missions. We used fighter aircraft flying at higher height to act as a relay station. With returning missions on critical fuel configuration, this Sparrow control was a useful method in assisting recoveries.

We were attacked thrice during the night but there was no damage and the bombs fell way off from our unit. After second raid, we decided that AD guns would open fire at night only if there was a proper radar lock-on to avoid giving away the exact location of the VP.

04th Dec 71: Full-fledged operations started from dawn of 04 Dec and strike missions took off and CAPs were mounted on all the bases. Ops room was buzz with activity with controllers detailed for various duties viz. carry out sector scanning on expanded scope to provide cover for our strike missions, to monitor enemy missions, to coordinate with PAD and Ack Ack command posts and for Movement & Identification (M&I) duties. Lack of proper info on own strike missions led to identification problems, dubious air raid warnings and impeded recovery assistance. There were heated exchanges and frayed tempers. It took a little while to smoothen the irritants.

501 SU was attacked in the morning and the search aerial (FPS 100) was damaged. So ours was the only radar available in the sector for next two days. Our unit was also raided thrice, once in the morning and twice in the afternoon but luckily there was no major damage except some minor cables got snapped which were repaired immediately. In the afternoon, a fighter sweep was executed under our control over Lahore to draw out PAF. The fighter carried out two orbits in the area but there was no reaction from the other side.

During the night, Amritsar and Pathankot were raided continuously, Amritsar nearly eight times and Pathankot more than twelve times. The nearest bomb which fell was just about 500 mtrs from the unit in a field and created a crater of nearly 20 ft x 20 ft. Railway network did an excellent job of reporting these raids. In fact we were able to establish a pattern that if a certain Rly Stn reported 'sound heard', the raid would proceed to Pathankot and if the other two specific Rly Stns reported, the raid would be for Amritsar and thus, we were able to alert the respective Ack Ack command posts and PAD staff accordingly.

05th Dec 71: The morning of 05th Dec started with strafing of the unit by two PAF 104 Sabres. By this time we were a little used to such raids and some of us even came out of the offices/ops room to watch the aircraft pull up, align and start firing. Luckily we jumped aside in time to escape getting shot. We cursed ourselves for being so foolish and stupid.

Four aircraft fighter sweep led by the Sqn Cdr, was launched and went well inside the enemy territory in the Pasrur bulge. On return leg when over Gujranwala, the formation leader requested to get down and do an orbit to have a look at his old home town before partition. The controller looked towards me for approval. I told him to let the leader do two orbits instead of one to have a good look. There was no reaction from the PAF.

Two Cat A controllers joined us on attachment. With the shared load we could provide some relief to other controllers.

We were raided again in the afternoon but this time one of the F-104s was hit by the Ack Ack fire and the pilot bailed out close to the FBSU perimeter. The pilot Sqn Ldr Amzad Hussain was captured by locals and was saved from the wrath of the villagers by OC (JW Greene) and another pilot of the Gnat sqn (AK Agtey) who were on their way to mess after ORP duties. As per the narration of the pilot, it was his third attempt to put 230 SU out of action. He had led the first pre-emptive attack on the evening of 03rd Dec and was confident that he had damaged the radar aerial but learnt at night that we were still churning. Next morning (04th Dec) he had carried out a raid over 501 SU and hit their search radar. On the afternoon of same day, he had once again led an attack on our unit but we continued to be operational. As per him there was no problem in sighting our radar from a distance but after pulling up and lining for attack, it would merge with the surrounding area which made exact pinpointing difficult. So, in his third attempt (05 Dec), he had planned to attack at a slower speed but realised that he was too slow.

It was planned to evacuate the PoW to Delhi the same day late in the evening and a Dakota had come to pick him up. When the aircraft lined up for take-off, we got a report of imminent raid over Amritsar. ATC was informed which in turn instructed the aircraft to get back and switched off the runway lights. The officer who was escorting the PoW narrated that the aircraft took off in pitch darkness and they saw flashes of Ack Ack guns all around. The PoW was shocked and screamed 'you guys are mad; I did not bail out to die like this'.

During the night, we picked up a few plots on a track in Pak area heading towards Pasrur and being guided to some target on which we had no pick up. We realised that the PAF fighter was being vectored to one of our strike missions about which we had no information. I instructed my controllers to give blank calls on all available RT channels for the mission to duck down and warn about the approaching enemy interceptor. After about a minute, there was a PAF transmission that pick up on the target was lost as 'the b*****d seems to have ducked down and it was probably a transport aircraft carrying out Para dropping, so the concerned army authorities in the area be warned accordingly'. While we were still trying to get information on this strike mission, we heard a Msn 206 calling our SU and asking if it was safe to climb. After authentication, we asked him to start a gradual climb and a little later picked him heading on the desired course. We learnt afterwards that it was an AN-12 which had gone on a special mission. Incidentally, it turned out that the Capt of AN-12 and I were together at an earlier station and knew each other well.

06th Dec 71: On the night of 6th Dec 71, I was controlling the **'Sparrow'** mission when we heard a PAF interceptor being guided to some target which was reported at 11 O' clock 55 miles. At that time there were four of our strike missions inside Pakistan and none of these was due back for another 25-30 minutes. There was no pick up on any of these aircraft and the PAF interceptor also. I asked 'Sparrow' to transmit this information for the benefit of our strike missions. The PAF interceptor continued to be guided with very precise information about the target. We were wondering why we were not picking up any of these aircraft and manipulated the tilt. When target was reported 30 miles, we picked a track east of Amritsar heading towards the 'Sparrow'. I instantly realised that the PAF interceptor was being guided to attack the 'Sparrow' and immediately instructed him to do a descending turn and put him behind the intruder. He gave a passing contact at 10 kms and started closing in. At that time we heard the PAF interceptor being warned that he had overshot the target and to immediately get down and head back. My fighter lost contact and we also lost radar pick up on the PAF interceptor. Later we came to know that PAF was under the impression that 'Sparrow' was a Russian AWACS and we were using it to guide our night missions to strike deep inside Pakistan. They had planned to eliminate the same.

08 Dec 71: A formation of six aircraft was picked up crossing the bulge and heading towards Pathankot. The CAP over Pathankot was alerted and keeping in view the strength of the raid, CAPs from Adampur and Amritsar were also diverted towards the hostile aircraft under our guidance. As soon as our fighters bounced the Pak formation, they split into three and turned back in three different directions without inflicting any damage. Two of our interceptors got a lock-on but the missiles did not fire. Our Gnat interceptors also made contact but the Mirages engaged reheat and got away.

09-16 Dec71: After 10th Dec 71, PAF was mainly used in defensive role and for close support missions only. They used to mount area patrols for defence of Sargodha complex. One day we monitored that a PAF aircraft had crashed close to the Sargodha base. One of our missions from TACDE had gone there for a recce cum strike mission around that time. I spoke to the pilot who had flown that mission and asked him about the target and whether he had fired his weapons during the sortie. After a little hesitation, he acknowledged that on the return leg he had spotted an aircraft right in front and let go his weapons and continued on his course without checking the damage. I told him about the monitored RT transmission which confirmed the 'KILL'.

A similar incident happened on 13 Dec. We monitored the following conversation of PAF Whisky formation:

> ***Whisky 4: Whisky leader, I see a Gnat.***
> ***Whisky Leader: Go and shoot the hell out of the b*****d.***
> ***Silence for some time.***
> ***Whisky 4: Whisky Leader I have been hit by the Gnat.***
> ***Whisky Leader: Then go and bloody well do an emergency landing at Lahore.***

I checked up with 501 SU and they confirmed that two SU-7 escorted by two Gnats had gone from Halwara for a close support mission in the Ferozepur sector around that time. I contacted the escort leader who narrated that after firing at the Sabre for about a second, his guns got jammed and he was not sure whether the Sabre was damaged or not. I told him about the monitored transmission and also sent a transcript of the same for confirmation. (All the above incidents including interception of 'Sparrow' being considered an AWACS were confirmed later by two Bangladeshi controllers who were deployed at Sakesar Air Defence Centre and later escaped from Pakistan.)

During all these days, the unit controllers continued to provide cover to almost each and every close air support and strike mission in the sector.

16 Dec 71: Pakistan Army in East Pakistan surrendered and cease fire was ordered in the Eastern Sector.

17 Dec 71: After the declaration of cease fire in the Eastern Sector, it was expected that soon it will be declared in Western Sector also. As a last minute push, a number of strike missions were launched to inflict maximum damage. Lahore was raided repeatedly, and large amount of ammo was dropped in a matter of few hours creating extensive damage.

As mentioned earlier, PAF used to mount patrols for defence of Sargodha complex. The distance, pattern and duration of each patrol was studied and calculated. A pop up interception was planned to attack the patrol when it would be about to take a turn. The formation leader was briefed thoroughly by a senior controller about the course, duration and time to pop up. It was expected that when the mission commenced the pull up, the target would be 12 O'clock 8-10 kms. The interceptors were to fire missiles and get back. In no case they were to get into a dog fight. The interception went perfectly as planned and the pilots gave contact at 8 kms just when they popped up. The leader was again instructed to fire missiles and get back, but unfortunately, they got into a dog fight with Sabres and No 2 was hit and had to bail out. Immediately, we heard the transmission of the Pak pilot that he has shot down a MiG 21. The pilot was so excited that he kept repeating the same nearly 10 times. After landing, the leader explained that they were so advantageously positioned that he did not want to take chance with missiles as these had not functioned properly a number of times earlier. He wanted to engage the Sabres with guns but they were out maneuvered during the turns. This was a case of a perfectly planned and executed interception which went awry due to other factors.

Cease fire was declared in the evening and the hostilities came to an end and I went home for the first time after the commencement of war.

Ours was one of the first units visited by CAS Air Chief Marshal PC Lal immediately after the cease fire. He congratulated the personnel and lauded the performance of the unit remarking that a small unit had achieved a great feat.

Veteran Gp Capt ML Bountra *was commissioned in the Adm Branch on 16 Dec 1961. Immediately after commissioning he was detailed to undergo the Fighter Controllers' course. He is a Cat A controller who had participated in the 1965 and 1971 wars. During the 1971 war, he was the Senior Operations Officer at 230 SU. He has vast experience as a controller with more than 8000 Practice Interceptions including 40 Live missions. He is the recipient of CAS commendation and was awarded "Mention in Despatches" during the 1971 war. He lives in Noida and is available on mlbountra@hotmail.com and 9811728545.*

12 Fairchild Packets in 1971 War

Shomir Choudhuri

For us the "Air Transport Support" and "Casevac" role for the 1971 War started on 27 Mar 1971, a day after the unilateral declaration of independence by Bangobandhu Mujib-ur-Rahman, which stretched almost every day to over nine months. I cannot compress all the incidents but can only highlight a few memorable ones.

Background: 1971: The height of Naxal trouble in the then Calcutta and surroundings and CPI cadres on the loose made travel in the city and suburbs dangerous. This intertwined with the need to provide air transport support to the Mukti Bahini in conjunction with the Army at Fort William fell upon 48 Sqn Packet aircraft to airlift a minimum of 75 tonnes per month of ordinance and other stores and men into Agartala from Calcutta. The Packet aircraft or C119G is non pressurised, did not have a weather radar and required special fuel 115/145. This fuel was available only at Dumdum, Bagdogra, and Gauhati and with a 5-tonne payload endurance did not permit a round trip. Therefore, it had to be refuelled at Gauhati or Bagdogra on the way back. At times, we had night halt also after refuelling. This info is necessary for an incident that will follow in the article.

OPS Plan: The CO decided to base one aircraft at Dumdum where the new terminal building (now junked) was just completed but unoccupied and could house the ground crew to service the kite for early morning take off as the weather later invariably packed up. Aircrew accommodation and transport from Barrackpore was a tiring 90-minute ride in a dilapidated 3-tonner. As a Squadron Captain belonging to Kolkata, I was detailed to operate throughout this period with replacement aircraft flown in from base whenever my aircraft was due for servicing or became unserviceable. This suited me fine. I shifted my wife also to Calcutta as she was carrying our second born. My scooter helped me commute. At times, the Co-Pilot or Nav took a ride with me and stayed with us.

Incident 1: The high twin booms and the rear clam shell doors of Packets open up to permit loading direct from an Army 3-tonner backed up. One careless driver ignored the directions given by the airman load supervisor and bumped into the fiberglass skids below the boom and damaged it. As a Captain, I had no option but to abort the sortie and seek a C of I. Frantic requests from the Army that the stores included weapons and ammunition and are urgently required could not move me. Those days there were no cell phones but the DQ from Fort William wanted to talk to me on the landline. He said, "Major Nandwani DQ". The name rang a bell and I interjected, "CQMS Kilo Sqn 20th NDA Sir?" "Yes, who are you." Flt Lt Shomir Choudhuri, 24th Kilo Sqn...I will take the stores but when I come back a day later and order the C of I, your driver should say that it happened today and not earlier." "Agreed, but please make sure that the stores reach Agartala today ". That was the trust and camaraderie we developed at NDA!

Incident 2: A Mukti Bahini Sector Cdr, Maj Khalek Musharaf had been hit by grenade shrapnel and required brain surgery at the Army Hospital, Lucknow, and I was ordered to pick him up and land at Bakshi-ka-Talab. I landed him with four Mukti Bahini escorts at 2 am. He recovered, joined the war effort and was decorated. After liberation, he rose to the rank of Maj Gen, was very close to PM Mujib-ur-Rahman but was annihilated during the purge. Years later in 1990, as a businessman, I was with the President of the Arab Bangladesh Bank for a loan when in walked Md Saidul Islam who was introduced to me as a freedom fighter under Khalek Musharaf. The Casevac topic came up and he tested me, "What time did you land him?" After my reply he hugged me and said he was one of the four escorts in my plane. Small world!

Incident 3: To blockade Chittagong and other harbours, the Navy wanted 4/5 tonnes of limpet mines airlifted from Mumbai to Agartala.

These mines are prohibited cargo in service aircraft (I was told they explode on contact). So I was recalled to Base and the CO offered to send another bachelor captain, since I was a family man. My arguments prevailed and I completed the task. Satisfaction...news came some weeks later...our Naval frogmen were able to scuttle ships at Chittagong harbour and render them inoperative.

Incident 4: The day after our Gnats ex Dumdum shot down two Sabres in Nov 1971, we landed as usual at Agartala. While unloading was going on, many airmen and Army jawans wailed that they had sneaked their families in and had no way to send them back, and war was looming. They requested me to take them to Dumdum. Both the return sortie refuelling stops were with duty crew in AF Stations and 70-plus ladies and children could not be hidden as the refuelling crew had to climb on the wing through the cabin and cockpit. One report and court martial was for sure! The crew also pleaded and my calculations showed that if we cut corners over Bangladesh at two places, we might just about make it to Dumdum. So we did. In those days, communication was limited to crackling HF and short range VHF. Just reported to Gauhati that bad weather was enroute so diverting to Bagdogra and then diverting to Dumdum. With fuel gauges almost empty when we landed there, one engine stopped. It was a civil aerodrome. So all the ladies and children walked away safely without anyone knowing as to who they were. Maybe some veterans reading this may connect now.

All through the monsoon we flew without radar until the task was completed. Fond memories.

An IAF tradition then: In peacetime, aircrew van would pick up the crew first and the Captain last. However, during emergency times, the Captain was first and then you collected the rest. I have shared this at management schools that there is no better test of leadership when the Captain, looking into the eyes of a young wife of an airman, with two small children, gives her the confidence that you will bring her husband back home safe. Not sure if this tradition still exists.

To conclude, our Packet instructor repeatedly stressed to handle the aircraft gently and lovingly since it was the only one with C in front and G behind, and "she won't let you down" ...no wonder it had been nicknamed "the flying coffin". I survived nine years and 3,700 hours to pen down these lines.

Veteran Wg Cdr Shomir Choudhuri *was commissioned in the Flying Branch on 18 April 1964. He actively participated in the 1971 war as a part of the Packet crew. He was based at Dumdum as a part of the Packet Dett. Keeping in mind the need of the hour and the urgent operational commitments at hand, he took certain daring decisions to ensure that the operations went unhindered. He is a recipient of VSM. He took premature retirement in the year 1984 and is now settled at Kolkata. He can be reached at shomirc1@gmail.com and 9433077188.*

13 INS Vikrant and the Air Force Avros

Akash Kumar Dutta

The Background

During the period 1970 to 1973, I was on the posted strength of NSS (Navigators and Signalers School), Begumpeth in Secunderabad after my conversion as Radio Tech-1. I was an LAC then. Training activities for navigators and signallers were being carried out with two Dakota aircraft at that time. I did not have any problem with maintenance of Dakota since experienced technicians were there to guide new persons like me. But Dakotas were getting replaced. Two Avros aircraft arrived in a short while. These were new to all of us. Experienced technicians were not available initially. Service manuals were the only hope for us till we received formal training. For me that also did not take place. That is another story which follows.

Training on Avros

Towards the end of October 1971, our training programmes were made. One aircraft with first batch of ten technicians left for training at Palam air base. CTO Sqn Ldr KC Gangopadhyay accompanied the team. I was scheduled in the second batch. After about ten days the second batch with about similar number of technicians left for Palam in the other aircraft. The first aircraft came back the same day. Captain of our aircraft Sqn Ldr Pedgaokar and other crew members took off from Begumpeth with all of us on board. Our CTO Sqn Ldr KC Gangopadhyay, who had come back from Palam earlier joined us again. Flight took off. I quickly got settled in one of the training stations. As the plane gained height I kept my eyes glued to the abundance of clouds of different shapes, sizes and hue. My joy had no bound with first ever flying experience. Fragrance of a new aircraft was a thing of life time memory for me. Throughout the journey I kept looking outside.

Darkness had already descended when we landed at Palam airport. We were taken to an almost near-abandoned transit block at Palam. It was a huge building, not being maintained regularly. Inside,it was dark too. No bulbs were glowing but we managed with candles that our senior team member Cpl Tripathy had carried with him. Fans were not working but that did not matter a bit since November night in Palam was cool enough to do without fan. However, we got settled without much of difficulty. Late in the evening our Captain and CTO came to see if we were settled properly. They saw things but did not say much. Next day when we came back during lunch break, we found everything in order i.e. all fans were working, lights were glowing, charpoys were debugged and rooms cleaned.

We finished our dinner and started discussing our schedule for the next day before going off to sleep. Around 1 am we were dislodged from our beds by none other than our Captain, CTO and other crew members. Before we could realise what was happening, our beds were rolled up, holdalls tightened and we were made to slip inside our khakis. The captain, CTO and other officers started picking up our luggage before we could reach them. Out on the road Air Force bus was roaring in the cool and quiet night. Driver sat alert on his seat with hands on steering. Off we started. The entire episode may not have taken more than ten minutes. Our training program ended before starting. Soon we were on board Avro and headed towards Begumpeth. Had the war been declared? We kept on guessing until we were told that we were going back to our base to remain stand by to move to some location at a very short notice. Thank God, at least one batch had completed the training.

In Support of Indian Navy

Towards the end of November or early December 1971 we moved to Naval Base at Vizac. We were accommodated in tents. We were to walk quite some good distance to reach for toilet and bath. However, we were comforted by our naval counterparts. They generously invited us to use their toilets, which were very close to our tents and also well maintained. We went for dinner with the anticipation of dal-ricechapati-samber-mutton combo; but were surprised with mug full of soup and few loaves of bread. They called it supper. We were surprised initially but soon got used to the system.

After supper our Navy friends used to come to our tents. We learnt a lot about life in waters, about ships, submarines, cruisers etc. We learnt a lot about INS Vikrant. We were praying for our luck to get an opportunity to step inside the gorgeous, unbeatable hero of waters, the one and only one INS Vikrant.

Our avros were deployed to carry out reconnaissance operation over Bay of Bengal to identify intruders, probably PNS Ghazi. Aim was to protect our ace carrier INS Vikrant from enemy attack. INS Vikrant was to work in close co-ordination with IAF to support our air strikes from eastern air bases to keep East Pakistan (now Bangladesh) air bases inoperative at all times, thus isolating East Pakistan. This was achieved jointly by IAF and INS. Presence of INS Vikrant enhanced our victory, as a Navy officer described later. To keep pace with the requirement, we needed to do our maintenance work in odd hours very often.

The war was on. Our daily roster was changing as per need of the hour. News bulletins on radio became the main source of information about war proceedings. Suddenly, one day (don't remember the date now) a very exciting news came. PNS Ghazi was drowned. The Pakistani Submarine was drowned while making a foray into the Bay of Bengal to reach INS Vikrant. It fell victim to depth charge carried out by our destroyer INS Rajput. INS Vikrant's safety was our task. So we felt jubilant. There was an air of victory all around.

Why destruction of PNS Ghazi gave us a sense of victory? A Naval officer described it is to us on a later occasion. I will try to put it from my 50 years old memory.

Pakistan realised that victory wouldn't be possible as long as INS Vikrant guarded Bay of Bengal. Knowing pretty well about its sophistication and striking power, they desperately wanted to get rid of INS Vikrant. PNS Ghazi, the US ship was the best bet for them. Ghazi had proven its worth during the 1965 Indo-Pak war. So Pakistan deployed PNS Ghazi for this task this time also. PNS Ghazi had two tasks to carry out. To destroy INS Vikrant and lay mines along the sea bed, whether destroyed Vikrant or not. PNS Ghazi was drowned with 90 Pakistani sailors on board.

A Trip onboard INS Vikrant

We continued with our operation over Bay of Bengal until the war was declared over. Naval authorities at Vizag awarded us with a life time gift for successfully completing our task. We finished our breakfast a bit early. Navy bus was waiting for us. We reached the dock as per schedule. A cruiser took us to INS Vikrant. Vast expanse of sea or wide spread war dock or anything worthy of catching attention became unimportant as soon as we stepped inside our great pride INS Vikrant. It stood authoritatively with its vastness and elegance. Water was calm and limitless. Sky above was clear and blue. Atmosphere appeared peaceful. One could not believe that only few days back the vast blue canopy over Bay of Bengal was torn apart ruthlessly by IAF fighters and bombers. INS Vikrant the hero of 1971 war strolled over Bay of Bengal majestically causing turbulence in the otherwise calm waters. We were totally drawn towards INS Vikrant's interior since we knew that this was the only opportunity, if lost would never come our way again. Everything inside looked new and challenging to us. They explained to us a lot, we grabbed very little. More than what we wanted to know, we wanted to feel. From the deck of INS Vikrant I saw calm water of Bay of Bengal. I saw clear blue sky above, spread like a huge canopy. I saw at a distance the humble sky bowing down to embrace the calmness of water of Bay of Bengal. Was it a message of 'end of war'? Was it a message of eternal peace for our Holy Earth?

We stayed there for over two hours and left for our next destination. PNS Ghazi, the Pakistani Hero was lying in silence but could not hide its presence. Long strip of diesel on surface was evidence of death of PNS Ghazi, the Pakistani Hero of 1965 Indo-Pak war. PNS Ghazi was lying dead with 90 Pakistani sailors on board. Life jackets were spotted by fishermen and brought to the notice of the Naval authorities; we were told. Officer who took us to the site explained a lot about the submarine PNS Ghazi.

We uttered every single word about PNS Ghazi with due respect that the Pakistani war hero deserved.

We saluted the 'Dead Heroes of Pakistan' before our departure.

Jai Hind

Veteran Sgt Akash Kumar Dutta *was enrolled in the Telecom Tech-1 trade on 12 July 1965 Subsequently, he went through a conversion training to become Radio Tech 1. During the 1971 war, as a young LAC, he was on the posted strength of NSS, Begumpeth. He served in the Air Force for 18 years and retired on 01 Aug 1983. He is now settled at Kolkata and can be reached at aakash46@gmail.com and 9937007073.*

14 A Squirrel's Contribution

AK Goswami

The Young Pilot Officer

On 03rd Dec 1971, I was working in the Equipment Branch (later renamed Logistics) of the IAF and had all of 11 months and 8 days of commissioned service to my credit. As a young Pilot Officer, I was supposed to be only seen and not heard. I did whatever my seniors ordered me to do. Yet, I had the satisfaction of contributing my wee bit to that magnificent 1971 War involving the entire Nation.

On 01st Jan 1971, I was posted directly from the AFAC to a forward stock holding unit in the Eastern Sector. All the operational bases depended on us for logistics support. By the time I joined the unit, war preparations were going on in full swing. The first task I was assigned was to check the entire stock of equipment and spares held by our unit and tally them accurately with the stock-holding records. We were a team specially designated for this task. Simultaneously, wherever reserves were short, we had to raise IOR demands on the respective mother depots. This exercise, successfully completed, ensured that we would not run short of stocks at the time of actual hostilities.

Logistics Support

A Logistics Control Centre was established in Air Headquarters, New Delhi. It had records of holding and locations of all equipment, stores and spares in the entire Air Force. Air Headquarters had created an intricate system like the Speed Post Service of the P & T Department, to rush equipment and spares from one corner of the country to another at the earliest where it was required. A tremendous volume of energy was pumped into the whole system. A fleet of Dakota aircraft was dedicated to this 'courier' service. They would cover the whole of India flying from one unit to another picking up items and delivering them to a central point at Nagpur. As a result, stores meant for the Eastern

Sector would be segregated and delivered to Gauhati (later renamed Guwahati) airport. Whenever the stocks arrived at Gauhati, we had to rush our trucks to pick them up and take them on charge.

A fleet of Class 1 trucks was earmarked for delivering equipment and spares in the quickest possible time to operational units. The allocation of stores to different flying units under the EAC used to come in encrypted signals. When such a signal was received in the Signal section, we would be summoned to go to a highly secured cryptographer's room and quickly decode them in plain language, irrespective of the time of day or night. The decoded signal would then be rushed to the Demand Control Office (DCO).

The DCO would raise demands on behalf of the unit concerned and pass those vouchers on to the Stock Control Office (SCO). After verifying the stock, the SCO would forward the approved demand vouchers to the related stockholding site. The site, in turn, would take out the items and forward them to the Transportation section, where they would be packed and made ready for dispatch. By that time, a truck would arrive there to receive the items along with vouchers and gate pass, it would head for the consumer unit right away, irrespective of the volume/dimension of the store or distance involved. This work would go on day and night. With such an energetic and all-out effort, all the Stations under EAC continued to receive robust logistic support. For example, a spare part lying in Yelahanka, Bangalore, would reach Jorhat in the minimum possible time for immediate use to push up the serviceability state of the aircraft held there.

Those days the local markets in the Eastern Sector were neither well-stocked nor were there industries worth the name to manufacture items required by us. Air Headquarters would authorise us to locally purchase stores from the Calcutta (later renamed Kolkata) market. I belonged to Calcutta and knew the place well. Therefore, my Commanding Officer sent me a couple of times to Calcutta. The urgency was such that he would authorise me to travel by civil airlines to do local purchase of urgently required stores for stocking up. The windfall opportunity of staying with my parents at home for a day or two was a big bonus for me.

Challenges and Thrills

Sometimes some unusual situation would crop up leading to serious tension. For example, in a hired civilian truck we had loaded 1000-lb bombs to its full capacity and dispatched it to a fighter/bomber base. Shortly we received an SOS message from the escort with the truck. He informed us that in the hill section enroute, the heavy bombs had rolled over to one side of the truck. As a result, it had tilted dangerously and was hanging on the brink of a deep precipice, threatening to topple into the forested valley below. We left everything and rushed there with wooden logs, sisal ropes, pulleys, crowbars and whatever equipment we could lay our hands on. Fortunately, we could rescue the truck and it resumed its journey with more caution.

The IAF devised an innovative method of carpet-bombing enemy positions by dropping AN-12 loads of napalm bombs. The incendiary semi-liquid used in the napalm bombs was manufactured in our unit. A large mixing machine was erected in a vacated scooter garage. The volatile semi-liquid sticky material was produced by mixing petroleum with other inflammable ingredients. It looked exactly like fresh jaggery. We nicknamed the device a 'Gur Making Machine'. Technicians would fill the semi-liquid stuff into drums locally purchased by me from Calcutta and send them to operational Wings. In the flying units, the armament guys would fill up large bomb-like metal containers with the petroleum jelly to prepare napalm bombs for dropping by AN-12 aircraft, specially modified for the purpose.

In addition, we used to take part in Passive Air Defence at night. This was done to prepare us to protect our unit against enemy saboteurs/paratroopers who could sneak in through the miles of the barbed-wired periphery. The area was full of uneven land covered with thick growth of elephant grass and treacherous marshy land infested by insects and snakes. Thus, we used to be on duty at night as well. When the war was declared, the Army moved in to take over the defence responsibility of our unit. We were thankfully relieved.

In the Officers' Mess, only one officer possessed a transistor radio. I still remember the brand. It was Telefunken. All of us would huddle around it to hear the newscast on the progress of the War. On 16th Dec

1971, Pakistan surrendered. An impromptu victory party was organised in our unit.

My Miniscule Part

Those were heady days. I was a minuscule part of a massive war effort. It could be well compared with the mythological squirrel of the Ramayana. When Shri Ramchandra's Banar (monkey) Sena headed by Shri Hanuman and Jamboban were dropping huge boulders into the Indian Ocean to build a bridge to cross over to Ravana's kingdom, Lanka, Shri Ram noticed that a squirrel was continuously wetting itself, picking up sand on its wet body by rolling on the beach and then dusting the sand off on the bridge under construction. Shri Ram Chandra was surprised and asked the Squirrel as to what he was doing. It replied that it was trying to fill the gaps between big stones. Shri Ramachandra appreciated the squirrel's dedication by gifting stripes on its back.

Our unit received accolades from the higher-ups for providing excellent support to the flying Wings. We were greatly encouraged as a team. For the young officers like us, the appreciation was as good as the stripes on the back of the squirrel. However, we were personally proud to have been entitled to hang the Poorvi Star Medal and General Service Medal on our uniforms on the right side of our chests at a relatively young age. Those medals are still with me.

Veteran Wg Cdr Amit Kumar Goswami *was commissioned in the Logistics Branch on 26 Dec 1970. He was a young Pilot Officer with just one year of service during the 1971 war. He served a pivotal role during the war in the stores management especially the movement of AOG items to the operational bases. He is presently engaged in writing and publishing books. He has three books to his credit. He is based at Noida and can be reached at authorgoswami@gmail.com and 9810559543.*

15 Modification to the Electric Plug: My Little Contribution

Shanti Kumar Jain

I was commissioned in the IAF on 04 Jul 1966 soon after completing my M Tech from IIT Bombay. After completing my abinitio course training at AFTC on 03 Dec 1967, I was posted to 16 Sqn at 17 Wing AF. During the period upto 1971, I had gained sufficient experience on a number of systems including Canberra aircraft, on which I had done MCF at 4 Wg AF.

1971 War

In Jun 1971, I was posted to 4 Wing AF from 16 Sqn AF. However, my CO took up the case for cancellation of my posting. At the same time CTO of 4 Wing was pressing for my reporting. Finally, I was relieved in Sep 71 to move to 4 Wing. After reaching 4 Wing I was detailed to undergo a course at 505 SU. The course was suddenly ceased in Nov 71 and all trainees were asked to report back to their respective parent units. On reporting back I was asked to work in 5 Sqn AF due to my previous experience on Canberra aircraft. Hectic activities in the Sqn started. I, as O i/c DSS, was tasked to ensure maximum serviceability of aircraft and to follow up on AOG demands. On 3rd Dec 1971, the war finally broke out. During the initial bombing missions assigned to our Squadron it was found that a large percentage of bombs could not be released and it was a matter of concern for Air HQs. An Air HQ team comprising of Air Cmde Singha and Wg Cdr K Balakrishnan, DD Aeronautics, Ministry of Defence was tasked to study the cause and suggest remedial measures at the earliest. On detailed study and investigation, it was concluded that the cause of hang-up of bombs was due to a faulty electric plug in the bomb carriers.

The Suggested Mod

I, on my part also studied the system and suggested certain remedial innovative measures to solve the problem. Keeping the urgency of operations in mind and also the non availability of plugs for replacement, I had to think of an alternate solution.

While discussing the technical issues I suggested locking of the plug and socket with a collar fitting on the plug with locking wire. This involved de-soldering of wires in the plug of every carrier. It was not feasible due to the urgency at hand. I then offered to make a specimen wooden collar in the workshop which would obviate the need to de-solder and re-solder wires in the plug. This was done by cutting the collar into two halves and joining the halves around the cable.

This contraption, though simple looking, effectively made launching of successful offensive operations possible during the war. I perfected the modification/contraption which worked very satisfactorily and the IAF was able to launch effective offensive operations. This fact has been well documented by HQ CAC.* Subsequently all other bases operating Canberras were instructed to incorporate the same modification. That was my small contribution to the 1971 War which helped in successful dropping of the bombs.

*Note: The Author had supported this fact with a letter which was issued on the subject by HQ CAC, IAF. As the letter is 50 years old, the same was not quite legible. Therefore, the same has not been attached here with the article.

Veteran Wg Cdr SK Jain *was commissioned in the Aeronautical Engineering Branch on 04 July 1966. During the 1971 war, he was on the posted strength of 4 Wing, AF. He actively participated in the war and was instrumental in designing a modification which resolved the issue of bomb hang ups in the Canberra aircraft. He served in the Air Force for 27 years and retired on 31 August 1993. He is a certified Lead Assessor for ISO 9001 certification. Post his retirement he worked as a consultant with NSTL Vizag and GE. He is now settled at Hyderabad and can be reached at shanti_kjain@yahoo.co.in and 9885190238.*

16 MEMOIRS - 1971 WAR

Parvez Jamasji

I was commissioned in Oct 1965 as a Helicopter Pilot. Before the war, I had served in 111 HU and 115 HU as a helicopter pilot and gained experience by operations during the Mizo insurgency of 1966-1967.

On 20 July 1971, I was deputed to the ARC (Aviation Research Centre). Being deputed there and working with the "Special Frontier Force" (SFF) in itself meant that we would probably be the first to enter East Pakistan. Thus, our preparation had begun in September 1971 with our first task being Hi and Lo recce of the Western borders of Mizoram. The main aim was to get orientated and to know the area like the back of our hands, including memorising peaks, topography, and variation in height of the topography. This knowledge would be our 'saviour' during ingress and returning. This then graduated into further ingress into enemy territory for recce and planning future drop zones.

Our next job was trial and error with armaments and reinforcing our Mi-4s. We had to derive the best permutation combination between carrying men and armaments for the chopper and chopper armour protection.

It was also clear that most, if not all, missions would have a solo pilot, especially in the initial days of ingress. This made me more conscientious as any miscalculation or error would give away our strategies that were shrouded in secrecy. We also made it clear to our superiors within the ARC and SFF to convey to the IAF hierarchy that flying within service-laid down rules would not be possible if our planning was to be put in play. We were told to try and stay as close as possible to the laid down flying rules but keeping in mind that the operational requirements were paramount. We were also known to fly in civvies at times and at times in uniform with a laid down excuse of straying from Mizoram air space by mistake in case of capture.

Being a solo pilot ferrying troops, added a sort of an extra challenge, as their survival would depend on my evading radars and ground fire while their own mission would depend on safe ingress and dropping without being detected. Being detected on my return flight path would also mean that I could have endangered the ground troops that I had just dropped.

Thus, I had the responsibility of the troops of the Special Frontier Force in a way.

First Ingress

My First ingress to East Pakistan was on 30 October 1971. We were using 1/2" and 1/2 million maps of West Mizo and East Pakistan. As we progressed, we learnt and improvised on many things; the ratio between troop weight to chopper, armament to chopper. Escape routes were studied and even recceed. In some missions, armament for the chopper was substituted with better protection against ground fire. Sand bags were strapped as armour protection too. We set up field hospitals and infrastructure in appropriate places along the mountains. Each step forward was paralleled with setting up infrastructures as safe havens in case of problems. Air and ground crew sleeping quarters were cut into the hillside.

War Declared

Once war was officially declared, there was not a single day where I was not ingressing into East Pakistan. The operations involved using every inch of space within the chopper and maximising the weight lifted. All flights were with me as a single pilot ferrying troops of the Special Frontier Force and medi-evacuating the injured. Our drop and pick up zones were marked with coloured flags. Troop dislodging was conducted with the chopper moving slowly on nose wheels on the ground. Drop and pick times were minimised and takeoffs were with max power to avoid enemy troops realising the location of drop/pick-up zones and to be out of range of small arms fire and mortars, with a full load of injured soldiers from within the enemy territory.

Hit

Counting bullet holes on the chopper was an initial pastime that faded away as operations began becoming more and more aggressive. The words of Gen S Uban of the SFF written on my VrC recommendations are: ***"This Officer brought back his helicopter with bullet holes every time. This officer's cool courage was a source of inspiration to others".***

From 30 Oct 71 to 10 Dec 71, I was lucky not to be bodily hit but ground fire made its mark on 11 Dec 71. A shrapnel from one of the guns pierced my leg. Luckily, it missed the bone and made a clear exit wound on the other side of the calf. While I felt a pain in my leg throughout the flight, I realised that I had been hit only when I removed overall that was stuck to my leg with blood. The makeshift field hospital had a nice civilian doctor working for the ARC and he patched me up all through the night for me to be fit to fly the next day.

A flight that will always be etched in my mind

It was then, to keep the motivation high, Maj Gen SS Uban himself accompanied me on a mission into East Pak. Talking about the mission, he wrote:

> ***"I personally accompanied this brave officer to show him that his life was as precious to me as my own."***

That flight as a young Flt Lt will always remain etched in my mind as the fact of having on board the Head of "Force 22" on an operational war mission has its own peculiar importance.

Post War

The war over, I visited my family on 10 Jan 1972 whom I had last seen in September 1971. I remained deputed to the ARC until 1973 to fly into Bangladesh often. I had the privilege not only to channelise East Pakistan into Bangladesh but also play my role as a pilot of the IAF deputed to the ARC to aid the new country in its early days.

Veteran Wg Cdr Parvez Jamasji *was commissioned in the Flying Branch on 16 Oct 1965. He participated actively in the 1971 war. He was a part of the Special Frontier Force which had only one helicopter on its strength which was manned by him. During the 1971 operations his helicopter was hit on four occasions. He had an engine failure also on one of the occasions while flying over the enemy territory. On all the occasions he brought back the helicopter safely. He displayed gallantry and devotion to duty of a very high order. He was awarded a Vir Chakra during the war. He retired from the IAF in 1985. He is now settled in Mumbai and can be reached at rustomjam@yahoo.com and 9833241037.*

17 1971 War Experiences

Suresh Damodar Karnik

Canberras in the 1971 War

We were operating Canberra aircraft (both Bomber and Interdictor role). As a Flight Commander, I was responsible for planning and execution of operations in the Eastern Sector and the other Flight Commander was responsible for the Western Sector under the Squadron Commander.

Some Interesting Missions

Mission 1: On 3rd December 1971, in the evening at about 2000 hrs, we got orders to carry out offensive missions as war had been declared. Accordingly, four aircraft aircrew were detailed by me and the ground crew (Engineering Officers + Technical Airmen) were ordered to prepare the aircraft with appropriate ammunition, viz., each to be loaded with eight 1,000 pound bombs. We took off at about 0000 hrs midnight led by me for targets in East Pakistan, which was Kurmitola Air Force Base. Having reached there, we dropped our bombs on the targets. It is interesting to note that my aircraft had developed a snag on the ground itself before take-off in that one of the two generators was non-functional; yet, I took off with only one functional generator that was against Flight Safety Rules, more so, since it was night and one generator might not have taken the load. This was an exceptional decision in itself.

Mission 2: In another mission, we were four aircraft led by me, for the target, which was Chittagong airfield that was heavily defended. This was a daylight mission. We took off at around 1400 hrs when one of the aircraft had to abort the mission due to a technical snag developed in Indian Territory itself. Hence, the remaining three continued with the mission. On reaching the target, we were subjected to a barrage of anti-aircraft firing from the ground. However, I did not deter, but continued in the bombing raid and destroyed a large POL (Petrol Oil Lubricant) Bulk Installation. This was recorded on the wide-angle camera fitted on the aircraft, which operated automatically once the bomb doors are opened for the bombing run. Additionally, this was also observed by the other aircraft. However, due to the heavy firing by the ground anti-aircraft guns, one of our aircraft had to drop its bombs away from the intended target. The third aircraft could not drop any bomb and had to return to Kalaikunda due to heavy ground fire by ack-ack guns.

Mission 3 - A real daring one: In yet another mission in East Pakistan, I detailed myself to undertake a single aircraft daylight mission, the targets being the gunboats operating on the Meghna river ferrying Pakistani troops from the West to the East to augment the ground forces at Dacca to ensure that it did not fall into Indian hands. In this mission, I destroyed about 7-8 gunboats each carrying about 30 enemy soldiers with their equipment consisting of LMGs and MMGs. While they were firing at me, I was firing at them with my rockets (T-10) and four front guns (20-mm calibre) which was recorded by my front camera automatically. In the process, my aircraft was hit resulting in malfunctioning of the main compass and altimeter. In order to give a false impression of ending my firing, I steered west and flew about 50 km away from the battle zone and did a left semi circle and this time changed my attack direction keeping the sun at my back and once again carried out a couple of surprise attacks on the gunboats. As the enemy could not see my aircraft because of the sun in their eyes, I got the maximum 'Kills'. I then returned to Dum Dum Airfield where I requested for a priority landing as I was running short of fuel. This was refused as the famous 'Tangail Operations' was in progress and the airfield was saturated. I told the controller that as I am short of fuel, I am coming overhead and bailing out. Immediately, he consulted the Army Operations Room whereupon I was allowed to land.

A Daring Flight Back to Base

On inspection, the ground engineers told me that the aircraft had been damaged by bullet holes at a number of places that could not be counted, as it was dark by then. They advised me that it would take at least four days for the aircraft to be airworthy. Additionally, I realised I would be non-functional until I got back to my parent base (Gorakhpur). I instructed the ground engineers to get the aircraft refuelled and let me know if there was any leakage. When they told me that it has been fully refuelled with no leakage, I contacted the radar units via telephone hotlines informing them that I am taking off to proceed to Gorakhpur and I required total help in guiding me as I was blind in the air without my main compass and altimeter. Additionally, my aircraft had bullet holes and might not be aerodynamically fully stable. More so, since it was in night hours, the requirement of radar guidance was much more. I took off notwithstanding the negatives of undertaking the risky flight. Fortunately/Mercifully, I landed at Gorakhpur safely.

Mission 4: Having gained air superiority in the East, I participated in offensive missions in the West. One such mission was a single aircraft bombing attack at night over Murid Operational Frontline Pakistan Air Force Base in West Pakistan. I took off from Gorakhpur and proceeded to Chandigarh for a refuelling halt. Thereafter, I routed via Batala near the border in Indian Territory where the IAF had installed a rotating beacon to guide us to exit accurately from our territory into enemy territory. On entering West Pakistan, my route was over Dab airfield in Punjab, which was non-functional. However, on entering Dab, there was a barrage of ground fire by anti-aircraft guns, which was unexpected. This airfield had been activated by Pak just a day earlier, which our intelligence was unaware of. I dived to about 100 feet so that the anti-aircraft guns could not be lowered to less than 30 degrees to target me, as they would then be firing at each other. Luckily, I got away without hitting any microwave towers. I proceeded towards Murid and on the bombing run, dropped the bombs on the runway/ airfield area. Earlier, before take-off, I had ensured that all the bombs were fitted with delayed fuses, which would explode at various random timings varying from 3 minutes to 12 hours. Therefore, the enemy defusing teams would be unable to render them ineffective. By then, I would have left the target area and their air defence radar would have picked me up on their screen and activated their night capability aircraft to chase me. I got an audio signal fitted on my tail (called Orange Putter). Simultaneously, I got a relay message from our Experimental Wireless

Units located on our border to warn me about two F-104 aircraft chasing me. I changed my direction, and instead of flying east, turned north towards the Himalayas and descended low so that the enemy missile radar could not locate me due to the ground clutter on their screen by which time I had already entered the valleys of the Himalayan Range. Thus, they had to call off the chase due to their limited fuel. My bomber aircraft carried much more fuel. I turned towards Chandigarh, landed safely there, and after refuelling, returned to Gorakhpur.

Mission 5: Another night operational sortie was to West Pakistan where my target was enemy armoured tanks that were harassing the Indian Army in Khemkharan sector during the day but were unseen at night. Actually, those tanks, as per our intelligence, were hiding in Changia–Mangia forest for cover at Kurianwala village in West Pakistan where their Sui gas plant was located. Having located the area where the Tanks would be hiding, I carried out area bombing somewhat blindly. I dropped the bombs and turned towards India when I realised that one 1,000-pound bomb was stuck under the wing and not dropping. I tried a number of others methods to open the lug holding the bomb, i.e., via standby electrical supply, manually, and subjecting the aircraft to violent shaking in the hope that the lug would open and release the bomb, but, every effort failed. I returned eastward towards Gorakhpur. About 40 km from the base, I once again (half-heartedly) shook the aircraft whereupon the bomb was released and landed about 2 km from a village in a field and exploded. Luckily, no damage was reported.

Recognition and Awards

In the year 1990, the Maharashtra Govt conferred on me the 'Maharashtra Gaurav Puraskar' for lifetime noteworthy service to the nation beyond the call of duty as a citizen.

In December 2013, I was invited as State Guest by the Bangladesh Govt. for their Victory Day, 16 December Celebrations in Dhaka as a member of the Indian military delegation as the only one invited/ selected from the Air Force for carrying out significant professional tasks as a fighter pilot in various battles of the 1971 War.

In November 2014 at Air Force Station, Bhuj, in Gujarat, the main central hall was named 'Karnik Hall' as a tribute for the professionalism and dedication exhibited when in service in the IAF—a rare honour for a living individual.

Veteran Wg Cdr SD Karnik *was commissioned in the Flying Branch of Indian Air Force on 14 Jan 1956. He was actively involved in the 1971 war and flew a few very important missions by day as well as night in the Western as well as Eastern Sector. He was instrumental in causing extensive damage to the Pakistani assests which included Chittangong airfield and a large POL dump. He was awarded a Vir Chakra during the 1971 Ops. He is now settled at Pune and can be reached at sdkarnik35@gmail.com and 9422015138.*

18 The 'Helicopter Guys' of Silchar

S Krishnamurthy

Prologue

The 1971 War, on paper, was very short but for us in Silchar, it had started as soon as the rate of influx of refugees increased. If I may say so, it was ultimately cut short because of the performance of our Tech and Air crews and the helicopters that were flown, in the Eastern Sector throughout the war. The air and maintenance crews vied with each other in contributing to the success of the "airlift" or "Special Helicopter Borne Operation (SHBO)" of the troops to cross various rivers and rivulets and finally the mighty Meghna.

We were a lone helicopter unit positioned in a worn-out WW II airfield called Kumbhigram. While the blast pens (open concrete structures to save the parked aircraft) were intact, the runway itself was a rundown affair. The Dakotas (simple, two engine transport DC-3 planes, also of WW II vintage) which used to come from Jorhat to carry out air maintenance sorties in Mizoram, Manipur and Nagaland, could operate there after a bit of resurfacing of the tarmac.

In a place that was far from us, the P staff of Air Hqrs may have had a premonition to post a staggering number of young pilots to the helicopter unit here. So, we were about twenty-odd pilots barely out of our teens that had congregated, ready for any kind of adventure. If that action by the Directorate dealing with postings of pilots could be termed as careful planning, we may also say that it formed a foundation for a trained set of military pilots to fly Mi4 helicopters and fight the war that was to come two years later.

Meanwhile, the people of East Bengal who were under the near tyrannical rule of the Martial Law administrators of West Pakistan started revolting. The Late Sheikh Mujibur Rahman, who was spearheading the renaissance of ancient Bengali culture, gave the clarion call for a "free" Bangla Desh and declared independence. Many things happened; among them, a massive crackdown occurred in March 1971.

At the end of March, the East Bengalis were attacked and murdered in 'Op Searchlight' as per the order of West Pakistan leaders. This wrong move ended hope of any kind of compromise; instead, it gave way to resistance or declaration of independence. On 26th March, Bangabandhu Sheikh Mujibur Rahman declared Bangladesh independent. He called upon the people of Bangladesh to resist the 'Army of Occupation' to the last. The fight was to go on until the last soldier of the Pakistan Occupation Army was vanquished and final victory was achieved.

We, in Silchar or on detachment at Agartala heard the speech on Bangla Betar Kendra, in Bengali and the English translation. History says that once again, on 27th March 1971, Maj Zia-ur-Rahman declared the independence of Bangladesh.

History is replete with how the 1971 War between India and her neighbour started and how India won the war. I was a young officer then and flew all the missions whenever planned by my seniors. I shall just give a brief summary on the preparations for the war and the way we participated in it.

(a) Two guys belonging to Rajasthan, both kingpins in their own sphere with independent thinking and capable of orientating quickly to the prevailing situation, saw the wisdom in utilising their greatest asset in the form of Mi 4 helicopters from Silchar to keep leap-frogging to the unplanned destination—to the capital city of Dacca.

(b) Lt Gen Sagat Singh displaying his usual foresight and intiative had got the maps required for IV Corps sector printed at the Survey of India Press in Dehradun several months before the war. He had also got the maps, which covered the area from Brahamnbaria to Dacca and included our next objective across the Meghna, which was the Landing Zone at Raipura. IV Corps was not to cross the river Meghna, so getting those maps printed was again a premonition.

(c) The operations had originally started with 110 HU and subsequently helicopters and crew from 105 HU and 111 HU also joined. So we formed a team of "Helicopter Guys of Silchar".

(d) We were twenty-odd pilots barely out of our teens but we had the coveted Wings on our chest and Rings on our shoulders to show we were 'Flying Officers' posted at Kumbhigram airfield.

(e) We had no structured training on night SHBO; we, no doubt, practised plenty of night flying and performed beyond expectations in the actual war. We were forced by the prevailing situation to flout 'SOP' when we carried fuel barrels and refilled from them without the mandatory 48 hours settling down time for the sediments to settle. We did night flying with UVL (ultra violet lights that were necessary for night flying) going off or falling off at critical landing times due to the increased vibrations.

(f) All of us spent many nights in the 'open air' sleeping in the paddy fields that were our temporary landing grounds among rodents and the snakes chasing them!

(g) The "Helicopters Guys of Silchar" performed exceedingly well and contributed in a very big way to hasten the Victory of India.

(h) The Unit did have three forced landings but none in the battlefield! One was a write off on its way back to Kumbhigram base for servicing. It was flown by the Late BLK Reddy and Sukhi Hundal. No harm was done to the pilots or other occupants but the helicopter caught fire and was destroyed.

(j) What is really amazing is that the entire heli-borne operation was an impromptu improvisation in the heat of the battle, and not a well thought-out or rehearsed military manoeuvre. Not then or ever. The Meghna heli-lift is what changed the course of war and by 9 Dec 71, just nine days from the time 4 Guards crossed the border, Dacca became an achievable objective.

(k) One night, Gen Sagat wanted to go to Brahmanbaria for an urgent meeting and Sqn Ldr Singla was told to get the Allouette ready. Singla asked Sandhu to loan him a pilot, as he had not been to B'baria. 'Lambu' Ali was detailed to be his navigator. It was a dark night, but the weather was good. However, due to the blackout, no villages were lit, no traffic on road. Lambu just went by 'time and course'. Then, he asked Singla Sir to switch on his landing light. The 'H' of the helipad was right in front of them. Such was his professional capability!!

(l) On 15th and 16th Dec 71, All India Radio was asking the enemy forces to surrender; there was heavy traffic on the Army signal routes asking the enemy forces in East Pakistan to surrender. The fall of Dacca was imminent, but when, was unknown.

(m) On 16th December, it was anticipated that the enemy forces would surrender; we were told to be ready to fly all the helicopters to Tezgaon airport for the surrender ceremony.

SPECIAL NOTE: Details of the operations undertaken by the three helicopter units viz 110 HU, 105 HU and 111 HU have been covered in detail in this book in another article written by Gp Capt CS Sandhu who was commanding 110 HU during the 1971 War.

I will now give some snippets of the Surrender Ceremony at Dacca. I was a young Flying Officer and fortunate to be one among the few to be physically present there witnessing the surrender ceremony. A copy of the Instrument of Surrender is placed at page 232.

Note: **Though in the photograph given in the Instrument of Surrender, then Fg Offr S Krishnamurthy is not visible, however, he can be very clearly seen in another photograph which is printed at the back cover of the book.**

(a) On board the 'lead' helicopter piloted by Flt Lt Pushp Vaid of 110 HU; seated in the pax cabin were Gen Sagat Singh (Cdr IV Corps), Gp Capt Chandan Singh (senior-most AF officer in IV Corps Sector), Col Himmeth Singh (CO 4 Guards) and Major Chandrakant Singh (2 i/c). There were fourteen MI-4 helicopters lined up and all were without the rear clam shell doors. This was to facilitate easy boarding and disembarking. Precisely at 1600 hrs, four helicopters carrying a platoon plus a few Mukti Bahini boys forming a loose formation took off simultaneously. The helicopters had to do a running take-off, after taxiing a small distance, as they were overloaded.

Flt Lt Pushp Vaid who had made a daring landing at Sylhet only the previous day was decorated with a VrC.

(b) Col Himmeth Singh and Gp Capt Chandan Singh had already carried out a recce of our landing zone earlier in the morning along with Gen Sagat Singh and Brig Mishra. Their helicopters had been shot at on their way home. Gen Sagat Singh received a bullet, which passed through his beret grazing his forehead. A lesser man would have been perturbed but Sagat being Sagat, it made no difference.

(c) When we were headed to Dacca for the surrender ceremony, Gen Osmani who was the chief of the Mukti Bahini, wanted to visit his mother in Sylhet. Accordingly, RV Singh and Chitnis flew him there. However, Sylhet had not surrendered on 16 Dec 71; they were still holding fort and shot at the helicopter. A bullet hit the helicopter reductor sump and RV made a forced landing at Shamsher Nagar. The next day MM Ali, along with Chippy D'Souza took Osmani from Shamsher Nagar to Sylhet but landed on the outskirts near the Sylhet railway station instead of entering the stronghold of the enemy. Maj Zia-ur-Rehman (He later became the President of Bangla Desh) was accompanying Osmani.

(d) It was a daring decision to take all the helicopters to Tezgaon airport. Nothing untoward happened. The 'pistol' was handed over as a mark of surrender. The surrender of the century by several thousand men.

(e) The winter sun had set at Tezgaon, Dhaka, when the helicopters got airborne for Agartala. There was much jubilation at the birth of Bangladesh. We slept peacefully that night. Our small personal three-day kit had been of great help to us, but we were ready to repack yet again!

At the Agartala arrival hall, tired armed forces personnel occupied all available space. The next day, the first flight to Agartala from Calcutta brought the newspaper of the day. It carried news of the surrender in detail. It also carried a special photograph that had a helicopter pilot representative, along with the brass hats, telling the world about the Helicopter guys of Silchar and their three-day kit who flew simple mercy missions and logistic support sorties enabling the forces to win a war!

We 'peace loving' Silcharians had got together and joined hands with the Army to hasten the surrender bringing the war to a closure. Then surrender of 93,000 Pakistani soldiers and officers was unprecedented and a new country was born!

Air Marshal HC Dewan (AOC in C, EAC) had stated that helicopter operations deserved to be written in golden letters in the annals of IAF history.

Awards

The efforts and valours of "The Helicopter Guys of Silchar were definitely well recognised. All the three helicopter units which participated in the 1971-War were awarded the Presidents' colours (No 105 Helicopter Unit, AF in March 2009, No 110 Helicopter Unit, AF, in March 2011, No. 111 Helicopter Unit, AF in March 2012) in recognition of the exceptional service rendered by them to the nation, both during the war and in peace.

Everyone, without fail, displayed gallantry, professional skill and leadership of the required level. We loved the machines we flew. They gave us the best output despite being overloaded and severely overworked. They did not let us down or complain. We loved our Mi4 helicopters; rightly so, as they lived up to their reputation.

AVM Chandan Singh who planned and executed the Sylhet Airlift was decorated with an MVC. The Unit was decorated/awarded two Vir Chakras and two 'Mention in Despatches'. The Commanding Officer and the Flight Commander of No. 110 HU, AF were awarded Vir Chakra for successfully landing troops by night repeatedly, during 30-odd hazardous missions.

Veteran Wg Cdr S Krishnamurthy *was commissioned in the Flying Branch on 02 June 1968. He participated in the 1971 war as a young Flying Officer with little more than three years' service. He was a part of 110 HU which was based in the East. During the short 14 days war, he flew across to Bangladesh many times including the one during the surrender ceremony. He has been a keen mountaineer and was a part of the IAF delegation to Antarctica. He took premature retirement in the year 1990 and had been leading an active life including taking up Flying assignments. He has been a ground instructor also. He is presently settled at Mumbai and can be reached at sukrani46@yahoo.co.in and 9820069195.*

19 THE 4TH OF DECEMBER 1971

Harish Masand

I was a Flying Officer with less than four years of service with 37 Squadron, the Black Panthers, in Hasimara in December 1971 with just about 240 hours of flying on the Hunter. We had been on alert for over six months from the summer of 1971 due to the political and military situation in East Pakistan.

Mission 501 over Tezgaon

On December 04, ours was the first mission, 501, against Tezgaon airfield in Dacca, 181 NM away. The CO, 'Suppi' Kaul was the leader with 'Billoo' Sangar, 'Mascy' and me with a ToT of 0705 hrs IST. The mission was in a lo-lo profile with four 100-gallon external tanks and just guns, as ordered by Command HQ. Even in this configuration, we were 14 miles beyond our calculated radius of action and had no combat fuel. I had raised this issue earlier and we had debated going just with guns at low level but orders were orders. Due to this, two MiG-21s from Gauhati were to RV with us over the target to protect us during the attacks and we were briefed to disengage, if bounced.

Our boss on the flight line, Flt Sgt 'Chiefy' Choudhary gave me my favourite aircraft, BA-291, which I had used for all my reconnaissance missions earlier and which had brought me back without a scratch every time. Suppi Sir's aircraft did not start and Mascy's had a hydraulic leak. Suppi Sir quickly jumped into the standby aircraft to carry on with three aircraft. After take-off, streaming behind as Number 3, even my favourite 291 let me down initially and I could not raise the undercarriage. I kept falling behind Suppi Sir and Billoo while trying to push the undercarriage button in. Finally, before I lost contact with Suppi Sir, I decided to use the emergency override since this was an operational mission and I did not want to miss out or let Suppi Sir go to war with just two aircraft even though with such use, there was no certainty of getting the gear down for landing. Fortunately for me, that decision paid off in the end, on both counts.

Soon, I was in position on Suppi Sir's left abreast at about 1500 yards with Billoo on Suppi Sir's right in battle formation. Two minutes short of Tezgaon, as we left the Initial Point (IP) at 420 knots hugging the deck below 100 feet, I spotted two Sabres on the right, 3 O'clock high about 5 miles. When I reported them, Suppi Sir called up the MiG-21 leader who asked Suppi Sir for our position. While this conversation of 'where are you' was going on with no visual contact between the MiGs and us, the two Sabres closed in with the lead one behind Suppi Sir and Billoo at about 2500 yards and the other moving in behind me, obviously guided by their radar, AR-1.

Subconsciously, we accelerated to 480 knots with the radio thick with calls between Suppi Sir and the MiG leader when I heard a "swoosh' under the belly of the lead Sabre now about 2000 yards. While it was actually fuel spray due to dropping of tanks by the Sabre in an effort to close the distance, I thought it was a missile launch since Pakistani Sabres had reportedly been modified to carry Sidewinder missiles. Instinctively, I ordered tactical action with a 'Hard Right'. In my eagerness to get to the lead Sabre behind Suppi Sir while looking out for the one behind me, I hauled 8g or more with my neck hurting from the effort of craning under this g-load. The lead Sabre turned slightly left towards me to cross at high angle off to avoid a passing shot from me. As expected, just before 90 degrees of turn, I lost contact with Suppi Sir and Billoo under my belly.

How I got Him

Rolling out on the course home of 350, I initially did not pick up Suppi Sir or Billoo on my left as expected and asked Suppi Sir for his position. Looking further back, I found two Hunters in a lazy turn at about 0730 to me with a Sabre 3-400 yards behind them firing its guns with puffs of black smoke from its nose. I yelled "Hard Right, he is firing at you" and mindless of the fuel and the instructions not to engage, hauled my aircraft into a hard left followed by a sharp reversal to the right while looking for the Sabre behind me. Due to the lower speed of these three aircraft, I quickly fell 400 yards behind the Sabre in a right turn with my gunsight pipper right on the Sabre's cockpit. All this was as practised in mock combat so many times in peace but, unfortunately, the same habit made me press the camera button first. Cursing myself for this stupidity, I lowered the gun-trigger by which time, due to my closing-in speed, I was less than 100 yards from the Sabre. At this stage, the Sabre sharply reversed to the left, perhaps having been warned by the one behind me. In this reversal, I put the cross on the Sabre's spine and pressed the trigger. The Sabre just stopped dead in its flight and blew up while I flew right through the centre of the explosion, fortunately without any debris damage while yelling, "I got him". Immediately, I heard one of the MIGs say, "Well done, he has ejected".

Time to get Back to Base

There was no time to dwell on anything due to the other Sabre still lurking behind me and I went back into a hard right looking for this second Sabre rolling out on the course home while yelling at Suppi Sir to turn harder on to 350 and look for me inside his turn. Initially, I kept the speed high while looking for Suppi Sir and Billoo but again did not see anyone. I was now even lower on gas. So I zoomed up to 15,000 feet and flew back at range speed. Fortunately, I had just enough gas to land in a glide from 15,000 feet with the fuel gauges showing empty. After landing when I came out of the aircraft to a cheering crowd of airmen led by the Chiefy, despite the winter my G-suit was soaked with sweat.

Epilogue: The mystery deepened when I found neither Suppi Sir or Billoo's aircraft were hit nor did they see any Sabre or me after the initial turn. However, my course mate 'Buster' Bains from 17 squadron, also in Hasimara, had returned at the same time with 42 bullet holes and multiple-system failures due to the ball ammo used by the Sabre. Buster was Number 2 to Lele, with Neb and Bajwa as 3 and 4. We pieced it together to confirm that I had shot down the Sabre behind Buster. Chiefy Chowdhary later told me that I had just fumes left in my tanks and had fired only 18 rounds, less than five rounds per gun, or a quarter second burst. The next morning, we went hunting for the Sabres in the air with eight aircraft but I never saw a Sabre in the air again during the war, my kill being a small contribution to air superiority.

Veteran Air Marshal Harish Masand *was commissioned in the flying Branch in Dec 67. As a young Flying Officer, he participated in the 1971 war while serving in a Hunter Squadron based at Hasimara. He participated very actively in the 1971 war and flew two very important missions. In the first one, he shot down one Pakistani F-86 Sabre Jet and in the second one he was a part of the formation which attacked the Governor's house on 14 Dec 1971. For these acts of gallantry, he was awarded the Coveted Vir Chakra. He retired in 2006 and is now settled in Mhow (Madhya Pradesh). He can be reached at harishmasand1@gmail.com and 9993037797.*

20 MILK RUN TO DACCA

VM Mayadev

Background

In 1971, I was posted as an instructor to the Flying Instructors' School at Tambaram and was on leave around Diwali with my wife and son when I was recalled. That trouble brewing in East Pakistan was a common knowledge and a general recall of servicemen indicated that we were heading for a second round. I returned immediately to Tambaram where an order to move to Air Force Station Kalaikunda awaited me.

I had been away from a squadron and not flown a MiG 21 for over three years. My worst fear during the train journey was that due to my long absence from active duty I had been sent to AF Station Kaliakunda to be put on a ground job which I resented and reluctantly reported to the Station HQ. I jumped with joy when they directed me to report to No 30 Sqn based there to fly MiG 21 aircraft.

From Instructional Flying to Operations

It felt great to be back in the familiar environment of a vibrant fighter squadron crew room, pilots' notes and manuals, morning briefings, frequent cups of tea during lively discussions including briefing and debriefing and, of course, the refresher flights on MiG 21 that got me ready for operations faster than I had anticipated.

Thereafter, I was sent to Panagarh on attachment with four aircraft to secure the airfield there where a Su-7 Squadron was based. I was the senior-most officer and by default became Detachment Commander with an unexpected degree of freedom and authority. Without any hiccups, we settled down to the job of defending Panagarh airfield.

We had our aircraft armed with air-to-air missiles at all times and were on alert 24/7. Our allotted tasks were to man the Operational

Readiness Platform (ORP) and carry out Combat Air Patrols over the airfield. I was a past master at such work. I did a couple of live scrambles and was directed towards the border when air intrusions were detected but enemy aircraft returned to the safety of their airspace much before we could catch them. Most of the month of November passed in such activities and in anticipation of greater excitement.

Air Combat Training

Notwithstanding a state of alert, we also had to carry out air combat training amongst ourselves and with the SU 7 aircraft co located at Panagarh to remain combat worthy. Carrying out mock dogfights armed with live missiles was totally against the SOPs; on the other hand, we could not remove the missiles for air combat training due to the prevailing threat. It was a Catch-22 situation. Any ordinary Base Commander would have nipped this idea of air combat training in the bud but Base Commander Panagarh, Wing Cdr Chotu Bakhale was made of sterner stuff.

He discussed the feasibility of carrying out air combat training with the boss of the Su Squadron and me; the Sus were without missiles, so the ball was in my court. I had no doubt in my mind that weapons/ missiles cannot self-launch themselves as the pilot was required to put on a couple of switches to get them ready and finally press the trigger to launch them. Therefore, I suggested that it was safe to carry out training dogfights with live missiles with proper precautions and briefing. The decision-maker was gutsy enough to trust me and boldly permitted us to carry out air combat training with live missiles which we did without any untoward incident.

Air combat practice between MiGs and Sus made our adrenalin rush and broke the monotony of waiting. Not only had I been away from MiG flying for over three years, I had flown just about a hundred hours and had not done air-to-ground gunnery when I went for the Instructors Course. Therefore, I exploited this opportunity to carry out dummy air-to-ground weapon delivery practice at Panagarh and got ready to strike the enemy with rockets and bombs. As they say, all is fair in love and war, and we continued to sharpen our combat skills attributable to bold field commanders like Wg Cdr Bakhale and were better prepared for the shooting war that ensued.

The War Breaks Out

On 3rd December, the PAF launched airstrikes on our airfields in the western sector and the wait was over. Air action commenced the next morning when our Sukhois mounted airstrikes on the airfields of Tezgaon and Kurmitola near Dacca while we mounted Combat Air Patrols to guard our base against enemy air raids, but the PAF did not oblige. I also carried out a few sorties as escort to aircraft that went to attack enemy airfields. We circled above and gave air cover as the aircraft with bombs dived through the barrage of heavy ack-ack to release their bombs at the runways. I was itching to contribute.

My Induction into the War Zone

One fine morning I rolled down Panagarh runway with a heavy MiG 21 loaded with two 500-kg bombs in place of two light missiles and headed for Kurmitola airfield with Flying Officer J S (Jassi) Mann with two more bombs. We cruised at about 9 km on a route which was quite familiar and reached the target area with effortless ease. I descended and positioned myself for the attack while Jassi held at a safe height above ack-ack range.

I put on the weapon switches, readied the trigger, attained the recommended speed, height and power setting and carried out a descending left turn ending in a steep dive towards the target and steered the aircraft towards the aiming point two-thirds way up as guided by the gunsight, all the while keeping an eye on increasing speed and reducing height. Ack-ack shells whizzed past and burst above but concentration had to be on the gunsight, aiming point on the runway and release height and speed which was approaching rapidly.

At the precise height, I pressed the trigger and the aircraft jumped with joy as it became a thousand kg lighter helping me pull out of the dive and enter a steep climbing turn to get above the bursting ack-ack barrage. It felt as if my aircraft had sighed and whispered to me, "Thank God, we are in one piece and I can take you back to Panagarh". At about the same time, No 2 called "Good bombs, Sir" making me smile inside my mask. I spotted Jassi and got to his height. Checked all clear at a safe height above the ack-ack and told Jassi to go for it. He descended and with precision added two more craters to the runway getting a "well done, Jassi" from me. I still remember the pieces of concrete thrown up by exploding bombs.

A runway appears to be a big target and easy to hit; it may be 3,000 yards long but it is only 50 yards wide and any crater out of the runway is a bomb wasted. Putting an unguided, free-falling bomb released at about 900 kmph, at a height above a kilometre from a steep dive, within those 50 yards separated the men from the boys who rendered the two airfields at Dacca out of commission by bombing their runways at regular intervals and prevented PAF activity over East Pakistan that gave it the well-deserved prefix of "erstwhile". This ruled out any movement of Pakistani ground and naval forces and enabled our ground forces to move freely, swiftly and securely with impunity towards their goal.

I am sure that the present crop of fighter pilots would be amused to read about the primitive way in which free-falling bombs were dropped before computers, laser guidance, etc., added spice to air warfare. Incidentally, the first bomb was carried by a pilot in an open cockpit and hand-dropped on enemy positions.

Search and Strike Missions

I also got a chance to carry out search-and-strike missions with rockets over enemy territory. On one occasion, we spotted some trucks near Jessore in Bangladesh and dived in for the attack. As we approached them, I realised that they looked like our Tata trucks and called off the attack. We later learnt that they were indeed our trucks and that our forces had already reached Jessore. This information had not reached us and I was happy that a little alertness and quick thinking saved our own troops who were sitting ducks for our rocket attack. We went further and attacked a ship in Khulna port with the rockets so saved. Many years later memory of this attack was rekindled by an Indian Naval officer who was active in the vicinity of that port during the war and remembered having seen an accurate rocket attack on a ship in Khulna by MiG 21s of the Indian Air Force.

The USA, as an ally of Pakistan, was not happy at the turn of events leading the latter towards a huge military defeat. It was an open secret that their Seventh Fleet was rushing at full speed towards the battle zone but it was coming for a wrong cause and luck favoured our rightful cause. The Seventh Fleet moved slower than the Pakis could resist our advance and turned out to be an empty threat much to the discomfiture of the Paki brass and the Nixon/Kissinger duo.

The final nail in their coffin was hammered in by an accurate rocket attack by our MiG 21s on the Governor's House when he was huddled with the Pak Army brass. So devastating was the effect of this attack that he resigned forthwith, vacated his official residence that was more vulnerable than in his wildest imagination, and took shelter at the UN Hotel in Dacca. Under such compelling circumstances, Pakistani Commander Lt Gen AAK Niazi surrendered with 93,000 able-bodied fully armed soldiers to our Armed Forces. After their abject surrender, a new nation named Bangladesh was born. Pakistan, as they say, was cut to size.

After this historic surrender, I moved with our detachment to Pathankot on the western front where No 30 Sqn was relocated. Soon, a ceasefire was announced with Pakistan swallowing the bitter pill of losing a part of its territory. I had to be content with a few Operational Readiness Platform duties and a few CAPs at Pathankot.

Visit to Pakistan without Passport

In the west too, our forces had made deep ingress into Pak territory. Pathankot was under the command of Air Commodore LM Katre (one of our finest officers who rose to be Air Chief later) who was not only an operational commander to the hilt but also an unassuming and friendly one with excellent contacts across the Services with a flair for life. Brigadier Handu, his batchmate from the National Defence College, had moved in with his brigade deep inside Pakistan and, for old time's sake, invited the AOC with a few Air Force officers to enjoy his hospitality in Pakistan. I was privileged to be included in this small group which flew in a helicopter from Pathankot to a pick-up point from where we drove into Brigadier Handu's operational mess. Besides their warm hospitality, I remember and cherish the memory of a signboard put up by our army which proudly declared:

> ***"You are now entering Pakistani territory without a passport, kind courtesy the Indian Army."***

We tended to credit Pakistan with better intelligence-gathering and decision-making as a military state. However, they always messed up interpreting intelligence and arrived at wrong decisions ending up in a mess bigger than the previous one. It looked as if, after usurping political power, a General was neither capable of running a government nor a war machine.

Back to Instructional Flying

In or around the end of January 1972, with the satisfaction of having made a humble contribution to the war effort in spite of a long absence from a fighter squadron I returned to instructing at the Flying Instructors' School with a green and red flag of Bangladesh given to me as a memory of the historic event.

On the way back from Pathankot to Tambaram, I picked up my wife and son from Nagpur where they had spent the better part of the trying time with my parents, for whom it was the second experience of a son being at war. They fortified each other, and I am sure their prayers kept the ack-ack shells at Dacca airfields away from my aircraft on the numerous occasions when I dived in through their barrage to drop my bombs.

Veteran Wg Cdr VM Mayadev *was commissioned in the flying branch on 26 May 1962. He has flown Gnats and MiG-21 aircraft and has participated in the 1965 as well as 1971 war. He was a Prisoner of War during the 1965 war and spent four months in Pakistan. He is now settled at Mumbai and can be reached at vmayadev@gmail.com and 9323277708.*

21 1971: The Indo-Pak Air War - As I Saw It

Narayan Menon

Prelude

I saw the 1971 war from Adampur air base. Adampur Air Force Station, Punjab, was fully ready for the war by mid-November 1971. All of us, pilots, technical and non-technical personnel, lascars, civilians and families had been briefed and trained about what to do and what not to do—when and not if—war commenced. During the process of this build-up to war, this key fighter base of the IAF had been a target of an unintended live but friendly rocket attack too!

Training standards were as high as our adrenalin levels, and our fingers longed to press the aircraft's trigger as we waited in anticipation. The 'we' included me, a Flt Lt in 26 Sqn, which was equipped with the recently inducted Su-7 fighter-bomber aircraft. 101 Sqn was operating from the adjacent loop. No 1 Sqn with MiG-21 FL fighters, in the southern dispersal, were tasked for Air Defence.

Preparing for the War

I was posted to 26 Sqn in Feb 1970 and rapidly progressed through the laid down syllabus to be declared 'fully operational' by March end that year. The aircraft serviceability was excellent and under the command of then Wing Commander MS Bawa; we flew a lot. The Flt Cdr could order the Daily Servicing Section (DSS) as to how many aircraft he needed the next day and Flt Sgt Krishnan, who ran the DSS with an iron hand, produced the required number of aeroplanes. We operated from the 'loop' out of the concrete blast pens. The area within the loop was 'leased' to one Sardar Mohan Singh for agriculture and the Sqn profited from this by getting our wheat and milk free. No 'aircrew rations' were available those days. Mohan Singh regularly hunted jackals, which were plenty in the loop area, and reportedly consumed their meat. His offer to send us some jackal meat was politely refused!

Command of Adampur, 8 Wing, was taken over by Air Cmde Randhir Singh on 14 July 1970, a no-nonsense commander with a focus on operations and his imprint on the station showed almost immediately. The problem in East Pakistan had been slowly building up and by Apr-May 1971, we were aware that something out of the ordinary was in the offing. By Jul-Aug the AOC ordered all squadrons to fly loaded aircraft on all the training missions. Accelerated training commenced to get pilots their 'fully operational' status. Armament delivery sorties were increased and low-level strikes became the norm. I remember flying hi-lo-hi missions during Aug-Sep with targets in Rajasthan. The AOC ordered that the missions be planned as per war orders but to operate within our airspace. All three squadrons maximised their flying effort. At one time Adampur was lifting more aviation fuel than Chandigarh, which had three transport squadrons. Airmen were looked after well and facilities for them improved so that they could concentrate on their tasks. By August, Adampur came to be called 'Randhir Air Force' (RAF).

Friendly Rocket Attack

Both the Sukhoi squadrons were to fly all missions armed with live ammunition and 57 mm rockets. We were briefed not to touch the trigger during simulated attacks. In late October, 26 Sqn planned a 'dawn' strike with Adampur base itself as the target. The four-aircraft mission members were allotted individual targets on the base. During the simulated attack, Flt Lt Wahi, in the heat of the moment, pressed his trigger. Two 57 mm rockets took off and impacted the ground with a deafening blast. There was commotion all round. Safety vehicles started up but did not know where to go. Some panic was created in the residential areas, as people were shocked out of their sleep. Telephone calls jammed the Base Ops office, which had no clue about what was happening. When the AOC was informed that someone had fired munitions onto the base, he took his jeep and came to the 26 Sqn loop.

By that time Flt Lt Wahi had reported the incident. No damage was reported from any part of the station. The AOC, Sqn Cdr and Wg Cdr Ram Batra waited in the pen for Wahi to exit the aircraft. The CO was quite livid with anger. When Wahi came out, the AOC questioned him, "What was your target?" Trembling a bit Wahi answered, "The Base Ops Sir." The AOC asked Wahi, "Why did you not hit your target? I can excuse you for the mistake of pressing the trigger, but your not hitting the target is inexcusable." It was later learnt that both rockets had hit just outside the Base Ops along the rail track running from Jalandhar to Hoshiarpur. Two Defence Security Corps jawans had some minor injuries due to flying stone pieces.

Post this incident, the AOC carried out an inquiry. He summoned both the jawans to his office and some officers/airmen waiting outside the AOC office overheard snatches of the questions and answers inside the room.

AOC: Jawan, batao kya hua?

Jawan: Saheb main aur Param Chand lota lekar Sham Churasi gate se baahar nikal rahe thay.

AOC: Phir kya hua?

Jawan: Hum gate se baahar hi thay ki peeche se bijli si chamki aur dhoom dhadaka hua.

AOC: Aage batao kya hua?

Jawan: Aage kuchh nahin hua.

AOC: Jhoot mat bolo. Kaho kya hua

Jawan: Saab, our rear orifices burst (far more descriptive in local lingo) aur hum vahin gir gaye.

The AOC laughed and let them go. Wahi was given additional duties as Orderly Officer and reprimanded.

Inter-Services Communication

We also trained for 'Close Air Support' or CAS missions. This involved obtaining targets from the Indian army and directed by a 'Forward Air

Controller' or FAC to reach and attack the target. Targets assigned by the army were generally tanks, gun positions, bunkers and enemy ammunition or supply dumps. As the terminology used, map types and scales and the perception of the target from ground and air were quite different, the FAC, a pilot, moving with the land forces would use air force terminology and language while guiding the CAS missions. Similarly, there was a Ground Liaison Officer or GLO from the army based at Adampur who would interpret the army's operational requirements and inform the mission leaders. Our GLO was Major Poonia from the JAK Rifles. We carried out many small and large-scale exercises with army formations to rectify communication glitches and fine-tune procedures. In short, the IAF had identified weaknesses in the system and weeded them out through training and exercises; procedures and tactics were refined and a sense of purpose and coordination permeated the pre-war planning.

Services at our Door Steps

In mid-November the squadron was instructed to carry out 'night patrols'. These single-aircraft missions required aircraft to fly along the IB at low levels and pop-up at pre-designated points. While the Sukhois flew these sorties, the MiG-21s from 1 Sqn, armed with Ka-13 air-to-air missiles, patrolled deeper inside to shoot down any PAF interceptors. This exercise carried on throughout the night to keep the PAF on constant alert without our crossing the IB. We slept in the crew room and had to wake up bleary-eyed at odd hours to fly these missions. The bitter cold that grips Adampur in November-December compounded the difficulty factor. However, hot cups of chocolate milk and chocolates cheered us up somewhat. Our stock of these foods was plenty as the central and state authorities sent truckloads to all armed forces units. When we told the AOC that it was very cold in the crew-rooms where we slept, he promptly instructed the Senior Logistics Officer to issue the aircrew with sleeping bags. These made our nights comfortable. Nobody asked for these sleeping bags at the end of the war and I still have mine with me. It was during this time that the Defence Minister, Babu Jagjivan Ram, with a large retinue of officials, visited the base. He spoke to all of us and promised to make sure that all we needed was made available in the shortest possible time. Later, I was given to understand that he delivered on that promise.

Security Awareness of the Sorrounding Villages

Right from November there was partial blackout in Adampur and security had been tightened. The AOC summoned the 'mukhiyas' of the many villages around the airfield, talked to them about infiltrators and spies and the damage that could be caused to our war effort. All of them must have been highly impressed because one day some villagers brought a family of four trembling members to the Main Guard Room near the gate. It transpired that this group had, during their early morning journey from Jalandhar to Hoshiarpur, stopped beside a culvert at a point past Khurdpur village to stretch their limbs and eat what they were carrying for breakfast. That was the time of maximum take-offs from Adampur base and all aircraft passed directly over the place where they had stopped. They were looking up and pointing at the aircraft as they passed overhead. A villager, fired up by the instructions of Air Cmde Randhir, concluded that these were Pakistani spies counting IAF aircraft. He summoned back-up forces and literally dragged the family to the AFS and handed them over to the IAF (Police). The Security Officer informed the AOC who came to the scene. He gave a big 'shabash' to the villagers and sent them back with 'gifts'. He explained the situation to the frightened family and sent them off with a warning not to stop near military bases.

Hush-hush Activities

Some days later we saw unusual activity near 'Sun-n-Shade', a semi-VIP room opposite the Officers' Mess. There were many civilians and IAF personnel not belonging to Adampur who became regular visitors to 'Sun-n-Shade'. Some aerials sprouted from the building and we were warned not to go anywhere near that place. A few days later the entire caboodle shifted to a house in the married accommodation area. We learnt that a Pakistani spy had been caught near the SAM-2 battery deployed about two km to the NW of the base. He had been transmitting information to his handlers in Pakistan. Our Air Int, RAW and IB probably coordinated and used coercive methods (my conjecture) to turn him into a double-agent. It was learnt that he was made to transmit fake info to Pakistan throughout the war. Probably this was one of the reasons why Adampur was never attacked during those 14 days of war.

Commencement of the Operations

The commencement of war for me was rather non-dramatic. It was the 3rd of December 1971 and I had strapped up in the front cockpit of the Sukhoi-7U trainer aircraft with the rear cockpit occupied by Squadron Leader Jiwa Singh, Flight Commander of 26 Squadron, for my 'dark night' dual clearance sortie. We were in a hardened RCC aircraft shelter called 'pens', 16 of them located on either side of a taxi track that formed a huge teardrop loop at a distance from the runway. Outside, dusk was fast disappearing into the pitch black that envelops the fertile land of Punjab on moonless nights.

I pressed the R/T button on the throttle and transmitted. Rockline was the confidential call-sign of Adampur ATC. "Rockline Control from 202, request permission to start-up." "202 from Rockline Control, standby for permission." "202 from Rockline, permission denied, vacate cockpits and contact on land line." When we returned to the crew-room and I asked air traffic control the reason for not granting permission for the sortie, it came to light that the PAF had carried out pre-emptive strikes against many IAF airfields and that Pakistan had initiated war against India. No one was surprised, as such action by Pakistan had been anticipated, because only a few days earlier, on 22 November a 4-aircraft Gnat mission, led brilliantly by Flt Lt Roy Andrew Massey, had shot down 3 Sabres intruding into Indian airspace at Boyra near Calcutta. Roy and I had been squadron-mates in 23 Sqn before my posting to Sukhois.

The situation in the then East Pakistan had been worsening with atrocities of the Pakistani army against the predominantly Bengali-speaking population there. The flow of refugees across the border, fleeing the brutality of what was considered an 'occupation army', had put India in a difficult humanitarian and political situation. As we were to learn much later, a decision to intervene militarily had been taken but postponed due to the insistence of General SHFJ Manekshaw, the Indian Army Chief, on more time to prepare. Another operational reason was that the riverine terrain of the area would not be negotiable by tanks and armoured vehicles of the Indian Army till November-December when winter set in and the ground hardened. In the pre-emptive strikes on 3rd December evening, Adampur airfield was not attacked, though it was fully prepared. The probable reason why the PAF did not strike Adampur was the fake information passed on by the captured spy to his handlers in Pakistan. It was rumoured that one element of this misleading intelligence transmitted back was about the impregnable air defence weapons network in and around the Adampur base. Whatever the reason, the PAF found it prudent to leave out Adampur from its strike plans. Throughout the duration of the war from 3rd December to 17th December, our base was not attacked, with the exception of an aborted raid by a PAF Canberra, which dropped its bomb load at least 15 km away injuring a villager who was walking with a lantern in his hand. The PAF pre-emptive attacks were a failure, as lessons had been learnt by the IAF from the 1965 conflict, when the PAF was able to cause a fair amount of damage during its pre-emptive strikes in the eastern sector, including at Kalaikunda air base, where I was posted as a Pilot Officer during that war. In 1971, all IAF aircraft operated out of hardened shelters resulting in the PAF's pre-emptive attacks not achieving their objectives.

The Sukhoi-7

The Sukhoi-7 had a fuselage 16.8 m long, wingspan of 9.3 m and height of 4.99 m. Its wings were sharply swept back at 60 degrees. It was the first Soviet aircraft to use an all-moving tailplane and had a movable cone in the air intake for managing airflow into the engine at supersonic speeds. Its engine, AL-7F1, developed a thrust of 6800 kgf in a dry regime and 9600 kgf with afterburner and was the most powerful fighter engine of that time. Heavy fuel consumption, however, affected its radius of action. It had two hard points under the fuselage that could carry weapon loads or fuel drop tanks of 950 or 600 litres. Four hard points were under the wing. The inner ones could carry a weapon load or 600 litre fuel drop tanks while the outer could carry only weapons up to 250 kg on each side. Two cannons were at the wing roots, each with a maximum of 80 x 30 mm gun ammunition. Some aircraft were also fitted with AFA-39 cameras for photo reconnaissance missions. It was on this fighter aircraft that I flew eighteen missions during the 1971 war code-named Operation 'Cactus-Lily'.

Missions and Targets

Our allotted area of operations was mostly in the 'bulge' sector, north of Lahore and south of Sialkot. The terrain in this area is suitable for armoured vehicles to operate and Pakistan launched offensives here during 1965. My first mission was as No 2 to Sqn Ldr Jiwa Singh to assist a Madras Regiment unit near Husainiwala. We came over the target area as instructed by the FAC, but there was a complete undercast and we could not spot the target. After descending to almost 100 m, and still having clouds below us, the mission had to be called off. While returning, we expended our rockets against the alternative target. The same day I flew two more missions, to Chander airfield and to Dera Baba Nanak (DBN) area. Chander base had been evacuated by the PAF and we hit the air traffic installation and other structures. At DBN, the attack was against gun emplacements. The entire area of interest to us used to be covered in the dust thrown up by convoys and tanks on the move. Target acquisition was difficult but under the guidance of the FAC we were able to accomplish most of the allotted tasks. There was intense activity on the ground and the entire airspace was full of lead ejected from guns of various calibres. After the first day's missions were over, 13 out of 16 Sukhois of the squadron had small arms bullet damage, all of which was repaired overnight and the fighters were ready early morning the next day. The airmen slept in the loop area and worked throughout the night refuelling and re-arming the aircraft. Their devotion and commitment was outstanding.

During those fourteen days from 4th to 17th December, I carried out missions against targets at Wagah, Shakargarh, Zafarwal, Darman, Nainakot, Nurkot and Narowal. The targets were Pak army installations, gun emplacements, troop concentrations, tanks and armoured vehicles. The routing out had to be in a specified manner to permit easy identification of friendly radars. Similarly, the return procedures were clearly stipulated. All this was to reduce the risk of fratricide. On the ground too, there was a method agreed upon so that IAF pilots could clearly identify Indian tanks. However, in war one has to accept losses and carry on fighting. The Sukhoi-7, because of its size, presented a large target to anti-aircraft artillery and to the enemy small arms. The IAF lost a total of 19 Sukhois during this war.

Role of 26 Sqn

26 Sqn lost Sqn Ldr DS Jafa, on attachment from the office of the CAS, on 5th December near the Ichchogil canal. He ejected safely. Sqn Ldr Jiwa Singh was killed in action (KIA) on the 7th, shot down by a Sabre or MiG-19 near Zafarwal. Flt Lt RG Kadam, on attachment from the squadron to TCDTS, was hit by ground fire near Risalewala; he failed to eject. Flt Lt DK Parulkar ejected after being hit by anti-aircraft fire near Zafarwal. He was taken PoW and returned a year later. Flt Lt KK Mohan was KIA after being hit by a wire-guided missile near Shakargarh. On 14th December Flt Lt L Pereira, an FAC with 8 Tactical Air Centre, was killed on the ground when attacked by a Sabre. From 8th December onwards, many of the missions were 'escorted' by MiG-21 aircraft of 1 Sqn. One felt sad at losing colleagues, but there is no time for emotions during war.

On 16th December, Wg Cdr RK Batra, the Sqn Cdr, led a four-aircraft bombing mission to the railway yard at Narowal. Flt Lt TS Dandass, a classmate of mine from Delhi, was No 2, Flt Lt Ravish Malhotra, who later trained as a cosmonaut, was No 3, and I was No 4. The mission was flown late in the afternoon, and visibility conditions were poor. The aircraft were heavily loaded and it was to be a steep glide attack from 4.2 km height for greater accuracy as the intent was to destroy the Narowal rail yard, a prime interdiction target. Due to a navigational error, the formation drifted left of the track and when we pulled up the target was displaced well to our right. The speed had dropped during the pull up and we were lazily turning right to get into attack mode when the sky was filled with anti-aircraft fire. Despite our altitude, the ack-ack shells were bursting around and above us. The barrage of fire came from Chinese-built quads. We rolled into the attack through the ack-ack fire and went into steep dive individually. Being the last, I saw

No 1 pulling out after bomb release and No 2 in the dive. A few seconds later No 2's aircraft appeared to continue in the dive until it impacted with the ground. I saw a huge ball of fire followed by a plume of smoke. By now I had achieved release conditions—bombs were released and I pulled out of the dive. Later, when the formation was gathering up, the leader asked for check-in on the radio. All but No 2 checked-in but the time was not right for me to volunteer any information as the images were still fuzzy in my mind. On landing I related what had happened. I could not confirm an ejection as I did not see any. Later it was conjectured that the aircraft could have taken a direct hit on the cockpit disabling the pilot.

Suspense and Thrill

Earlier in that week, a four-aircraft mission was ordered to destroy a large conical tower in the Zafarwal sector which was suspected to be a lookout from where artillery fire was being directed. The mission was being led by Flt Lt Pant and we were instructed to carry out a single pass attack, two aircraft with rockets and the remaining two with bombs. A second pass was not to be attempted as we had lost three aircraft in that sector. The attacks were carried out and we turned towards base.

As no instructions came from the leader, as deputy leader, I ordered 'reheat on' to accelerate. However, the radar reported that the track behind was gaining on us. We descended to about 50 m and the landscape below flashed past at near supersonic speed. We reduced speed only when approaching over our home base, which had been put on air raid alert. We had to orbit nearby and then the mystery unfolded. The 'chase aircraft' revealed itself to be our leader who had carried out a second attack and was trying to catch up with the rest of the formation. He had erroneously also changed over to another radio channel. After landing, he had to literally run away to escape our combined wrath. This observation tower or whatever it was remained an enigma as even after many attacks by different missions with varying weapon loads, it continued to mock at us by just being there. This information was passed on to Western Air Command operations centre. One day when we passed that area on another mission, the entire area around the tower appeared to have been carpet-bombed. This was carried out at night by an AN-12 squadron. However, the tower still stood erect until the end of the war and we did not find out its purpose.

On the 11th, while returning after a CAS mission, my No 2, Fg Offr Chonker, spotted a Pakistani army Bird Dog observation aircraft. We tried our best to manoeuvre and shoot him down, but his low flying and the aircraft's agility did not allow us to get close. We tried for about 3 minutes and as fuel was running low had to abandon the chase.

Experimentation and Innovations

During the war 26 Sqn also did some 'experimenting'. On 14th December, very large crates arrived at the squadron dispersal. They contained the powerful S-24 air-to-ground rocket projectiles. No literature was available about these weapons. We did not know much about them. Command Hq was equally ignorant. Something in Russian language was marked on the crates. Some of the officers and airmen, who had trained in the Soviet Union and knew the language, deciphered the instructions, which also contained release conditions for these missiles. With such scant information, attack plans were formulated. Instructions came down to send a 2-aircraft mission to attack Sulaimanke Headworks. Sqn Ldr TJ Fernandez and Flt Lt JS Ghuman carried out the mission. This was a first, when without any prior training or practice, completely new weapons were employed for live missions. The S-24 proved to be a deadly weapon.

There were some brilliant innovations during the war. Su-7 and MiG-21 aircraft of the Tactics and Combat Development and Training Squadron (TCDTS, later TACDE) would transit through Adampur on their night missions. They attacked PAF airfields deep inside enemy territory. Fuel limitations dictated that the route out and in to be direct. Such return at night at extremely low heights required the single aircraft mission to be given 'homing' or bearing to get back to the closest IAF base. While the control towers or radars monitoring these missions would get faint indications of their transmissions, their reply could not be heard by the returning fighter as it flew at very low heights. It was then that 'Sparrow' control was established. This required an aircraft, mostly MiG-21 of 1 Sqn, to climb and orbit overhead Adampur at about 8-10 km height and transmit the homing to the TCDTS aircraft on its return leg. This worked very well and these night strikes caused considerable attrition to aircrew and aircraft of the PAF. After the war, Pakistan accused Israel and the Soviet Union of supporting India with AWACS aircraft!

The Surrender

The Pakistani forces in East Pakistan under General AAK Niazi, along with 93,000 army, navy, air force, para-military personnel and 'razakars' surrendered to General JS Aurora, GOC-in-C of Eastern Command, Indian Army, at 1631 hrs on 16th December at Dacca and the new nation of Bangladesh was born. The next day we heard General Yahya Khan, President of Pakistan, in a drunken, rambling speech accepting an Indian offer of cease-fire on the western front also. The Air Force called off all offensive action on the evening of 17th December 1971 and the war came to an end.

Experience and Feelings

Many have questioned me about my 'feelings' when I first crossed the border with hostile intent. Yes, there was some element of fear or apprehension, but the requirements of flying an aircraft, of looking out for enemy interceptors and delivering the weapon load pushes all 'feelings' into the background and one's professional training takes over. There is sadness at losing your colleagues, but then they have died for a cause. In this war, the IAF and Adampur did exceedingly well. Many from 101 Sqn and some from 26 Sqn were awarded gallantry medals for exceptional valour. Compared to the stalemate of 1965, the Indian armed forces were the clear winners in the 1971 war. Jointmanship was evident in all operations and the forces were given clear objectives and allowed full freedom to attain them.

Planning Pays

Subsequent analysis revealed that meticulous planning and preparations carried out by Air HQ and WAC in the western sector had paid rich dividends. In the eastern sector, our helicopters played an extremely crucial role in the air battle. The IAF had achieved total air domination after the first two days and its paradrop operation and accuracy of air attack are legend. This accuracy was demonstrated during the strike against Governor's House in Dacca on 14th December morning resulting in the Governor abandoning the building and taking refuge in a hotel under the UN flag, and hastening Pakistan's abject surrender. Nearly 93,000 Pakistanis laid down their arms during a 'surrender ceremony' broadcast live all over the world. Pakistan has yet to live down this humiliation.

In the west, the objective was to force the PAF on the defensive and permit 'hold' operations to remain unhindered. Capturing Pakistani land was not an objective in the west except as a bargaining chip. The aim of the IAF was to cause attrition and prevent the PAF from interfering with our land operations. This objective was achieved as 70 per cent of PAF missions were flown to protect its own bases.

Future wars will be different. There has been a revolution in military affairs. Advancements in aerospace technologies have brought warfare to a different plane. The electromagnetic spectrum will be harnessed to one's advantage while denying it to the enemy. The advent of nuclear weapons in our neighbourhood has added another more sinister dimension to war. Nevertheless, some things will remain the same, and these are training and preparations during peace for the next war.

Veteran Air Marshal Narayan Menon *is an alumni of the prestigious Modern School, Barakhamba Road. He was commissioned into the Flying Branch on 25 Dec 1964. He has flown various types of fighter aircraft which includes Hunter, Gnat, Su-7, MiG-21, Jaguar Trainer, MiG-23 and Mig-29. He has participated in both the wars against Pakistan. During the 1971 war, he was on the posted strength of Adampur and flew 18 missions in SU-7 against various targets in Pakistan. A highly decorated officer, he is now settled at Bengaluru, Karnataka and can be reached at nana_menon@yahoo.co.in and 9880438267.*

22 Ghosts from the Skies: Audacious Night Air Raids by the IAF in 1971

DR Nadkarni

The Context

During WW II, heavy casualties were inflicted on aircraft bombers, as many were shot down by fighter aircraft and ground ack-ack. This forced both the Allied Forces and the Luftwaffe to switch to the safety of darkness. Night bombing became the norm. The fearsome blitzkrieg unleashed by the Luftwaffe devastated most of London and other industrial areas. The Allied Air Forces retaliated with the '1000-bomber' raids on German industrial complexes in a bid to halt their war machine. Apart from just destruction, the night bombing caused a severe psychological impact on the people who lived in constant fear of the sound of military airplanes.

This was the trigger for rapid development of radar to detect these bomber missions as they were flown at high altitudes of 15-25,000 ft. Detection could lead to interception.

After WW II, faster and potent jet fighter-bombers were developed. They could ingress into enemy territory at low levels, thereby avoiding detection by radar. Such low-level attack missions were very effectively employed in 1967, when the Israeli Air Force destroyed most of the Egyptian Air Force on the ground. However, the point to be noted is that all these missions were flown by daylight, not by night.

Did you know that it was the Indian Air Force that mounted the world's very first low-level attack missions by night?

This is a story that is worth telling.

The Setting

In December 1970, when general elections were held in Pakistan, the Awami League in East Pakistan won the majority. Its leader, Sheikh Mujib-ur Rehman, rightfully staked his claim to become the Prime Minister of Pakistan.

However, the "military-landlord-business" nexus of West Pakistan balked at the idea of Bengali domination and hesitated to accept the new dispensation. As violent protests grew in East Pakistan, Gen Yahya Khan ordered a military crackdown on the hapless civilian population, even resorting to the use of air power to crush the rebellion. Genocide was perpetrated, and a mass exodus resulted with millions of refugees pouring into India. India's then Prime Minister, Mrs Indira Gandhi, appealed to the big powers to prevail upon Pakistan to stop the genocide. When her appeals went unheeded, she decided to support the quasi-military resistance organisation in East Pakistan—the Mukti Bahini. As history tells us, this resulted in the Indo-Pak War of 1971 and culminated in the creation of a new nation, Bangladesh.

The Run Up

In February 1971, the Indian Air Force (IAF) formed a new specialised unit—TCDTS (Tactics and Combat Development and Training Squadron). It was based at Ambala and consisted of a mix of six MiG-21 and six Sukhoi SU-7 aircraft. They were manned by highly experienced and competent IAF pilots.

I was then posted at the Aircrew Examining Board (AEB) at Hindon AF Base. By the very nature of my job at the AEB, I was getting plenty of flying, which kept me in top operational trim and always raring to go. Two of us, perhaps in better operational readiness, were attached to the TCDTS. All we knew was that this was to be a crack unit that would develop special tactics to surprise the enemy.

The TCDTS was, in fact, the precursor of the IAF's current TACDE (Tactics And Combat Development Establishment). The TACDE is in many ways the IAF's equivalent of the US Navy's Top Gun. At least, their mandates are the same—to sharpen and develop new air warfare tactics.

Back to mid-1971. The TCDTS was tasked to develop tactics for night counter-air attacks over PAF airfields. This was different from the routine counter-air missions planned by day. Low-level day strikes were expected, but not by night. They were not the norm in warfare. Not yet, anyway.

The task to carry out "night" counter air strikes deep into enemy territory in single aircraft missions was an audacious concept in those days. **In the history of air warfare there was no such precedent. It would be the first-ever attempt by any Air Force.** There were very little cockpit aids for such missions. It would be intimidating and daunting to fly at night, at extremely low levels, over hostile enemy territory, onto blacked-out and heavily defended targets, mainly PAF airfields—all in deathly silence. These were literally 'Ghost Missions'.

We took on the challenge and started developing special attack profiles. A training module was worked out which involved some aggressive handling at low level by night, low-level navigation and practice bombing at Sidhwan Khas range. While low flying itself did not pose any problem, map reading at night while flying at low level threw up some difficulties. We made and fixed a makeshift clamp in the cockpit. It could hold a torch that looked downwards into the cockpit. The illumination from this torch was inadequate to read a map of 1:1 million or, for that matter, any other scale. We then selected routes involving linear features (railway lines, concrete highways and waterways like canals and rivers), which would reflect moonlight and could be made out at night. We then memorised the route and noted down the major pinpoints as a back-up measure. Next, we dimmed the instruments, switch panels and the PKI gunsight till the aiming index was barely visible. We were merely improvising to address the problems and ensure a successful strike on the target.

It was briefly decided to experiment with target illumination. Two of us were sent to Jamnagar on 2nd December to carry out trials by night with M-6 flares over Sarmat Range. These trials were not very effective or conclusive and were to be continued the next night. However, the following day, around noon, the Station Commander sent for us. He told us to discontinue further trials and return to Ambala as soon as possible.

Ghost Strikes

We reached Ambala on 3 December with hectic activity. Clearly, war clouds were peaking. Sure enough, the same evening there was a pre-emptive strike by PAF Mirages over Amritsar SU (Radar Unit) and some of our airfields in the Western sector. We at Ambala did hear jet noises overhead, which must have been PAF B-57s, but no bombs were dropped. Had they missed the target? Anyway, India retaliated against Pakistan. It was a go, with no holds barred. And we were ready.

Let me step back with an analogy here. Think of a boxer who gets hit first, who then gets super-charged to hit back. Even after 50 years, I remember the charged feeling to go in for a few rounds with the PAF after their pre-emptive strike on us. It was the same feeling with all of us in the IAF.

Sure enough, the IAF retaliated with full force. We put into action our night raid plans on PAF airfields like Shorkot Rd, Risalwala, Sargodha, and Chaklala. These airfields had various degrees of difficulty in locating them. I personally found Sargodha relatively easier to locate as a hill feature called Kirana at the beginning of the runway was visible from quite a distance when flying at low level at night. It was left to the individual pilots of the TCDTS to decide on the type of attack to be executed in the terminal phase. Some pilots preferred a timed turn at low level to return to the runway for a second pass. I preferred to climb overhead keeping out of the brilliant display of ack-ack fireworks and dive down through it to execute a steep glide attack along the runway, with precision effect. The unpredictable attacks by each aircraft, due to the differing individual profiles followed, kept the PAF ack-ack gunners guessing from where our aircraft would appear for the second pass. Unpredictability also accorded us mission safety.

These raids continued daily as we went every evening from Ambala to Amritsar (which was the launch base, to get more range and strike deeper), refuelled, and mounted raids throughout the night into Pakistan. We returned to Ambala in the mornings to rest and be ready for the next night attacks.

One night when I had just returned to Amritsar airfield from a raid, a PAF B-57 made a "low pass" over the runway and I instinctively lay down near the blast pen and covered my ears to brace against the bomb blast that would follow. However, nothing happened. Was it a hang-up or a switch selection blunder (unlikely in a two-man B-57 crew)? Within minutes, this aircraft returned for another low pass over the runway for another attempt at dropping its bombs. However, this time it perhaps flew slightly higher and as it eased up, one L-70 gun battery locked-on and scored a hit. The B-57's two-man crew ejected successfully and was captured by our Army. For them, of course, the war was over. If the PAF was trying to match the IAF, they sure found the going tough and their attempts ended there.

While the effect or success of our own night raids over enemy airfields was generally known to us, there was no LLTV (Low Light TV)/FLIR to provide us real feedback on the efficacy of our attacks. The first real confirmation of our audacious strikes emerged during the interrogation of (then) Sqn Ldr DS Jafa (whose Su-7 was shot down during a day attack mission) by a PAF Air Commodore who made pointed enquiries about the IAF's night flying capability and navigation aids on board IAF fighter aircraft. When Jafa replied that they were like in any other aircraft, the PAF Air Commodore insisted that some of the MiGs and Sukhois must have been specially equipped for night operations. When Jafa replied, "Not the Sukhois that we have", the Air Commodore asked, "How are your chaps then popping up over our airfields with such unerring accuracy? How are they finding these targets so accurately in the dead of night that they just press a button, drop bombs, and vanish?" Jafa replied, "So far as I know it is just the compass for direction, steady speed and a good wrist-watch!" The Air Commodore exploded, "You expect me to believe that you have some very superior hot-shot pilots who can pop up at any place, anywhere, at the dead of night without any target-finding device in the aircraft? You better tell me what it is. I will give you until tomorrow." This particular episode is cited in a book titled "Death Wasn't Painful" written by Dhirendra S Jafa. In the same book, Jafa also mentions the visit by an American pilot who met him and made pointed enquiries on how Indian pilots were so accurate and wondered if they were using some new Russian targeting aids that the Americans did not know about! Jafa, of course, stuck to the same answers that he gave to the PAF officer.

Together, the PAF interrogation and the Yankee visit alluded to the fact that the TCDTS pilots must have been hitting their targets accurately. This must have put the PAF airfields under pressure and demoralised the Pakistan military and population. All this, by our incessant ghostly strikes through the night.

Conclusion

This, then is the story of, possibly the first ever counter air bombing missions by night at low levels by single aircraft anywhere in the world. It was executed to perfection by a team of highly dedicated and professional pilots selected to undertake one of the most difficult and daring tasks of the Indo-Pak War of 1971. The team that spooked and tormented the hearts of the PAF consisted of six MiG-21 pilots and five SU-7 pilots. The MiG-21s were flown by Sqn Ldr OP Sharma (later Air Cmde), Sqn Ldr 'Natty' Nadkarni (later Air Mshl), Sqn Ldr 'Ben' Brar (later Air Mshl), Sqn Ldr 'Deshu' Deshpande (later Air Mshl), Sqn Ldr 'Frisky' Verma (later Air Mshl) and Sqn Ldr Teshter Master (later Air Mshl). The SU-7s were flown by Sqn Ldr 'Dice' Dhiman (later Air Cmde), Sqn Ldr 'Doru' Doraiswamy (later AVM), Sqn Ldr 'Pat' Patney (later Air Mshl), Sqn Ldr 'Bum' Bamzai (later Air Cmde) and Sqn Ldr 'Mac' Basra (later Air Mshl).

Needless to say, the team was extremely special, and I was proud to be a member of the elite professionals who executed 'Ghost Strikes' in 1971.

The calibre and professionalism of Indian Air Force pilots lives on today as we witnessed in the daring Balakot strike emulating, I dare say, the legacy left behind by us.

Veteran Air Marshal DR Nadkarni *was commissioned in the Flying Branch in Dec 1958. He is a fighter pilot with more than 4500 hours of accident-free flying. He has participated in both the 1965 and 1971 wars. He has the distinction of being a proud member of the first team that flew "nine aircraft aerobatics on the hunter aircraft". He retired in Oct 1995 and is now settled at Gurugram. He can be contacted at dinadkarni@gmail.com and 9811213201.*

23 BANGLADESH LIBERATION WAR - 1971

Mantosh Kumar Nag

During the Bangladesh War, I was on the posted strength of 70 Squadron (SAM-II), Salt Lake, Calcutta-West Bengal.

On January 1, 1972, after the exchange of New Year Greetings, I was called by the Unit Adjutant to his office. I was asked to proceed to Calcutta International Airport (then under the control of IAF), en-route Dacca International Airport in Bangladesh immediately and was given a movement order. Not much briefing was given to me. Nor did I ask the reason for such a move. As I was born at Dacca, I was too happy since I was getting a chance to visit my birth place. At first, it appeared to be a dream only. By afternoon on the same day, I reported to Calcutta Airport which was at that time guarded by the Indian Army. I was taken to the Air Force authorities there.

Within an hour, I was given an Air ticket from Calcutta to Dacca by Indian Airlines in Aircraft Fokker Friendship. On the morning of January 2, 1972, I was ready but the flight got delayed because of the movement of Mr Sheikh Mujibur Rahman (Founder of Bangladesh) who was to land at Calcutta enroute his journey to Dacca.

Mr Sheikh Mujibur Rahman was released by the Pakistan Army and flown to London and handed over to the Indian Embassy. From there, he was flown to India at Palam Airport and received by the Indian Prime Minister, Mrs Indira Gandhi. After a formal exchange of greetings at Palam Airport, he was flown to Calcutta and from there his aircraft took off for Dacca around 9:30 am. The aircraft was escorted by two Hunter Aircraft which had taken off from 6 Wing Barrackpore. After his aircraft landed at Dacca, our aircraft took off and landed at Dacca at around 10:30 a.m. I was taken to the Orderly Room by IAF Police and introduced to the Adjutant, Flying Officer Singh who welcomed me.

The Adjutant knew that I was born in Dacca and was partially brought up there. I was well conversant with the local colloquial Bengali language and had migrated to India in March 1950 and joined Indian Air Force in May 1960. The Adjutant too happened to be a native of West Punjab and he too had migrated to India as a child with his parents after partition.

He assigned me the job of interpreter from English to Bengali language and vice versa to interact with Mr Edward Kennedy (Youngest brother of President John F Kennedy) who was leading a UNO team to assess the damage caused by the War, so as to get relief from UNO for the affected people.

I was introduced to Mr Edward Kennedy who was standing by the side of Chetak helicopter of IAF along with his wife, Mrs Kennedy and son of Robert Kennedy (President designate who was assassinated in 1968).

I was flown along with Mr Edward Kennedy and we landed at three different places and interacted with the local people. As already mentioned above, the purpose of Mr Edward Kennedy's visit was to assess the damage and determine the quantum of relief to be given to the locally affected people by UNO.

My stay at Dacca was for 11 days from 02 January, 1972 to 12 January, 1972 both days inclusive. During my stay, I had the opportunity to visit Dacca Mitford Hospital where I was born. The local people and the police gave me a big welcome and treated me like a VIP. On January 12, 1972, I was flown back to India by IAF Dakota and landed at 6 Wing Barrackpore. Though I had no role in the 1971 war yet I still cherish the memories of that visit to my birth place.

Veteran Hony Flying Officer Montosh Kumar Nag *was enrolled in the Elect Fit trade on 21 May 1960. During the 1971 war he was on the posted strength of 70 Squadron which was based at Salt Lake. The Veteran played an important role post the 1971 war. He was hand-picked to be an interpreter with the UNO team which had come to assess the damage that had occurred at Dacca during the war. He was born at Dacca and that is the reason for his having been picked up for this job. He is settled at Chandigarh and can be reached at nag_mantosh@yahoo.co.in and 9876733211.*

24 CROSSING THE RUNWAY DURING BLACKOUT

K Mohanchandran Nair

I was an under-trainee in Bangalore (Now Bengaluru) in 1971. Suddenly our conversion training was ceased. Reason was well known to all, disturbance with our neighbours along the Western border.

We were instructed to pack our belongings and be ready to move at a short notice. Soon we were airlifted in small batches to move to various locations. I landed up at Allahabad from where I was routed to Bombay (Now Mumbai) to work with the Air Force Liaison Cell at Santacruz airport. Our section had five airmen with one officer as Officer-in Charge. Our task was to issue Air Defence Clearance (ADC) to all the flights operating from and through Bombay.

I was accommodated at the old Kalina camp along with a few army personnel. The camp is located right in the middle of Bombay City just near the rear gate of the aerodrome. Our mode of conveyance to our workplace was through the State owned transport buses.

I was just 22-year-old, fresh from training centre with unfinished training. I had no knowledge about the working of a normal Air Force Station as I had hardly seen any Air Force Station. The work was quite interesting, and I was thoroughly enjoying it and that too at the biggest airport in India.

Things suddenly changed on 3rd Dec 1971 when the Pakis attacked a few of the Air Force Bases in the North. The situation changed immediately with counter attacks from our side after the war was officially declared by our Prime Minister. Meanwhile, the Pakistan army was moving into our territory. Life changed with seriousness everywhere. High alert was sounded and strict security measures were imposed immediately along with night black-out. In a big city like Bombay, it was not practical to have total black-out. Airport security was further tightened. All of us were instructed to keep a strict vigil on the surroundings. During such observation, we caught certain suspects from the Kalina camp area and handed them over to the civil Police.

Good news was pouring in daily as the Indian Armed forces were causing massive destruction for the Pakis. Adding fuel to fire the Pakistan citizens were getting agitated on their leadership and their armed forces started losing morale. It was a short war of just 14 days and on 16th Dec 1971, Lt Gen Niazi alongwith 93000 soldiers surrendered. It was big victory for India. We did lose many personnel during this war. My big salute to all of them.

> ***"The country owes a lot to you, and you shall always be remembered".***

On one of the days when I was to go for night shift, I missed the bus to our work place. The only option was to enter from the rear gate of the airport, cross the big runway and reach the office. I did not want to be late to relieve my colleague. So, crossing the runway, though unauthorised, was the only option. Thus, I entered through the rear gate and walked towards the runway. It was around 6:30 pm and it was dark. From the edge of the runway I started walking towards the other side with long steps. All of a sudden, there was sound of Blackout siren and all the lights went off. I was moving forward into pitch darkness like a blind man. I made a fast walk to cross the runway as quick as possible. I had hardly walked a few meters and there was thunderous sound behind me. It was a jet plane that had just landed. A lightening effect of a shock went through me which arrested my movement for a few moments. Then I ran as fast as I could to the other end of runway, and I fell as I hit some fixture. I got up quickly and dashed in the direction of ATC. I had some bruises but could reach in time for duty. Memory of this incident still brings back to me a feeling of guilt and then the God's grace too, or else I would not have been there to tell this story and war time experience of a 22-year-old LAC in this lovely Air Force.

Veteran Sgt K Mohanchandran Nair *was enrolled in the Radio Fitter trade on 04 Apr 1967.During the year 1971, he was undergoing conversion training at Bangalore. The training was suddenly ceased and all the trainees were routed to different locations to meet the operational commitments. He was routed to Allahabad initially and then to Mumbai to work with the Air Force Liaison Cell at the Mumbai International Airport. He was associated there with issuing the ADC clearance. He was discharged from the Air Force on 30 Jun 1983. He is now settled at Thiruvananthapuram and can be reached at nmohanc@yahoo.com and 9847258682.*

25 AN-12s of ARC and When We Strayed into Pakistan

NS Nathan

I was on deputation to ARC as the AN-12 Crew. As a team, we were extremely busy in undertaking support missions for Mukti Bahini. It started sometimes in summer of 1971, much before the actual war and we continued till Feb 1972. We were flying day and night, with no or minimal rest and periodic short naps on the tarmac during loading/ offloading and refueling halts. There was a fixed crew for each aircraft, and we flew from far and wide to Agartala, the routing would be normally from bases in Rajasthan and Madhya Pradesh via Bagdogra/ Guwahati to Agartala. The schedule was so hectic that we were mostly in overalls.

On one of such flights with jam packed Mukti Bahini troops, may be around 150 passengers on board, we did a refueling halt at Guwahati enroute our flight to Agartala. Monsoons were at their peak. We were flying at around 12000 feet. We could not climb higher as the passenger/ cargo cabin was not pressurised. We got caught in the middle of huge CBs with thunderstorm and lightning. The transport crew encounters such situations often while doing cross country sorties but this one was really tough. The Navigator finally gave up the lateral guidance for weather avoidance. We finally managed to land at Agartala with torn redome, damaged engine cowling, dirty cabin with vomits and to crown it all with bullet holed control surfaces.

Apart from airlifting troops, we did some critical Elint and Surveillance missions along the Western Border. In one of such missions on the intervening night of 12/13 Oct 1971, we had apparently strayed inside Pakistan near Rahimyarkhan. We strayed for almost 18 minutes. We were sure sitting ducks for the PAF 104s which I am sure would have scrambled after learning about our ingress into their territory.

Thanks to two of our scrambled MiG 21s who came to our rescue. That was probably the reason for PAF 104s to turn back. We were escorted back to India by these MiGs with total protection in the air. That was probably the first and last time I saw the belly of a Mig-21 so close in mid air.

We were escorted back to Ambala where we landed. Our Old Man, Air Commodore MS Aulakh, who was away to Delhi, was woken up in his sleep and asked to proceed to Ambala to give us the much-deserved dressing down. Sure enough, we were given all kinds of sweet Punjabi abuses by Aulakh Sir who was otherwise usually a very gentle and nice person with kind words.

Later on, we were shocked to see our AN-12 tracks inside Pakistan near Rahimyarkhan. We were sure to have been shot and captured by Pakistanis that night but for the timely intervention and the help from our MiG 21s which had probably scrambled from some of our bases in Rajasthan.

Memories of that incident send shivers down my spine even today. I thank God, the Almighty, for saving us.

The 1971 Operations were too good to cherish. Hats off to the entire team of Pilots, Engineers, Technicians and the ancillary support staff. Each and everyone played his/her part very well culminating in the great success of operations.

Veteran Wg Cdr NS Nathan *was commissioned in the Flying Branch on 16 May 1965. During the 1971 war, he was on deputation to ARC as a part of the AN-12 crew. He was actively involved in the 1971 war wherein he flew a few important ELINT missions. He took premature retirement in 1984 and continued with civil flying with Air India and Singapore Airlines. He has more than 18000 flying hours to his credit. From 2006 onwards, he is an instructor with the Boeing simulator. He is settled at Chennai. He can be reached at 777nathan787@gmail.com and 8951141033.*

26 THE 1971 WAR

AK Nijhawan

As Seen by a Final Term Cadet of NDA

When the war broke out in Dec 71, I was still a cadet at the NDA. Our Course, the 42nd NDA was into its fifth term and the 41st course was to pass out in early December. Most of the uniformed officers at the Academy who were medically fit had been asked to join their units, squadrons and ships in November itself. The last days of that term were managed by the leftover skeleton staff. The cadets' activities were restricted to digging trenches in the battalion area, covering cabin windowpanes with black paper in anticipation of air raids, practising for the POP and preparing for the end-of-term exams. The POP was a lukewarm affair with no outside guest and the salute being taken in-house by the Commandant.

By the time the term ended, the war had started. After the POP, we cadets dispersed for the term break in the usual manner. I was to take the NDA Special train to Delhi in the evening from Kirkee (now Khadki). The Special departed around 7 pm and headed towards Bombay (now Mumbai). Traversing the rugged Deccan Plateau to Lonavala and then downhill the Western Ghats to Karjat, it reached Dadar at Bombay around midnight. The powerful electric locomotive that brought the Special from Kirkee was replaced by a huge steam Iron Horse and the train switched over from Central Railway to the Western Railway. Hereafter, it followed the Western Railway route to Delhi. It was almost 2 hours of shunting and changing over at Dadar before the Special left for Delhi.

As mentioned earlier, the war had already started and the whole country stood in support of Armed Forces. One could see and feel patriotism oozing out from every corner of the country, at least from Kirkee to Delhi wherever the train stopped enroute. Nobody considered it to be an NDA Special but took it to be a Military Special, full of troops being relocated to border areas. Even when informed that the train was full of cadets, people would not believe us and thought that due to security reasons we were not telling the truth. Passing through Surat, Ankleshwar, Bharuch, Baroda, Godhra, and Dahod we were greeted by enthusiastic crowds at every station. We reached Ratlam in the evening just after dark around dinner time. The platform was full of volunteers, male and female, mostly young, from the Lions Club. They had come to know that a military special, full of young soldiers heading north, was passing through. They had organised dinner packets for us and had come to the railway station to hand them over and, of course, have a glimpse of the warriors. Patriotism was writ large on their faces, hearts going out to each one of us, wishing us victory and a long life. The whole atmosphere at the platform was charged with patriotic fervour. After the halt, as the train moved on its onward journey, umpteen hands could be seen waving and some girls blowing flying kisses. In that din, one could hear sympathetic adjectives like "bechare" and "poor" guys.

Overflowing Patriotism

Next morning, before reaching Delhi, the train stopped at platform number 1 at Faridabad. It was full of open kitchens, preparing breakfast and meals for soldiers passing through. Any soldier could just walk in and eat to his heart's content without paying a penny. As the train moved north, the patriotism was more and more evident. On reaching Delhi, when we were trying to get to our homes, the auto rickshaws would not charge us anything. We were not in our uniforms, but the haircut and the unmistakable black fauji trunk was enough to reveal our identity. That's how the general public was supporting the Armed Forces. That was the ground reality personally experienced and witnessed during the 14-day war.

There is another aspect of the war I would like to mention here. After the term break, I did not return to the Academy by the Special. Being an appointment cadet, I was required to report a week earlier at the NDA. So three of us travelled to Bombay by the Frontier Mail from New Delhi and then onwards to Poona (there was no direct train to Poona those days). The war had ended by now and India had clocked a comprehensive win over Pakistan. We were travelling by first class and had another co-traveller in our compartment. He happened to be a young captain going on leave after the war. His face was glowing with pride. Pride, because he had actively participated in the war, probably his first time, handsomely won it, survived it, and was now going on a well-deserved leave to unite with his family. We could see a peculiar glow and a sense of achievement on his face. I still remember his words, "I took part in the war, am going home now". Though slightly injured, he was bubbling with enthusiasm, ever eager to pour his heart out to receptive ears. He had umpteen stories to tell about the battles he took part in. The pride and the glow on his face is unforgettable. Though there was some remorse too at losing some of his comrades, the sense of achievement was unmistakably visible. We cadets could only hope to be in his shoes later in life.

Lucky to be with the War Heroes

After passing out from the NDA we landed up at EFS, Bidar, in July 1972 to train on HT-2s. Six months later, having conquered the snaky HT-2, we moved to AFA in Jan 1973 for the intermediate stage on the Texan Harvards. Many of the instructors at the training institutes were 1971 war veterans, and a few out of them had also been PoWs. To name a few, I clearly remember Roy Massey and AM Ganapathy, both VrC awardees. Among the ex-PoWs, we had Dilip Parulkar, Vikram Pethia and HND Mullaferoze, as far as my memory goes. One could still see the physical scars on both Parulkar and Pethia, but they always had an unmistakable aura of invincibility. Not everyone of us could fly with them, but I had the unique privilege of flying a few sorties with Parulkar at AFA—I still cherish those moments. Being a soldier in uniform, that is the only little connection with the 1971 war I can recollect.

Veteran Wg Cdr Ashok Kumar Nijhawan *was commissioned in the Flying Branch on 09 Feb 1974. During the 1971 War he was a Cadet at NDA. He has given a good account of his memories of the 1971 war. He held a number of key appointment whilst in service including the Command of 106 Sqn. He took premature retirement on 31 Oct 1996. Post retirement he continued with various flying assignments. During his 48 years of long career in the aviation, he clocked around 14000 hours of flying. He is settled at Gurugram and can be reached at ashoknijhawan@hotmail.com and 9818708205.*

27 Views from Low Level Observation Post

Rajinder Singh Padda

During the 1971 war I was on the posted strength of FTW Hakimpet. I was a Sgt and looking after the Instrument Trade.

In the month of Oct 71, I was on leave as my wife was on family way and the baby was due in the last week of Oct 71. I was staying locally at Hakimpet.

Somewhere in the middle of Oct 71, a signal was received for routing plenty of airmen to various locations under Western Air Command and Eastern Air Command. We were informed on 18th Oct 71 to be ready to move at short notice. On 19th Oct 71, it was Diwali. Two AN-12 aircraft arrived and picked up plenty of airmen and headed towards their respective destinations.

I was also to move. I was called by the Station Adjt. I explained to him my personal issue at hand. The adjutant was kind enough to listen to me. He told me to be ready in the next 4 to 5 days to move with the next lot. With the blessings of the God, the delivery took place during this period and now I was ready to move. To my further good luck, there was no movement for next three weeks. By this time my wife was back home with the baby. I was lucky to be allotted a new SMQ which was very close to the SSQ. I was a much relieved man now.

On 13th November we were called and asked to be ready for movement next day by train. I, along with some more airmen, was routed to 19 Wing on 14th November evening. On arrival there, we were attached to 19 Wing AF. Every day we used to report to Stn Headquarter and wait for further instructions. Finally, on 2nd December we were told that we will be sent for LLOP duties. Six batches were made consisting of one Sgt and three Cpls each. We were briefed about operating the Walkie-Talkie sets. We were asked to be ready next morning for move. Next morning on 3rd December we were given Walkie-Talkie sets, some utensils and dry ration for 3 to 4 days. In the afternoon, we were dropped at our locations by helicopter. It was a State Govt building having 2-3 rooms and one chowkidar was looking after those rooms. We were given one room for our stay. We cooked rice and dal on a make shift chullah with fire wood for our dinner. Next day morning two of us stayed there for operating the set and myself with one more airman went to buy mustard oil, potatoes, onions and some condiments from a small shop which was about 2 kms away. As we reached the shop, we saw four aircraft heading towards East Pakistan at a very low level. We bought our items and rushed back to our post. When we reached our post, the aircraft were coming back at a very high level away from our place.

This routine continued for many days. Whenever, we saw any aircraft movement, we would inform the same to 19 Wing, AF. Over a period of time the batteries of our sets became weak. Now we were not able to contact our base but we could communicate with the others posts. The frequency of aircraft movement started reducing slowly and, in a few days, became negligible.

One fine day we got a message from the next LLOP that a chopper is coming for picking us up. We packed our items and the chopper came. We came back to Base. We stayed at 19 Wing till 30th December. On 30th December we were routed back to our unit and we celebrated the New Year (31st midnight) in the train while travelling from Howrah to Secunderabad. We reached Hakimpet on 1st January 1972 in the evening. Families took a sigh of relief and welcomed us.

The memories of 1971 are still fresh in my mind. I shall always remain grateful to Air Force as all my personal requirements were met. And I was lucky to participate in the war also.

Veteran MWO Rajinder Singh Padda *was enrolled in the Instrument Fitter trade on 15 Dec 1959. During the 1971 war, he was on the posted strength of FTW Hakimpet. He was attached to 19 Wing, AF and assigned to man an LLOP with the help of three more airmen. He is backed by rich experience and has worked on various types of fighter aircraft. He superannuated from the Air Force on 31 Jan 1997. He is now settled at Bule Nangal (Amritsar) and can be reached at rajspadda@yahoo.com and 8146989993.*

28 ON THE 1971 WAR

KC Parik

On the morning of 10th Nov 1971, a detachment consisting of six Vampires (two T-55 and four MK 52) took off from FTW Hakimpet with eight pilots led by then Wg Cdr WH Marshal.

Initially, we were based at 12 Wing, AF and on commencement of hostilities, we took off for Halwara on 9th Dec. Two Vampires MK52 were sent to Srinagar. Until then, we were not told about our role. The day after our arrival at Halwara, we learnt that we would carry out night attacks on assigned targets. All six of us were fully ops day and night. Navigation at night in blackout conditions, using only compass and vintage clocks in a Vampire was a challenging task. With permission from the Detachment Commander, I took two MiG-21 clocks on loan from the Equipment Section, improvised the clamps at the Station Workshop and fitted the clocks, one each in the two Vampire cockpits at a suitable place. They proved very useful during ops.

We were assigned targets inside Pakistan at places near Multan, Okara, Patoki, Changa-Manga in Multan–Bahawalpur sector. All of us flew our night missions and achieved a high rate of success with no casualties. We mostly used T-10 rockets and 4 x 20 mm Aden guns for the attack.

On 14th Dec 1971, I was on standby for a night mission along with Flt Lt Girish Mehra at the Base Ops. We were summoned by Wg Cdr Sabherwal, the COO of the Station. He assigned us a target, i.e., a goods train at Khudian Khas railway station, reportedly loaded with heavy ammunition. After immaculate flight planning, we took off from Halwara at about 2330 hrs. We had 8 x T-10 rockets and guns. We had got used to navigate in dark blacked out nights by now. I was in the right (Captain's seat) with Girish on the left one. I had planned to do right hand attack. We flew at an ultra-low-level of 200–250′ AGL at night to avoid detection by PAF radars, flying initially at 300 knots.

Khudian Khas railway station was located on the Bahawalpur-Kasur railway line running nearly North-South. We were approaching almost at 90 deg to the railway line from a Westerly direction. At IP, we increased our speed to 360 kts and at pull-up point, I pulled up for a right-hand attack on the target. As I gained height, I could see railway line shining a bit in the moonlight. I noticed a dark patch on the railway line. Obviously, the goods train was parked at that spot. I went in for an RP attack and fired four T-10 rockets. As I pulled out, Girish confirmed a direct hit. I turned right and climbed for a second attack but saw secondary explosions on the train. As it was loaded with heavy ammunition, bogie after bogie exploded in a chain reaction. Debris were flying quite high, making it impossible to carry out another attack. In fact, the explosions were spectacular, and we circled over the site watching them. Realising that we had spent too much time over the target, I headed East, dived to ultra-low level and flew at high speed.

As we were entering Indian territory, we saw an air-to-air missile going past us on the left and slightly above that exploded some 2–3 km ahead of us at 11:30 O'clock. I was flash blinded by the explosion and could not see the instruments for a while. We continued towards Halwara not actually knowing as to where did that missile come from. We were on track. Smog was hanging over the airfield at 150 to 200' AGL. We had difficulty in sighting the flare path. We did a timed circuit and landed.

I was awarded Vayu Sena Medal (Gallantry) for my participation in the 1971 war with Pakistan.

Veteran Wg Cdr KC Parik *was commissioned in the Flying Branch on 09 Mar 1963. During the 1971 war he was a member of the operational detachment formation which was given a special role. On 11th Dec 1971 and 12 Dec 1971, he carried out two missions at night causing extensive damage to the installations at Pakistan. He carried out both these attacks with extreme precision. He was awarded Vayu Sena Medal (Gallantry) for his contribution during the war. He retired in Sep 1989. He is settled at Baroda and can be reached at kailash.parik@gmail.com and 9824279928.*

29 An Attack on Peshawar

CV Parker

Background

Until sunrise on 04th Dec 1971, the well defended PAF rear air base at Peshawar could only be reached by our twin–engine Canberra light bombers that had attacked it by night during the 1965 Indo-Pak War. In the late 1960s the IAF had acquired the updated Hunter MK 56A aircraft which, with its larger fuel capacity (230 gllns on the inboard pylons) increased its radius of action and range. Operating from Pathankot, it was now possible to cross the width of Pakistan and reach Peshawar low level but with no external weapon load i.e a gun strike with only 4x30mm cannons. As a Wing Commander I was in command of No. 20 Squadron, one of the two Sqns equipped with the new Hunters and relocated to Pathankot in early 1971. My war orders included Peshawar air base as one of my counter air targets. We trained accordingly. Owing to its location close to the border, Pathankot was vulnerable, hence all our serviceable aircrâft, pilots and supporting technicians went for night harbour to Ambala. On 03rd Dec 1971, when the PAF carried out its pre-emptive strike on Pathankot at 1715 hrs, my Sqn was away in Ambala and I was alone at base with two young pilots. I was told to carry out a two-aircraft gun strike on Peshawar at sunrise on 04th Dec 1971. When I reminded the higher-ups that my aircraft would only return much later, I was ordered to take two aircraft from our sister Sqn, but ToT had to be sunrise Peshawar time.

Attack

I took Flt Lt CS Dhillon (Channi) as my wingman and briefed him thoroughly. When we reached our sister Sqn's tarmac at 4:30 am on 04th Dec 1971, I was upset to see that the two aircraft prepared for us still had their rocket projectile (R/P) rails fitted though I had asked for clean aircraft + four tanks + full ammo. A quick calculation told me that we would lose about 500 lb of fuel carrying these rails, but as there was no time to remove them, I would have to forgo my combat fuel. Since Channi was not currently night qualified, I kept my nav lights ON for him to do a formation take-off in the dark. He coped well and we stayed low and in our own territory as long as possible before I came in from the West for our first pass over Peshawar air base. We seemed to have taken them by surprise; no ground fire was experienced as I went for an aircraft parked on the tarmac while Channi opened up on what appeared to be an airfield fuel dump. On our second pass made from the South I realised that there was no gun fire from the ground as the airfield was being capped by their aircraft; two Sabre aircraft crossed me diagonally but the early dawn visibility was not good and we set course for home, low level and high speed with an indeterminate number of Sabre aircraft in chase

I opened up our pair and placed Channi about 600 yds to my port so that we gave each other cross cover and forced the Sabres to divide their attention. They closed in very slowly and, as Channi and I were in R/T contact, I was able to break him to the port and into our own air space calculating that the Sabres would not follow him too deeply. I now had two or three Sabre aircraft behind me and as they opened fire, I broke into them and reversed, taking advantage of the Hunter's turning radius, around some high ground. One Sabre could not hold the turn and overshot me right in front. I fired but very few rounds must have been left after my two long bursts at Peshawar so, though the camera gun captured the enemy aircraft, I was not sure as to whether I had hit him or not. By now we were approaching Akhnoor area where a fierce land battle seemed to be taking place and both sides opened up on me as I was travelling West to East

I knew I had been hit and was very low on fuel as was also Channi who was one minute behind me. Pathankot gave us a direct approach and landing from the North and both our aircraft engines flamed out on the taxi track back to the aircraft pens. Our attack had been successful but my aircraft had 22 hits while Channi's had four. Minutes later, the SASO HQ WAC New Delhi was on the line for an immediate repeat attack. I strongly advised him to defer it to a later time but he insisted that the pressure had to be kept up so that the PAF could not use their Air Force in Peshawar to attack our ground forces. Since these were direct orders and my own aircraft had returned from Ambala, I had no choice and sent off the next pair after briefing them thoroughly to carry out the attack but not to get involved in air combat over the target. Their attack went through but unfortunately, we lost one aircraft and a pilot.

An Attack on Attock

Background

Among the Pakistani 'targets of economic value' allocated to my Sqn was the Attock Oil Refinery not too far from Islamabad. Based on intelligence inputs, we visited our own refineries to learn their vulnerable points. We arranged for our firing range near Jamnagar to place steel sheets of differing widths behind the Front Gun targets. With my Flight Commander as my wingman and the gun packs in our aircraft fitted with varying sequences of HE (High Explosive) and ball ammo, we made a practice Lo-Hi-Lo flight from Pathankot overflying Ambala and Ahmedabad and carried out a gun strike on Sarmat Range, target firing all four guns. The results helped us determine the optimum belting of ammunition to penetrate steel. It was our intention to start a fire and allow it to do the damage.

Attack

On 06th Dec 1971, I led a four-aircraft gun strike with Attock Oil Refinery as our target. Intelligence had briefed us that it was heavily defended with AD Arty. Since such guns were normally controlled by an Air Defence Control Centre, and the nearest one was at the PAF air base at Chaklala, I decided to attack Chaklala first to cause disruption. This diversionary attack paid off and our first West–East attack on the refinery drew no ground fire but our second on the South–North axis drew considerable ground fire. However, none of us were hit and we saw the unusual sight of a refinery on fire! The blaze was still visible to our Canberra aircraft crew on their night bombing raids. We repeated the attack two days later when I led another four–aircraft strike but there were mainly charred remains and debris. Along with the IAF attack on the Karachi Oil Refinery on 04th Dec 1971, Pakistan was now running short on fuel which intelligence told us was being trucked into the country overland.

Veteran AVM CV Parker *was commissioned in the Flying Branch in 1952. He is a fighter pilot and has flown various aircraft on the inventory of IAF and has more than 4000 hours of flying to his credit. During the 1971 War he was Commanding 20 Sqn, AF. He excelled in the 1971 War and was awarded the most coveted award "Maha Vir Chakra". He is a recipient of Vayu Sena Medal also. He is a prolific writer and has been regularly contributing to the AFA magazine, "The Eagle's Eye". He is settled down at Hyderabad and can be reached at cvparker22@gmail.com and 9810099874.*

30 A Desk Warrior

PP Pawar

At the War Front from Air HQ

Strange as it may sound, but this is the contribution of a Ground Duty Officer to the 1971 Indo Pak War. When the war fever was gathering momentum, I happened to be ADPO 1(b) at Air Hq (called the 'P' Staff) dealing with Postings & Promotions of all ground duty officers (Tech & Non-tech). My colleague Air Commodore Jasjit Singh VrC (then Sqn Ldr) was handling the postings of Flying Branch officers. We were housed in Room No. 335 Air HQ. We prepared our war plans by collecting details of all officers employed on staff duties at Air HQ, Command Hq, and other non-operational units. The details pertained to their flying experience, type qualification courses undergone etc.

This was a very laborious task as it involved all units of the AF including far-flung tech depots, training units, etc. The main aim was to have information readily available in respect of all officers in the reserve those could be drawn to man frontline Wings and Squadrons if the need arose. Both of us prepared this data manually in those days.

The war, as expected, did break out and the operations got underway. My friend Jasjit, a true Air Warrior as he was and a fully ops pilot on Mysteres was eagerly wanting to go to his squadron based in the north. He was certain that the DPO would never agree to his request unless I took on the responsibilities of his work. He was confident that I had sufficient knowledge of his work and could handle it well in his absence.

We met the DPO with Jasjit's request and after a short discussion, he agreed to his flying for his ex-squadron. The ball was now in my court with the only help available being our Statistics Officer, Flt Lt D Bakshi. The war gathered momentum and requests from the field commanders began pouring in for aircrew and technical officers to augment their existing manpower. I could meet their requests with the help of a well made out reserve list. With the help of our transport squadrons from WAC, we were able to position the officers in quick time.

All was going on well and we were in constant touch with the Ops Dte at Air Hq that was coordinating the requirements. Air Mshl Denzil Keelor (then Sqn Ldr), the hero of the 1965 War, was then in the Air Defence Dte and would call every day with a request that he be sent to his squadron at Adampur. I could not oblige him as there was an unwritten rule that officers from operational Directorates at Air HQ were not to be deployed on active flying duties for fear of being taken as PoWs and the subsequent consequences.

A Daring Decision

One fine day, I got a frantic call from the Ops room that WAC wanted three fully ops MiG pilots to be positioned at Adampur immediately. I could muster only two from my reserve list but the third was just not available. Yes, my eyes did fall on Denzil, the best option available, but as per our internal guidelines he was barred from deployment. The pressure from the Ops staff was growing on me. It was evening and I thought I should get the DPO or DDPO to hold my hand to send Denzil. Unfortunately, both had left for home and when I returned to my office I found Denzil there. He said, "PP let me go." Without hesitation I said, "GO". With the help of 3 Wing and the Dakota Squadron based at Palam, I managed to send Denzil to Adampur the same evening.

Next morning was peaceful but when I was about to have lunch, I got a call from Air HQ Ops room to say that Denzil had been fired upon and had ejected across the border. My heart sank and I thought the whole world had come to an end. I got scared, mortified with strange thoughts crossing my mind of a court of inquiry, a court martial, dismissal from service and wife and child left unprotected. My colleagues returned from lunch and on hearing the news and seeing my condition tried to console me. One of them, a neighbour of Denzil, had just seen his family having lunch on the lawns. He wanted to inform Mrs Keelor but I stopped him telling him that she would be officially informed by Air HQ.

I gathered courage and informed the DDPO and DPO of having sent Denzil on my own. Both told me to relax and hope for the best. I spent the next few hours praying for Denzil's safe return and at about seven in the evening, my telephone rang. It was the Air HQ Ops room to say, 'PP, Denzil has walked back to Indian territory and is being brought to Adampur." I raised my hands and thanked the Almighty for what he had done. I ran out and informed every one of the good news.

The Awards

We won the war triumphantly and slowly things started returning to normal. All the Operational Command Chiefs wrote to the CAS thanking him for the support received from Air HQ and especially the prompt placement of manpower required by squadrons and stations as the attrition rate had risen rapidly. This was also mentioned by Air Chief Marshal PC Lal in his various addressees. My friend, Jasjit, returned having flown 22 operational sorties and was recommended for a Vir Chakra. The AOA recommended me for a VSM and Bakshi for a Commendation of CAS. However, the Honours and Awards Committee while processing the awards changed my VSM to a Mention-in-Despatch, a gallantry award. I was rewarded with suitable benefits from both the Central and State Governments.

Veteran Wg Cdr PP Pawar *was commissioned into the Administrative Branch on 31 May 1959. During the 1971 War he was on the posted strength of DPO at Air HQ. He was responsible for the augmentation of officers of Ground Duty Branches initially. Subsequently, his counterpart, then Sqn Ldr Jasjit Singh who was looking after the similar task for Flying Branch Officer, had himself to go back to his parent Squadron to make good the shortage of pilots. He took on the additional responsibilities of augmentation and manpower planning of Flying Branch Officers. He was awarded "Mention-in Despatches" for the same. He retired on 30 Jun 1981 and is presently settled at Mumbai. He can be reached at padmanabh_pawar@yahoo.co.in and 9920948070.*

31 DEATH WOULD HAVE BEEN LESSER PAINFUL

Aditya Vikram Pethia

Move of Flying Instructors to War Front

During 1971, I was on the posted strength of Flying Training School. In July 1971, orders were received for the Flying Instructors to be stand by to move out at one week's notice for operational flying, if and when the situation demanded. In September 1971, orders were received to be ready to move out at short notice for operational duty in the event of war.

In October 1971, a few of us were airlifted to New Delhi and later we reported to WAC. One fine morning, a few of us were asked to reach Jamnagar by the evening. How? Even if we were authorised to move by Indian Airlines Corporation (IAC) from Delhi to Bombay the earliest flight from Bombay to Jamnagar was only the next day. However, good sense prevailed and we were airlifted to Jamnagar. I was to join Target Towing Flight (TTF) at Jamnagar. If my memory serves me right, it was Diwali evening. We took off and landed at Jamnagar at night.

The next morning, I reported to TTF. Sqn Ldr VN Johri, Flt Lt V Mathur, Flt Lt D'Souza and Flt Lt Das Gupta were on the posted strength of TTF. Flt Lt SS Naqvi, Flt Lt Saluja and myself were on attachment. The CO, Sqn Ldr Johri gave a dual check and I was to carry out a handling sortie on a Mystere. After a few days, seven of us with seven Mysteres took off for Nal and a new Squadron was formed and numbered **120 Squadron Air Force**. At Nal, not much of an accommodation existed. There was a long barrack and the seven of us, Technical, Adm and ATC officers (Sqn Ldr Jain, later on AOA) were given cots and that was it. MiG Squadron Wg Cdr Anand, Sqn Ldr Salins, Flt Lt Bundle Tyagi (later CAS) were also accommodated there.

A jeep was given which was to be used by the CO as his vehicle as well as the air crew. A 3-tonner for the ground crew was all that we had to move them. The clutch lever of the jeep would come out and being the leanest person, it was my duty to go under the jeep and place the lever in the socket. Later, some of us would push the jeep while the CO sat at the controls. He would put it in the first gear and we would run behind and then jump into it. I remembered my younger days when the clutch cable of my scooter broke. That is how we used to reach the Squadron.

Preparatory Phase

A few low-level navigation sorties were flown with fully armed aircraft. After a few sorties, it was noticed that the caps of the rocket pods (57 mm) were getting scratched due to insect hits to the pods; as a result, the pods had to be offloaded.

The MIGs used to be ferried out to Chandigarh whereas the Mysteres went to Jamnagar for servicing.

War was imminent, but life gets funny—an auditor had come to Nal (3 C&MU) and was playing hell with the system—as we call it in the Air Force. One fine morning, the auditor sat behind a bush with a bottle of rum answering his natures call. A MiG was being ferried from Chandigarh and the pilot decided to go supersonic over Nal. With the sonic boom, the auditor ran towards the Officers' Mess. The waiters shouted, "Do not panic, pick up your pyjama, it's our aircraft only". By the evening, the auditor vanished from the Station.

Every day, it was the same routine—morning to underground ACRR, evening back to the barracks, elbow exercise with Hercules, dinner and then off to sleep. On 21st November, the CO was called to WAC for briefing. He took off in the morning for Palam in a Mystere. Early in the evening, the telephone of ACRR rang. I happened to pick it up. The CO was on the line and wanted to speak to Flt Lt Naqvi. He was told that Naqvi was flying. He insisted on speaking to Naqvi only. The CO was informed that it was not possible as he was in the air. He appeared to be agitated and asked me to tell Naqvi, *"Six no trump double re double"* (game of bridge), and banged the phone down. The first thing that came to my mind was whether the CO had gone mad otherwise why was he speaking of bridge. He was talking about a card game on the phone! I came out of the ACRR and looked for STO and asked him to load the pods and arm all the available Mysteres. When Naqvi landed, I gave him the message from the CO. His first reaction was, *"Where is STO?"* I told him that he was getting the aircraft loaded and armed. Almost at sunset, Johri landed and informed us that war may start any time. Three Sabres had been shot down in the east.

One fine day, CAS Air Chief Marshal PC Lal came and met us. A question was raised, target given for us was close to a Pakistan airbase, and we were worried about their interceptors. Answers given by the staff accompanying CAS—open full throttle and return. The CAS said they were not going for a milk run. He said, "Ensure that the Pakistani airfield is under attack when they go for a strike". Later, the engine of one of the Mysteres had to be changed due to damage caused by surge. An engine came promptly in a civil truck. How to offload it was another task.

Bridge Game Over: War Begins

Life went on. On the evening of 3 December, the CO, Naqvi, Das Gupta and myself were sitting on a cot playing bridge. Flt Lt Saluja with soap and towel in one hand and a transistor in another stopped by to watch the game. For reasons best known to him, he switched on the transistor, and we heard that Srinagar, Avantipur and Pathankot had been bombed by the PAF. That was the end of the game. Total commotion broke out and the wait for orders began. STO was asked to get the aircraft ready for take-off by first light. That night, the Prime Minister was in Calcutta, while we kept waiting in the company of Hercules for orders. That evening we had dinner and went off to sleep.

My Induction into the War

On 4 December 1971, orders to go came early in the morning. We had our maps ready, but we had no personal weapon or any Pakistani currency. We rushed to our aircraft with Flt Lt Das Gupta as my wingman. When I got into the aircraft, I saw to my horror that the battery was 18 volts. Not fully charged, as the civil authorities had turned off the power lines for blackout in the night. Somehow, we started and took off for Chistia Mandi, turned left and followed the railway line towards the south of Fort Abbas to search and strike.

Nearly halfway, we found a camouflaged goods train, turned around and fired one pod. We moved forward and as we reached Fort Abbas and turned left towards the base, we saw a few people running towards camouflaged tents. We turned and pulled up for attack, with Das Gupta to follow. We released our pods with 57 mm rockets. Dasu called "pull up, pull up" and then there was a huge ball of fire. Dasgupta fired a second pod. We made a hard left turn and headed towards base on full throttle. We saw an overhead tank of Chatargarh on the skyline. We knew now that we were close to the base. I gave a call and there was a response from ATC with Sqn Ldr Jain in control. I told Dasgupta to go ahead and land and that I would give him cover. There was an RT call in Hindi, *"Hum log upper kya...?"*. It was Bundle Tyagi. I quietly landed. I do not know whether Bundle Sir remembers this incident. On the second sortie with Dasgupta as my wingman, we did not find any important target except a goods train near Chistia Mandi railway station. In the evening, a third sortie with Mathur as a wingman was flown. We followed the canal road towards the South that runs parallel to the railway line towards Fort Abbas. There were plenty of green trees, but we could not spot anything, so we headed back and landed. Hell broke loose when it was noticed that there were holes on the left wing of Mathur's aircraft. I asked him if he felt any thud, he said "Yes, over the canal road near Fort Abbas."

Later in the evening, we reached our barracks. Did a little elbow exercise, dinner and went to sleep. My cot was near the door. Someone knocked on it. It was still dark. On asking who it was, the answer was "Station Commander". He asked for the CO, who was still asleep. The Station Commander said to wake him up. He told the CO that a search-and-strike mission had to go at the earliest. Instructions were to reach Chistia Mandi, turn South and look for targets along the railway line. The CO agreed and while they were discussing it, I got up. As both of them had flown three sorties, I said I would like to take on this one. I woke up Dasu, got into my G-Suit while Dasu too was getting into his and we were ready.

The Unfortunate Sortie for Me

I remember very clearly that when we were leaving, the CO, who was very fond of me, said in a jovial manner—"*Ja mar*". As dawn was breaking, we took off. Just short of reaching Chistia Mandi, I saw the shining railway line on the left. All of a sudden, it vanished. Then I noticed a huge goods train with tarpaulins and camouflage nets. I called up Dasu and did a hard left climbing turn. There it was, two engines pulling the train. I fired one pod. Dasu called up, no contact. I asked him to ask for more aircraft. In the last attack as I was pulling out I heard a thud and saw my left wing on fire. I pulled up and turned towards India. There was a bang and smoke filled the cockpit. I did not know whether I was right side up or upside down. I pulled the ejection handle. As I landed on the ground, I released the QRB and ran. Then I felt something hot on my right leg; I was bleeding. I fell down and before I could get up and run, some people caught hold of me and gave me a good reception with sticks and kicks. That was the end of the war for me.

I heard someone shouting, "*Parey hatt*" and saw a young man with a single barrel gun ready to unload it on me. An older man stopped him and said to hand me over to the police. My hands were tied behind my back, and I was put on a tractor after being blindfolded. I was taken to a place that appeared to be a police station. I could not walk as my stomach had swollen. Band-Aid was tied on my stomach. I could feel my ribs broken, and I was spitting blood.

Taken PoW

Later, I was put on a cot and tied and loaded on to a 3-tonner and taken to some place where I was put on a hard bed with my hands tied to the railing of the cot. The place smelt like a hospital. Someone hit my knuckles with either a pencil or cane. Later, I found myself in a building with a very high ceiling; my clothes were removed and I was administered third degree, Electric shocks by Mega (a small cranking device); Burnt by cigarettes (Wills); it was terribly cold.

I was handcuffed, taken in a bus chained to the seat and blind folded. Another person was also placed in the bus, as I could hear the sound of his chain. The bus ran out of fuel and stopped. After some time, we started off and were taken to a place where I found myself lying on a plinth that appeared to be a cell of a guardroom. After few weeks when I had met other PoWs, I narrated this bus incident. Flt Lt Hari Singh Jijhala said that it was he who was in the bus that had run out of fuel and that he had heard another PoW moaning with pain as the bus jerked over the bumpy road.

The first time I met two PoWs was when I was taken out of the cell. I recognised Flt Lt Parulkar who walked up to me and helped me from my cell to the open yard where three people were sitting. I was introduced, to Sqn Ldr Jaffa who had a problem in getting up. The other two were Pakistani personnel; one was Sqn Ldr Sarfaraz Mirr who was a doctor. A minibus came, guards escorted out one PoW whose head was covered with a pillow case, and who was limping. Later, we came to know he was Flt Lt Tejwant Singh. On December 25, I met other PoWs; we were a total of 12.

Flt Lt Grewal was the first to learn that there were 12 PoWs as he had seen a civilian lashkar with 12 soap cakes. When Flt Lt Parulkar was brought to the PoW (3 P&S Flight) camp, he was shouting that his brain had been damaged. The escorts told him that he had no head injury; Parulkar told them that he had a cut on his left knee and that we carried our brains in the knees.

The Sickness that Followed

I was taken to MH as I was spitting blood. There, I was almost lynched by the ladies. The escorts and other MH staff took me away and locked me in a room. It was shocking to hear the ladies abusing in a filthy language. I was declared TB patient, but no medication was administered. I was segregated and kept in a separate room. Other PoWs would come and meet me, but I was not allowed to mix with the group. We used to get one paratha and tea in a mug for breakfast, three chapattis and dal for lunch and dinner. Wg Cdr BA Cohelo and Sqn Ldr Jaffa spoke to the Camp Commandant and requested that I be taken to hospital and given medicine, as I was spitting blood. I was taken to Col Akram in MH, an x-ray was taken and I was informed that I was not suffering from TB and that I would recover with time.

There was only one bathroom in line with the guardroom. In the morning, a newspaper was delivered at the guardroom window. Any PoW going to the bathroom would try to come near it to pick up some news from the headlines. When we got together, the person would relate what he rembered from the newspaper headlines. Sometimes it used to be that another PoW had also seen the news. That's how we came to know that Mr DP Dhar was coming to Pakistan.

One day, a tall, fair person with few more people visited us at the PoW camp. This was Mr Tetsuzs, Vice President of ICRC. Another person was a Colonel of the Pakistan Red Cross. Mr Tetsuzs, asked, "How is life in the PoW camp?" I said in front of the Camp Commandment and the Pakistan Red Cross Colonel that the Geneva Convention was not being followed and how I was tortured with electric shocks, burnt with cigarettes, beaten up with table tennis bats, etc.

In March, I got Rs. 57 as pay for the last three months. All PoWs used to pool their money and get one egg each that we had to eat under close supervision. We had one razor set for all the PoWs and everyone had one individual blade, and that's how we got ready in the morning. We would be taken to a courtyard, where we sat in the open. We got our breakfast and lunch. Later, there was an improvement in the lunch and dinner that we used to get—tinda, roti and dal. To kill time, we killed the flies that hovered around the table where lunch was kept.

We had a few visitors to our camp. Flt Lt Rasheed and his friends came to meet the PoWs, a few of whom had flown Sabres in the USA along with Pakistani pilots. Wg Cdr John Corpiat (PAF) came with his wife. John had done his Staff College in UK with one of the Indian Air Force officers. A few others also came and visited us. Wg Cdr Hashmi came and told how one of his chaps had been shot down by an SU-7 over Risalwala.

The Torture Continues

One day, there was a commotion and we were locked in our rooms. PAF Air Chief Jaffar Chaudhray, along with his young ADC, visited us. He opened the cell gate, walked in and said a few words to say. He asked Parulkar as to which place did he belong to. Parulkar replied,

"Nagpur". To which the ADC commented that there was a zoo in Nagpur where tigers were kept behind bars. Parulkar answered that when they go out, they will see tigers kept behind bars here as well.

We received parcels from the Indian Red Cross, which did not seem to have any thought while they were put together—canvas shoes, sugar and tea leaves would have been well received and appreciated rather than the cashew nuts, completely ill-fitting sleeping suits and Lifebuoy soap. It seemed we had not learnt any lessons from 1962 and 1965 wars.

On 7 May 1972, Wg Cdr Coelho was informed I would be repatriated to India on May 8, 1972. On the 8th, information was received that my repatriation stood cancelled. In the afternoon, a minibus came and I was blindfolded and taken to the airfield. There Sqn Ldr Sarfaraz Mir along with Pakistan Red Cross personnel gave me a farewell gift (cigarettes, underwear and toothpaste). Currently, they are displayed in the Air Force Museum at Palam. I can go on and on, but at times it did come to my mind that **death would have been less painful** than suffering in Pakistan.

Back Home

I am thankful to our doctors in New Delhi in MH for looking after me. I was told that my ribs and collar bone had cracked and that my left lung had hematoma due to the beating. I was operated after many years in Gauhati as pus had formed in the left side of my chest.

Wg Cdr Phat Phat Bapat, had come for flying to Tezpur in 1985. He called on me and over drinks while talking he mentioned how he had attacked the train near the railway crossing at Chistia Mandi. I thanked him for "his good marksmanship", as I was lying in a cot in a 3-tonner when the escorts stopped the vehicle and ran away. That's when I had heard heavy gun firing next to the 3-tonner.

Debriefing started immediately after I reached India in the New Delhi MH. I informed the officers debriefing me that I was ill-treated and that third-degree methods had been administered and that I had informed Mr Tetsuzs, the Vice President of ICRC, of it. I was admonished and told not to repeat it in front of Mr Tetsuzs if he was brought to the MH. The next day, these officers came to my room followed by Mr Tetsuzs. One of them asked me to state what I had narrated the night before. Mr Tetsuzs immediately asked, "Why you are asking your officer what he has already told me in Pakistan about the third degree given to him". As a Red Cross personnel, it is his job to bring peace and not hatred as India had thousands of PoWs and they would have been ill-treated likewise.

> ***"Bade chain sey kabr mey so raha tha mein,***
> ***Aapne aa key kyon utha diya mujhe"***

The story of the escape of three of our PoWs is well chronicled in many books and was the topic of conversation during a program on NDTV. That was perhaps the part of our confinement that people can relate to most. However, the routine was not so exciting. I am given to believe that there is a document on escape and evasion. I hope the Air Force has revised it over the years. I was perhaps the last serving PoW in the IAF when Flt Lt Nachiketa was captured during the Kargil Ops. I was not a part of his debriefing. We could have compared notes across nearly three decades apart.

Have we learnt any lessons from these wars?

Veteran AVM Pethia *was commissioned in the Flying Branch on 18 May 1964. During the 1971 war he was on the posted strength of a Fighter-Bomber Squadron based at Nal. He participated actively in the war and was instrumental in destroying two enemy trains transporting tanks to the battlefield. He was flying very low and his aircraft was hit by the enemy ground fire and crashed. He was taken Prisoner of War and severly tortured. He displayed gallantry and devotion to duty of a high order. He was awarded a Vir Chakra. He is now settled at Bhopal. He can be reached at adityavikrampethia@gmail.com and 9993635171.*

32 My Experiences in the 1971 War at 7 Air Force Hospital

SS Phatak

Prelude: My Indirect Participation in the War

During the 1971 War I was on the posted strength of 7 Air Force Hospital as an Accounts Officer. Immediately after the ceasefire there was an increase in the patient influx at the Hospital. Unfortunately, our Admin officer and Logistics officer were not available. So I volunteered to take on the additional responsibilities so that the admissions to the hospital could be done smoothly.

Sometimes in late December 71, we received an information that a large number of amputees (165) were being sent to our hospital from Eastern theatre. The hospital machinery started getting ready for this massive intake. Our bed strength was increased more than threefold (from 165 to 565 beds). Due to paucity of space it was decided to occupy our next door neighbour Guards Regiment Camp for our expansion.

Within a few days, Gen Bhagat, GOC-in-C drove from Lucknow and amongst other instructions gave strict orders to me to shut all doors and to not to allow any visitor once we receive these battle casualties. I went to the nearby Ordnance Factory and collected all that was required to cater for our increased strength. War accounting was in place at that time. We were now ready to receive these patients. All patients and the amputees started coming by special train. We had to requisition ambulances from the civil to transfer these patients to our hospital. We started receiving a series of special trains and after due fumigation sent the trains back. There was an increased load on our patients mess, MT section, security, etc. News of this massive influx was already in civil streets.

Display of Patriotism by Public

With zeal and over enthusiasm on such occasions, we started receiving gifts and hundreds of local populations were at our doors since morning. I was very strict and did not allow anyone inside our premises and gave instructions accordingly. For every gift received from anyone we gave them official receipts from gift stores which was under me.

One fine morning, one lady, immaculately dressed, beautiful and in very formal attire, came and told me that she would like to give sizeable gifts to these 165 amputees and requested me if I could give some idea as to what kind of items she can give. I prepared a list which included bath towels, bed sheets, warm blankets, under garments, transistor radios, toiletries etc. I handed over this list to her and forgot about her visit.

After about 10 days one mini truck came to our gate and from the accompanying car this lady got down. She had gift packed 165 boxes with all the items as per the list which I had given to her earlier. She requested me to allow her inside our surgical ward to give these gift packs to atleast a few patients. In spite of strict orders, I used my discretion and allowed her to come inside. When conducted in the ward, while handing over these gifts to each patient she was crying like a child all the way. After handing over the items to a few patients, her patience exhausted and she came out. She thanked all members of our surgical team, Nursing Officers and ward boys and thereafter she quickly left. She remained anonymous till the end and walked out. I wanted to know her name and address etc. for my gift accounting but she came like an angel and vanished not wanting her name to be mentioned anywhere. I still remember her love for the patients and her commitment as a citizen.

Sometimes when I sit alone and think of this incident, I ask myself **"Woh kaun Thi"**?

The Infiltrator Patient

In another incident - One fine morning when we were busy in our routine work, one inspector from IB came to meet me and started enquiring about our admission procedure. I explained to him that the entry point is at MI room where all details are recorded and depending on the ailment Officer I/C would send the patient to the concerned ward after completing the basic admission formalities. He was interested to know about the records during the period when we had received battle casualties and as to who was the Officer I/C MI room at that time. Our radiologist was manning the MI room at that time. He was called and all procedures were confirmed again. He then asked for details of Officers ward and wanted to know what separate records at the ward were being maintained. We briefed him again. This was almost four to five months after cease fire. He then confided in me that one Officer of the rank of Captain from Pak Army had escaped and managed to get entry into our hospital for a few days defying all procedures. The famous prisoner camp was located nearby for all Pak prisoners. He had all false documents and ailment to manage this admission. After verifying our records and taking certified copies the inspector left. The Paki officer was however caught by IB and thus saved lot of embarrassment to our officers. But we became wiser and implemented strict procedure for admission. I played my part in improving the system although not trained officially.

I cherish the memories of those days even now and remember my contribution to the Hospital administration as an Accounts Officer.

Veteran Gp Capt SS Phatak *was commissioned in the Accounts Branch on 26 Dec 1965. During the 1971 War he was on the posted strength of 7 Air Force Hospital, Kanpur. To aid the hospital administration, he volunteered to take on the responsibility of monitoring and controlling the patient's admission to the hospital. There were lots of casualties during the war and there was a lot of pressure on the hospital. He streamlined the admission procedure and was instrumental in setting up the additional facilities to cater to the increased patient load. He is presently settled at Pune. He is looking after the Maharashtra Branch of Air Force Association as its President. He can be reached at afa.wzssp@gmail.com and 9421003200.*

33 THOSE 14 DAYS IN 1971

Mrs. Shobhana Raje

We all knew the war would take place eventually. It was just a matter of time. Our 222 Sqn was moved to Halwara from Ambala in August 1971.

Date:	3rd December 1971.
Place:	Halwara
Time:	6.30 pm.
Temp:	–3 degrees C

Pre-emptive Strikes by Pakis

My late husband, then Sqn Ldr Bipin Raje, came home in the evening, all smiles and excited, saying, "Hey the war is on. Pack up your bags and I will drop both of you at the station to go to Mumbai".

I had already decided to stay back and told him of my decision. He tried to convince me, and ultimately said, "Don't expect any help from me during the war".

My son, Rakesh, was then only one-and-a-half years old.

Bipin quickly ate something, and before going, said, "I don't know when I will be back but I will try to be home for lunch every day".

That evening, at 9pm, we waited eagerly for Prime Minister Mrs Indira Gandhi's speech. No sooner had it started, I heard danger sirens blowing signalling complete blackout in all the areas. At the same time, we heard enemy aircraft overhead. There was no time to reach the trench (dug in front of our house), so I hid behind the car, completely scared. They dropped a few bombs on the station. I do not know what was the extent of damage but there was some damage to the runway.

We later came to know that Pakistan had conducted pre-emptive strikes against a few forward airbases in the Western Sector.

The Actual War

The damaged runway was repaired almost overnight and the pilots of 222 Sqn hit back with full force the next day. We lost one of our officers the next day and on Day 5 Flt Lt Kuruvilla was taken PoW.

Bipin used to come home at 8 pm every day and leave the next morning by 4 am. The flying schedule was so well organised that every officer got one day off every three days. On the day my husband had an off, we would drive out to the beautiful countryside on the outskirts of Halwara and spend the day there.

The hospitality of the farmers was overwhelming. They would offer us 'Sarson-ka-saag' and 'makke-ki-roti' along with fresh carrots and 'mooli'.

Whenever my husband came home for lunch, I would make a big 'degchi'of 'Khichdi' with whatever veggies available. We named it 'Jungle rice' and soon other officers also started coming home for lunch. Everybody just wanted some company. Twice, during those 14 days, the kerosene got over and I had to collect wooden twigs to make the rice. All such experiences taught us to make do with whatever we had.

The maids had stopped coming from day one. Only our 'doodhwala' Major Singh' regularly brought hot milk in a thermos for my son. Such loyalty was humbling to see during the war. We had to go into the trench two to three times a day.

My drawing room window gave a good view of the fighter aircraft taking off on their missions and landing after 40-50 minutes. It became a habit with me to keep a watch on them with fingers crossed. It was indeed a very stressful activity.

The Dummy Guards

On the lighter side, one day there was a tip-off that enemy paratroopers had landed close by and that their target was the family living quarters. Immediately, we five ladies who were on the station, were taken to someone's house and five officers stood guard with arms outside the house to protect us. We served them black coffee every now and then. Ultimately, it turned out to be a false alarm. The next day we came to know that three of the five officers did not have cartridges in their guns!

Another amusing incident happened when, one night, I along with my son and our pet dog, Simba, was in the trench. It was pitch dark outside, but I could see two bright eyes staring at us at the end of the trench. I did not know what to do. Suddenly my son wanted his toy horse and became restless. I was scared since the 'all clear' signal siren had not been sounded and therefore, I remained in the trench. Thankfully, Bipin arrived from work and we all came out of the trench. The next morning, we checked the trench only to realise that the bright eyes were those of my son's toy horse!

Victorious Moments

Victory was declared on the 16th of December 1971 with the surrender of Pakistan Army and the blackout was lifted on 31st December 1971. By this time, none of us could tolerate electric lights and even had the New Year Eve party by candlelight!

My husband, Sqn Ldr Bipin Raje (Later Gp Capt) was awarded a Vayu Sena Medal (Gallantry) for his role in the Indo-Pak War of 1971.

I will always be thankful to God for keeping us all safe. **If at all there is a next life, I would very much like to be a part of the Indian Air Force.**

Late Gp Capt Raje *was commissioned in the Flying Branch on 25 Aug 1956. During the 1971 war, he volunteered to fly some of the most arduous and dangerous missions deep into the enemy territory. His personal ability in flying, capable leadership and his contribution to the Squadron, both in operations and otherwise, are of special significance to the Indian Air Force and he was awarded Vayu Sena Medal (Gallantry). Unfortunately, he is no more with us and passed away in Aug 2007.*

This article has been written by Mrs Shobhana Raje widow of Late Gp Capt Raje. She is settled at Pune and can be reached at rakeshraje44@gmail.com and 9594928555.

34 THE 1971 WAR IN THE EAST

TJ Reddy

The Background

Having served fifty years ago during the 1971 India-Pakistan war, which led to the independence of Bangladesh (then East Pakistan), the memories of the events remain not as distinct as I wished them to be. However, it is still fascinating to walk down the memory lane to recollect the operations at 507 Signals Unit (SU), Singharsi, where I operated from during the war.

Air Force station Singharsi is situated in the remote hills of Santhal Paraganas, now in Jharkhand. The only habitation in the region is small hutments of Santhal tribals. The unit was equipped with American Star Sapphire Radar. The Unit had played a vital role during the 1971 Indo-Pak War and provided round the clock radar cover to our combat aircraft engaged in offensive as well as Air Defence missions. Posting to this unit was considered a punishment posting those days

Putting Back Life into the Station

The morale on the Station was at its lowest ebb as two airmen had been brutally murdered in a short span of time. These men were murdered by the local santhalli tribals as the tribals had a feeling that the airmen had misbehaved with the local women who often used to visit the Station to sell their produce of vegetable and eggs etc. Normally, these women would be topless as per their culture. There are chances that the tribals would have got triggered. Anyway, that is all past, though it was very unfortunate to lose two precious lives.

The Station was visited by the AOC-in-C. Things were not found very encouraging, both on the operational front as well as the Admin front. The Unit had lacked many facilities. It was a hard area family Station. I was posted on the specific request of Station Commander. The task given to me was twofold - as then the only categorised fighter controller (Category 'B') to improve the operational preparedness, and find ways to improve morale through additional facilities for a happier living. With complete support and backing from the Station Commander, a number of facilities were put in place very soon and the living conditions improved considerably – Cinema, Co-operative stores, weekly vegetable sale transporting them from Kolkata, evening social gatherings in a common shopping-cum-entertainment area, coca-cola kiosk; a novelty then, etc.

The operational preparedness too steadily improved with sustained interception training of fighter controllers both by day and night. I was also the Training Director. The AOC-in-C visited once again to check the operational status and morale and was highly satisfied with the progress made in the intervening period. **The unit was now ready to effectively play the important operational role assigned to it in the sector.**

The Battle of Boyra, perhaps better called the Battle over Boyra, took place on 22 November 1971. It was a typical air defence in action. I was on duty that day and the PAF aircraft had been noticed in the area twice earlier in the morning time, and it was in the afternoon that the interception took place. It was within the area of operation of 253 SU based at Barrackpore. Fg Offr KB Bagchi was the Fighter Controller who handled the interception. This air encounter defined the first victory in the eastern sector in the 1971war. This battle stands out as worthy curtain-raiser to the famous victory of the Indian defence forces in the 1971 operations.

This air battle is significant as it was the first engagement between the Air Forces of India and Pakistan before actual commencement of the war in Dec 1971. This brings back my memories of Fighter Controller experience of 1965 Indo-Pak war at 16 SU, a Sector Operations Centre based at Ambala, and the interception handled by then Fg Offr (later Air Marshal) RC Mahadik from 311 SU at Patiala, again Gnats Vs Sabres.

December 3, 1971: I was in the afternoon shift of the day. The news of PAF carrying out pre-emptive strikes on the Indian airfields in the West reached the unit through air defence network around 1800 hrs. By about 2000 hrs, the unit was informed that Canberra bombers would be going on their night bombing mission towards Dhaka past midnight, that is early hours of 04 Dec 71. This later became a regular night feature for a few days, only the time slots were different. The PAF operated only Sabres at Dhaka, which lacked night fighting capability. Our bombers were opposed only by the guns of the Pakistani light ack-ack regiment.

Once the command over air was achieved by our Air Force in less than 48 hours, by quickly neutralising the small PAF contingent, nearly all air defence squadrons of MiG-21s and Gnats were operating in the role of offensive air support of the Army, in addition to Hunters. In fact, they continued with the multi-role tasking between sorties. The role of 507 SU was to monitor the movements and provide recovery assistance to the missions returning to Dumdum or Kalaikunda after counter-air, escort, interdiction and Close Air Support tasks over various installations.

I vaguely recollect two instances where the unit had a role. One was noticing on radar a PAF formation following our mission of four MIG aircraft returning after attacking Tejgaon airfield near Dhaka and when alerted the mission leader asking to be vectored for intercepting the Sabres. It was about 50-60 kms west of Dhaka. After seeing our aircraft turning back, the sabres retreated and it was not possible to chase and intercept them due to fuel constraints. The mission was then recovered under close radar control at Dumdum instead of Kalaikunda. Another incident is related to a mission on the return calling the Unit and stating Bingo condition. The mission was recovered again at Dumdum after alerting the ATC for emergency landing in the opposite direction. It was a touch and go. The role of the unit also included giving radar cover to the formations transiting through east Pakistan between Kalaikunda and Tezpur/Gauhati. The unit with locational advantage could pick up aircraft at a height of 5000 ft over Dhaka 230 kms away.

The Canberras were later used to repeatedly strike at night the strategic city of Jessore, which came under the control of our forces on 12 Dec 71. The next day I was moved to Ahmedabad by air to 258 SU as Senior Ops Officer. The unit had earlier moved from Bihta for providing air defence cover from air strikes over oil refineries in Baroda (now

Vadodara) and Ahmedabad region. There was a small detachment of AD fighters at Ahmedabad to provide air defence support/CAP as required. Just three days later cease fire was announced. I remained there till the middle of Jan 1972.

Veteran Wg Cdr TJ Reddy *was commissioned in the Administration Branch on 21 June 63. He went on to become a Fighter Controller. He actively participated in the 1965 and 1971 wars. He took up voluntary retirement in the year 1985. All his three sons also served in the Air Force and all of them retired as Wg Cdrs. He has been closely associated with the Air Force Association. He has been the President of AP & Telangana Branch of the AFA for the last nine years. He is settled at Secunderabad and can be reached at reddytj@yahoo.com and 9391027020.*

35 Reminiscences of a Helicopter Pilot during 1971 War

Sudhir Sah

As a young Flying Officer, I was posted in 109 Helicopter Unit, Jammu, from 1970 to 1974. Prior to the Indo-Pak War of 1971, the Unit had dispersed its Mi-4 helicopters to various locations around Jammu/Udhampur. I operated from an army camp at Jindra (near Udhampur). I flew several missions from this location, some memorable ones are recounted below.

03 Dec 71: I, along with my Co-pilot, Fg Offr RK Sharma, was operating from a dispersed location at Jindra, an army camp near Udhampur. On 03rd Dec 71, the day the war broke out, we got a mission order to evacuate casualties from Jaurian, near Chhamb.

Even as an Indian Army Engineer Regiment was laying mines at a forward location in the Chhamb/Jaurian sector, the Pakistani Army started shelling this location resulting in several casualties from the Engineer Regiment. Ours was the first helicopter to carry out a casualty evacuation during this war. At Jaurian helipad there were several casualties, both officers and men, some of them very serious.

A Mi-4 helicopter that can seat not more than 10 personnel, was loaded with 16 casualties, some lying down and some sitting on the cargo compartment floor, packed like sardines. The question was, would the helicopter take off with all the load. With our fingers crossed, I applied full power and started rolling and rolling and rolling...to get the required lift. The good old Mi-4 did not let us down, it got airborne. Meticulous fuel planning

Mi-4 Helicopter

helped. The casualties were offloaded at Bikram Park helipad near the Base Hospital, Udhampur. Subsequently, several such evacuations were carried out throughout the period of war in the J&K sector.

05th Dec 71: Chhamb-Jaurian Sector was a scene of pitched battle between the two armies. Therefore, it was natural for both the opposing Air Forces to also pitch in with full force. One could see the Su-7s and Hunters of the IAF and Sabres of the PAF crisscrossing the skies. Flt Lt Gurdip Singh's Su-7 while on a close air support mission was shot by enemy ground fire. He ejected over enemy territory. Using clever evasion tactics, he evaded the enemy troops and villagers and managed to reach Indian territory.

On 05th Dec 71, the third day of the war, we were tasked to evacuate Flt Lt Gurdip Singh from Jaurian. He had fractured his leg. While he was being loaded into the Mi-4, a formation of four Sabres was seen approaching us. The stretcher-bearers left Flt Lt Gurdip Singh near the helicopter and all of us dived into the trenches nearby. Nobody dared move out and carry Flt Lt Gurdip Singh, who was half out of the stretcher and shouting for help, to safety. The four Sabres could be seen attacking our gun positions nearby. A helicopter on the ground makes a lucrative target. An attack would have led to disastrous consequences. How could we allow our colleague to meet such a fate? Both Fg Offr Sharma and I gathered guts and jumped out of the trench, ran to where Flt Lt Gurdip Singh was lying helplessly, picked up the stretcher and carried him to safety. Twenty-eight years later in 1999, I met Flt Lt Gurdip Singh, a Gp Capt, retired and re-employed, at Air Force Station Adampur. We recognised each other and had a good laugh re-collecting the incident.

14th Dec 71: The mission was to evacuate an injured Forward Air Controller, Flt Lt Lawrence Pereira, from a location near Nainakot in Shakargarh Sector of Pakistan. The crew: Flt Lt RT Chandani and Fg Offr Sudhir Sah. After a quick briefing at the Tactical Air Centre at Samba and a rough indication of the position of the casualty, our Mi-4 helicopter was airborne. As the Indian Army's strike Corps was advancing rapidly in the Shakargarh Sector, the entire area was covered with a thick layer of dust raised by tanks and vehicles making navigation very difficult.

With poor visibility and no identifiable landmarks, we flew on course and time. After flying for 20-25 minutes, we were unsure of our position. Such a situation over enemy territory is not a comfortable feeling. Flying low and slow, with prayers on our lips, Lady Luck smiled. We saw a group of Sikh troops waving at us. A low pass was made over them to make sure that they really were our own troops. Indeed, they were troops of a Sikh Regiment. A quick recce and we landed the chopper on a restricted space nearby. Rotors running, I quickly got out of the chopper to the amazement of the troops, and asked a jawan *"Sardarji, Nainakot kithe hai"*—"Sardarji, where is Nainakot". He pointed vaguely in an easterly direction which led us nowhere.

After 15 minutes flying, we saw a built-up area, a small town. On landing, we were told we were indeed at Nainakot and that the Air Force casualty had been moved by road. However, they told us that one Army Krishak aircraft had been shot by a Pakistan Air Force fighter aircraft. The wreckage lay nearby. One of the pilots, Major Gaur had died, while Capt Punia was alive with burn injuries. We quickly placed Capt Punia in the helicopter and took off for Pathankot, the nearest airfield. Over Pathankot, owing to operational reasons, we were not allowed to land and told to divert to Udhampur.

Low on fuel and with darkness setting in, we set course directly for Udhampur, necessitating flying over hilly terrain at night. On landing at Udhampur, we heaved a sigh of relief. Relief, because the low fuel warning light had been on for some time, we had just five minutes of fuel left and, more importantly, Capt Punia was still alive.

He was immediately driven to the Base Hospital.

Veteran Air Vice Marshal Sudhir Shah *was commissioned in the Flying Branch on 02 Jun 1968 as a helicopter Pilot. He has flown almost all the types of helicopters that were there on the inventory of IAF during his service career. A highly decorated officer who was awarded "Mention-in-Despatch" during the 1971 War. He is a keen writer and has a book named "Reminiscences of a Helicopter Pilot" to his credit. He is now settled at New Delhi and can be reached at sudhirsah@gmail.com and 9811796593.*

36 Heliborne Operations – 1971 War

CS Sandhu

MI-4 Helicopters: The Work Horse

In 1971, I was commanding 110 Helicopter Unit based at Kumbhigram airfield near Silchar in South Assam. The Unit was operating 10 MI-4 helicopters of Russian origin, which had safe endurance of 2 hrs 30 minutes and carrying capacity of 12 to 14 fully armed soldiers depending on fuel on board. It had basic night flying facilities on board. Overall, it was a rugged and reliable machine and a good workhorse. All pilots in the Unit were professionally qualified for day operations. As a policy, the Air Force did not permit night missions on helicopters. Moreover, due to the proximity of hills and as a flight safety measure, night flying at Kumbhigram was prohibited. Hence, the aircrew lacked the desired night flying experience.

Preparing for Operations by Night

In June, I was informed by Command that the Unit would operate in support of IV Corps, commanded by Gen Sagat Singh. I was directed to meet him for a briefing and ensure that all his requirements are met. When I met him, he required me to induct a maximum of a battalion at a time across the border by night. He clarified that the flying time would be around 20 minutes one way and that the Unit should be ready as soon as possible. I explained that this was the first time that such a mission would be undertaken by the Air Force by night and that the air crew would require extensive training for such an operation. Secondly, the monsoon had begun and there was little possibility for night training during this period. I, however, assured him that every effort would be made to be ready as soon as possible.

Looking at a map it became noticeably clear that to move towards Dhaka our troops would have to cross the magnificent Meghna River, which is up to 13 km wide at places and flows from the North to the Southern end of the country. It presented a formidable obstruction; it would be a slow and daunting task to cross it by conventional methods. Gen Sagat Singh had, very wisely, conceived using helicopters to airlift the troops safely and speedily.

My first task was to get permission from Command for night operations at my base. Next was to work out the strategy and the format. We decided to go by the norm for such missions: fly low level, maintain radio silence and keep anti-collision lights off to avoid detection by the enemy. This meant that all the helicopters would, perforce, go in a stream separated by distance/time. Similarly, due to a likely blackout over the hostile area, navigation too was ruled in favour of flying by course and time combination to reach the target. Accuracy in maintaining speed and course was of prime importance for the success of this mission. Any deviation could cause a telescopic effect close to the target, perhaps leading to a collision. No doubt, it was difficult to continuously fly for hours together and maintain the desired separation, but it was certainly not impossible.

By mid-October, the aircrew were trained and ready for the operation. Meanwhile, Corps had established its HQ at Teliamura, an uneven area approximately 20-odd kilometres east of Agartala. They had prepared five helipads nearby.

The War Begins

On the morning after the war broke out on 3rd Dec, five helicopters were positioned at Corps HQ, while the rest were dispersed on helipads in Mizoram.

On 7th Dec morning, TAC (TAC is an Air Force element attached to an Army formation to co-ordinate their air support demands) directed me to move to Kailashahar airfield to airlift a battalion to Sylhet at the earliest and return by night. Kailashahar airfield is right on the border, had a noticeably short runway meant for small aircraft and did not have refuelling and communication facilities. I, therefore, requested TAC to arrange refuelling there and route the dispersed helicopters.

Night Operations Commences

With five helicopters, I landed at Kailashahar. Gp Capt Chandan Singh and the Div Commander were waiting for me there. After a quick briefing, we went to select a landing area around Sylhet. The aim of this exercise was to contain the Brigade-plus strength of the Pak army at Sylhet itself and prevent it from moving towards Dhaka. At this stage, it will be prudent to mention that from day one our Air Force had complete air supremacy over the entire enemy territory, and the helicopter force could move freely in the sky. A small ground capable of accommodating two helicopters between the south edge of the city and the Suma River was selected. Towards the west was a road bridge over the river approx 600 metres away, which was heavily defended. On the eastern side was a wide expanse of sarkanda grass. On landing back, we waited for the remaining helicopters until well past 2 pm, and finally it was decided to launch the airlift with the five helicopters present. After a quick briefing where the aircrew were advised to airlift the maximum men in each sortie, we moved to Kalaura, where the troops were located and the first shuttle got airborne around sunset, which was uneventful. The next two shuttles were at night and faced heavy firing by Pak troops. One helicopter had a total electrical failure due to a bullet hitting the electric system, but managed to fly back while the rest, despite suffering several bullet hits continued regardless and successfully landed the troops. After the last shuttle, all the helicopters returned to Kailashahar. Fuel had not reached yet. A little later two more helicopters ferried in. The ground crew went to work immediately to repair the damage sustained by most of the helicopters. Around midnight, the Army sought an immediate sortie to send a signal team with equipment, as there was no radio contact with the troops at Sylhet. Two helicopters with adequate fuel were despatched instantly and continued to induct more troops after dropping off the team.

There was jubilation when two refuellers arrived at first light in the morning. The ground crew worked tirelessly the whole night and surprised us by repairing all the damaged helicopters, including the one with electrical failure and that too with limited resources at hand, a commendable job indeed. Later, all the remaining helicopters arrived. The first launch encountered thick fog as it approached the landing area. Yet, the pilot attempted an approach for a landing but had to abort in the final stage due to his inability to spot the landing ground. As he turned around several bullets hit the exposed belly of the helicopter and three men suffered severe bullet injuries, resulting in one fatality later. Fortunately, he managed to fly back safely. Although we had been facing regular firing in all our missions so far, this was the first time that it resulted in such serious casualties and damage. We had to wait for quite some time for the fog to clear before resuming the airlift despite enemy action. It was sheer luck that all the aircrew were safe.

On 9th Dec morning we were directed to proceed to Agartala. Two helicopters from other units joined us to augment the force to 12. An hour later, I was in the air with the Corps Commander on an aerial recce for the next urgent airlift. Flying above the small arms firing range, we headed west towards Dhaka. As we crossed Meghna River I noticed that one span of the bridge at Bhairab Bazar had fallen and pointed this out to the Corps Commander. He decided to descend for a closer look to assess the damage. After inspection he decided to fly back to Agartala. While we were on our way back at a low level along the road, a burst of several bullets hit the helicopter injuring the co-pilot severely and most of us superficially by the splinters, but we managed to reach Agartala in one piece. After landing, on inspection, we counted 39 bullet holes in the helicopter, some awfully close to its vital parts. That was the time all of us realised how fortunate we were to get a second life.

Enormous Unending Task

In the evening, the Corps Commander met me once again wanting to induct a battalion to Raipura immediately across the Meghna. Since there was no time to waste on a recce, he deputed an AOP helicopter who had selected the landing site to lead our formation to the spot. I immediately got the helicopters ready and just before sunset we set off on course. As I landed at Raipura, the helicopter began to sink as the ground was uneven, wet, and soft. I applied power to lessen the weight until the wheels were just touching the ground, though it did cause the troops some difficulty in deplaning. The third shuttle was done in complete darkness. Keeping in mind that only a small number of troops were at the landing site to tackle the enemy if the need arose, I took the risk to attempt the third shuttle in complete darkness. The big problem was for the pilots to hover steadily before landing without any ground reference in the dark–an exceedingly difficult manoeuvre which we had not practised even during training due to flight safety issues. This involved strict discipline and an extremely high level of skill. Luckily, the risk paid off and we successfully completed the third shuttle without an incident. The remaining sorties were completed after moonrise.

Early morning on 10th December, two helicopters were despatched towards Bhairab Bazaar and one to Sylhet on casualty evacuation missions to retrieve wounded soldiers. This was an ongoing top-priority mission whenever there was a casualty requiring urgent evacuation. Later in the day, the Army demanded a heliborne operation the next morning to airlift brigade strength plus, an element with artillery guns, armaments, etc., across the Meghna to Narsingdi. This was an enormous task to complete in a day.

Next morning, we were on our way before first light. Unfortunately, we lost one jawan when he walked into the tail rotor in the dark. That day we flew more than 110 sorties nonstop into the night; yet it took all of the next morning to complete the task. In the next two days, another two battalions were airlifted to Daudkundi.

The Surrender and the Role of our Helicopters

On 16th Dec morning we got news that Pakistan had surrendered. In the final analysis, the use of helicopters turned out to be a masterstroke in hastening the surrender. It would not be out of place to mention that the strategy to use helicopters was planned much in advance. The Unit had taken three months to train for this specific task by night.

Throughout the war, the Unit flew more than 400 sorties airlifting around 6,000 men and tons of equipment with speed and accuracy in a short span of time. On an average, 17 men were airlifted in each sortie against 12 to 14 specified. In addition, we saved several lives through timely air evacuations. We had three forced landings–two during day and one at night. All the helicopters were recovered speedily and were back flying within hours. The success of the Unit in completing all its commitments admirably must be attributed to the ground and the air crew who worked tirelessly and handled every difficult situation with a high level of skill and professionalism. This was an unparalleled effort, indeed, in attaining 100 per cent results in all spheres. The helicopter too, despite being over stressed beyond its stipulated limits, lived up to its reputation of being a reliable workhorse. The Unit was awarded two VrCs and one Mention in Despatches.

After the war, the Air Chief, when on a visit to Kumbhigram, congratulated the Unit for its unbelievable and outstanding performance. Later, the Unit made the Air Force proud when it had the honour of receiving "The President's Standard".

This award is one of the greatest honours bestowed upon a Unit/ Squadron in recognition of exceptional service rendered to the nation, both during war and in peace.

Veteran Gp Capt CS Sandhu *was commissioned in the Flying Branch in Dec 1959. For the first two to three years he flew fighter aircraft. In early 1962, he switched over to helicopters on medical grounds. During the 1971 war, he was Commanding 110 HU which was based at Kumbhigram. He was given the special task to train the helicopter pilots on night flying. The unit excelled in its task during the 1971 War. The unit was awarded two Vir Chakras and one "Mention in Despatches". He was awarded Vir Chakra for gallantry, professional skills and leaderships of the highest order. He is settled at Chandigarh and can be reached at polucs@gmail.com and 9878311987.*

The Flight Commander of his unit Flt Lt Pushp Kumar Vaid was also awarded Vir Chakra during the 1971 war. We have received another article from him on the role of 110 HU in the 1971 War. As the contents of both the articles were by and large similar in nature, the article by Flt Lt Pushp Kumar Vaid has not been published.
Veteran Sqn Ldr Pushp Kumar Vaid is now settled in Scotland and can be reached at pushpvaid@gmail.com and 9871625479.

37 Ruling the Skies: Absolute Air Superiority in Bangladesh, 1971

Hemant Sardesai

The Background

In November 1971, I was a young Flight Lieutenant of the Indian Air Force who had just completed operational flying training on MiG 21 Type 77 aircraft to become a fully qualified fighter pilot to undertake day-and-night operations. My unit, No 4 Squadron AF, was located in Tezpur, Assam. With the war imminent, we were moved during the month to Guwahati, which was closer to erstwhile East Pakistan where our target areas lay. Once the balloon went up on 03rd December we were asked to gear up for action from the next morning. The strike plans for various targets were finalised by late evening.

My Induction into the War

I went out on my first-ever operational mission against the enemy on 04th December. It was a strike on a Pak Army Brigade Headquarters in Rajendraganj-Mahendraganj area. We were assisted by an FAC (Forward Air Controller), an Air Force pilot attached to the army units to assist them in selecting targets and guiding the attacking aircraft on to them when required. I remember reporting of flak coming at me as I went in for the first attack. "What did you expect?" Came the prompt response; "Chocolates?" An obvious rebuke for breaking radio silence; thereafter I learned to keep my mouth shut and get on with the job. Our mission carried out 3–4 attacks and each time the FAC reported number 2 (that was me) right on target. Therefore, we repeated the attack with all other aircraft too, homing in on where I was firing. The enemy Brigade HQ, by now more or less neutralised by the air attack, was captured by our army with comparative ease. They took 160-odd personnel as prisoners and captured a vast quantity of arms and ammunition.

Changed Tactics: Steep Glide Bombing

During 04–05 December we too suffered some casualties. Some of our aircraft were shot down or damaged while they went in for front gun and rocket attack on Tezgaon and Kurmitola airfields by ack ack and even small arms fire while some others attacking other Pak Army targets were brought down by intercepting PAF fighters. A number of casualties occurred while the aircraft dived for weapon delivery and pulled out thereafter flying as low as 300 – 500 feet above ground rendering themselves vulnerable to ground fire. Therefore, the tactics was changed from the next day, 06th December. We now went in for steep glide bombing attacks. Four of us, 3 other pilots and I, dived from about 12000 feet at 45 degree angle over Tezgaon runway and released two 500-kg bombs from a height of 3000 feet, thus staying out of the small arms range and remaining in the lethal range of the ack acks as briefly as possible. I carried out four missions of steep glide bombing attacks, two each over Tezgaon and Kurmitola runways. Overall, the strike turned out to be a resounding success. We had rendered the runways unusable by any aircraft and did not lose even a single aircraft. And PAF could no more operate their fighters from Tezgaon runway.

Unexpended Bombs

On 08th December we were ordered to attack an ammunition factory. However, on reaching we found that the target, didn't resemble an ammunition factory or depot. Our leader, therefore, chose not to destroy something that might turn out to be not lethal at all and could very well prove to be of use in the reconstruction of the country after the war. That left us with the option of flying back to base with the 500-kg bombs. Landing the aircraft with this additional load was a tricky business with the inherent risk of the bomb getting accidentally dropped on the runway which could cause havoc. Three of the aircraft landed safely (a rare instance of live bombs being brought back and the pilots executing safe landings with the load), but the fourth, running low on fuel, had to drop the bomb (in a safe state) before landing safely at Guwahati.

My Share of Flying

I did a total of 21 missions during day and one by night, striking a variety of targets. The night mission, carried out on 12th December, was undertaken to flush out a mercenary pilot who landed at an unmarked airfield at Narsingdi to the North-East of Dacca reportedly to fly Pak Eastern Army Commander General AAK Niazi and the rest of their top brass out of Dacca in their escape bid to get to Rangoon. We executed the mission with three aircraft flying one after the other at intervals of two and a half hours, each firing two air-to-air missiles in the general direction of the 'ghost' runway. The message was clear enough for the pilot who took off post-haste with no one else on board. The next morning I led a four-aircraft strike over this runway and rendered it unusable by any aircraft. On the following day, 14th December, we attacked the Governor's House with rockets. All four aircraft delivered 32 rockets each from different directions in four dives over the massive bungalow. There wasn't any more fight left in the enemy and on 16th December the world saw General Niazi with nearly a hundred thousand troops of his surrender to the Indian Army unconditionally.

I had played my role in the war; 11counter air missions including one at night, eight offensive air support missions and three air defence missions – part of the historic feat that crowned the Indian Air Force as absolute masters of the Bengal skies in the War.

Veteran Gp Capt Sardesai *was commissioned in the Flying Branch in May 1965. During the 1971 war he was on the posted strength of a front line Squadron. He participated actively in the war and flew a total of 22 sorties causing extensive damage to the enemy assets. He displayed professional skill of a very high order and was awarded a Vir Chakra. He is now settled at Pune and can be reached at hemusardesai@gmail.com and 9850212152.*

38 My Experiences during 1971 Indo-Pak War

Avinash Saxena

I Almost Lost my Son in Transit

During the 1971 Bangladesh operations, I was posted as a young Flying Officer at No. 2 Mobile Echelon Unit. The Unit was located at Hasimara, West Bengal. The role of the unit was to activate abandoned airfields/ to take over civil aerodromes and prepare them to operate as fighter bases for two squadrons, providing all administrative and technical support.

In August 1971, we received the orders to move to Roopsi, an abandoned airfield in Cooch Behar, just 5 km from the East Pakistan Border. It was evident that we would be away from base for quite some time. Hence I decided to send my wife Rashmi and our two-year-old son Rohit from Hasimara to Seoni (MP), where her parents were staying.

In those days, Hasimara was served by meter-gauge railway network and one had to travel to Siliguri, take a cycle rickshaw from Siliguri to New Jalpaiguri station, about 8 km away to board the broad-gauge train to Sealdah. There was no direct rail link from Siliguri to Howrah and even within Kolkata, there was no rail link from Sealdah to Howrah. Those who have moved with family from Hasimara to other places in Central and South India in those days will remember the horrendous journey. One had to carry food and water for at least three days !!!

I took my wife and child to Siliguri and arranged Ist class reservations to Sealdah and from Howrah to Nagpur by Howrah Bombay Mail leaving at night. In those days, travelling from Sealdah to Howrah was quite cumbersome, more so when one was carrying a lot of luggage. My wife and son somehow reached Howrah safely. The railway platforms of Howrah station were full of Bangladeshi refugees leaving hardly any space to move. My wife reached the compartment of Howrah-Bombay Mail, just ten minutes before departure. She had to leave the hand of our two-year-old son to pay the coolie and in those few seconds our son went missing. She immediately went to the Asst Stn Master and requested him for announcements to be made for the missing child. Without waiting for action on her request, she went to the MCO for help. The Duty Subedar Sahib sent two Jawans to look for the child. He advised my wife to wait at the compartment and search in the nearby areas. He personally went to the Station Master's Office and arranged for announcements in Hindi, English and Bengali several times.

It was time to depart. The engine blew the first whistle and our son was nowhere to be seen!

My wife ran back as fast as she could to the train Guard and told him, "Look here, my two-year-old child is missing from the platform. I am travelling alone with him. My husband is in the Air Force, posted on the Front. My luggage is unattended in the First Class compartment. You must have heard the public announcement of my missing child and if he has been picked up by thieves or boarded another train, I would never get him. I will not let the train move until my child is found". She held the train for the next one hour.

Apparently, Rohit, our son, was fascinated by a toy seller and went after him. When he realised that his mother was not there with him, he started crying. Luckily some gentlemen saw him and asked him why he was crying. Rohit told him, "My mother is lost!" The gentleman asked him "Where is your father?". He told him "Ladai ladne gaye hain" (He has gone for war). The gentleman asked him, "What is the name of your father?" Rohit told him "Fg Officer Avinash Saxena, hum Hasimara mein rehte hain aur Nani ke ghar ja rahe hain" (Fg offr Avinash Saxena, we live at Hasimara and we are going to Nani's home). The gentleman immediately understood the situation and took him to the 'Enquiry counter', where Subedar Sahib was already waiting. He escorted the gentleman and Rohit to my wife.

Teaching the two-year old kid his name, father's name and destination of the journey paid rich dividends. This way our son was saved, just because of brave steps and the presence of mind of my wife, and the support provided by the Railways and MCO Staff.

Today, Dr Rohit is a Sr Consulting Eye Surgeon in the UK.

Operations from Roopsi

Ours being a small unit, had a lot of work to do at Roopsi. We were only three officers, one Flt Lt (Navigator) OC, One Flt Lt AE (M) and myself Fg Offr AE (L) with 140 men of all trades. We prepared the airfield to receive fighter aircraft in record time and sent a signal to EAC to confirm our operational readiness. Immediately a "Hunter" Aircraft came and landed safely. It took off after a brief discussion and we were declared operational, as all our ATC, technical and administrative services were found exceptional. After a few days we were ordered to move to Agartala as Pakistani Air Force had vacated Lalmunirhat air base of East Pakistan, a bare 5 Km inside their border.

Operations at Agartala

Agartala, the capital of Tripura State, had a civil aerodrome whose Southwest dumbell was touching the East Pakistan border. We were asked to take over the airfield and convert it into a fighter base. Later on, one Gnat and one MiG 21 Squadron operated from our base. Wg Cdr Sanwal Shah was attached to our unit as Stn Commander Air Force Stn Agartala. Later Plt Offr Majumdar (Logistics) was also attached. Now we were five officers in our unit, to operate as an Operational Wing.

Our reception at Agartala was unique. On the first day in the evening when myself, Flt Lt Sahni and the Aerodrome Officer were standing on North East dumbell and discussing about handing/ taking over, suddenly Cpl Thakran our MTD shouted "Sahab, dushman ke jahaj!" ..... (Sir, Enemy aircraft!...) and he vanished. Aerodrome Officer also ran away. Flt Lt Sahni tried to go toward the jeep, but I caught hold of his arm and dragged him towards the nearest trench and as we dived in, I could see splinters of bombs coming towards us and passing over our heads. It was a close shave... a miraculous escape from certain death.

Commissioning Russian Radars

I was detailed to proceed to Poornia and Panagarh for repair of a Russian Mobile Radar. I had just completed the task given when I was asked to report immediately to the Air Force Cell at FORT WILLIAM, Kolkata. I was asked to proceed to HQ EAC, IAF immediately and meet Air-1. I was given an Indian Air Lines ticket for Guwahati. At Guwahati, one helicopter was waiting for me and I was with Air-1 in no time.

I was told, "Our Russian made Radar vehicle had met with an accident and is lying in the MT Section of HQ EAC, IAF. The vehicle mounted Radar is to be taken out, repaired, transported to Agartala, installed on ground, calibrated and made operational. Today is 29th Nov and war may start any time. You have very limited time. Whatever you want, CSO will help you". I requested Air-1 and CSO to provide me with whatever I needed, right at the work spot and leave the paperwork aside. My request was granted. I completed the task in the limited time and our direction-finding Radar was fully operational at Agartala Airfield before two fighter squadrons arrived there. This Radar was used throughout the War.

When Sam Manekshaw was Asked to Hold on to the Lightning Call

It was 16th Dec 1971 evening when I received a call from ATC that "Lt Gen JS Aurora is coming from Dhaka and immediately after landing he wants to talk to Field Marshal (then General) Manekshaw." In those days Trunk calls used to take a lot of time hence I immediately booked a lightning call, but to my surprise the call materialised within seconds. When I picked up the receiver, I heard a strong, deep voice "Sam here". I was shaken up but told him, "Sir, I am Fg Officer Saxena speaking from Agartala Airfield. I got the message from ATC that Gen Aurora is coming from Dhaka and he wants to speak to you immediately after landing. But the helicopter is not even in sight and will take about 20 minutes before landing". He told me, "I want to talk to you because you have actually fought the war and you must have been under pressure in the last 15 days". His tone was so warm that I felt comfortable within a few minutes. He took full account of

Agartala air base. He talked to Gen Aurora for 10 to 15 mins and finally called me and thanked me personally. A great Supreme Commander, indeed!

Managing the Prisoners of War (PoWs)

War was over and I was given a new task of handling PoWs. I used to receive PoWs in open trucks, count the heads, safeguard them and hand them over to the Captain of the visiting transport aircraft. We did not have enough space to keep them indoors and some of them did try to run away. It was not an easy task to handle them. This operation continued for many days.

Moving to New Nation Bangladesh

Wg Cdr Sanwal Shah and Plt Offr Majumdar left the unit immediately after the War.

Our unit was asked to move to Dhaka. Dhaka's Mohammadpur airfield was badly damaged. Runway and taxi track had large pot holes. All the services were completely damaged by our bombing. Pakistanis had destroyed every leftover thing before leaving. Even the fighter aircraft parked in the pens were fired by machine guns. Our unit was sent there to repair/replace every equipment for use and make the airfield fully operational.

I was produced in front of Air Cmde King Lee, AOC Air Force Station Dhaka of Indian Air Force. He told me that I was required to restore all signals and electrical facilities including ground to ground and ground to air communication systems and all navigation aids and other ATC arrangements.

He looked at my small pips and asked me "Will you be able to do it?" I confidently said 'Yes Sir'. He enquired "What is your experience?" I told him "My first posting was at 9 Squadron and I am in this unit for the last one year, but before joining Air Force I have been working at BHEL Bhopal for five years".

He was happy, satisfied and asked me to update him on the progress on daily basis. I could complete the task in four months. The normal air traffic had commenced. My name was recommended for VSM. However, it did not come through. May be there were more deserving people.

We returned to our base, Hasimara in April 1972.

Veteran Wg Cdr Avinash Chandra Saxena *was commissioned in the AE (L) Branch on 01 Apr 1968. Prior to the 1971 war, he was on the posted strength of No 2 MEU, AF. He was actively involved in the refurbishing of the civil airfield at Agartala from where two fighter Squadrons operated during the war. Post the 1971 war he was assigned the task of refurbishing the facilities at Mohammad Pur Air Field in Dhaka. The airfield was made fully operational in five-months time. He was awarded the CAS commendation for the same. He retired on 28 Feb 1993. He is settled at Sahibabad, UP and can be reached at avinashsaxena40@yahoo.com and 9873493600.*

39 VAMPIRES OF SRINAGAR

Manjit Singh Sekhon

During the period 1969-70, I was Flt Cdr HTS, Jodhpur. On my request, during the term break, in Jan 70, I was attached to FTW Hakimpet to undergo Vampire conversion where I flew nine sorties-dual/solos. Back at Jodhpur, I continued flying Bell-47 helicopters with HTS, T-6G/Harvards with AFFC and Vampires with C&R School. On 01 Jan1971, I was posted to C&R School.

On 18 Aug 1971, Air-1 WAC, Air Cmde Timki Brar and Ops-1A, Gp Capt Man Singh along with our CO, Wg Cdr OP Mishra walked into our crew room and said, "Gentlemen, war clouds are hovering; we are planning to use Vampires from Srinagar"

Five vampires from Jodhpur, two from Hakimpet and one from ATW Jamnagar arrived during Sep, Oct, Nov 71. Thus, we had a total of eight aircraft. This Dett was renamed, "No 121 Vampire Sqn" for Ops and armament roles. On 30 Nov 71, we were eight pilots with one engineering officer and 29 technicians operating from two softcover/ other open blast pens. The details are given below:

- Pilots: Flt Lt Sekhon, Flt Lt SS Kaushik, Flt Lt NK Kapur, Flt Lt SS Bains, Fg Offr BS Rathi, Fg Offr PPS Kawatra, Fg Offr AK Banerjee, Fg Offr Farais
- STO: Flt Lt AI Rajadnaya

Technicians: Chiefy Flt Sgt Dalvi and 28 Technicians and six more were attached later from R&SU Kanpur.

I had less than one year service at C&R with 200 hours of non-ops flying and I was still U/T on type. I had, never fired a bullet from air. By virtue of my seniority, I became the CO. And, now I was ready to lead and fight the 1971 war in the J&K mountainous region. A datewise record of various activities right from the prepartion of war to its end is given below:

30 Nov 71: Prime Minister of India, Mrs Indira Gandhi addressed all pilots of 18 Sqn, 121 Vamp Sqn & 114 HU.

03rd Dec 71: Four PAF Sabres struck Srinagar at 1730 hrs. At midnight, one C130 Tpt ac did a para drop of boxes containing communication sets for Pak informers/anti nationals. 93 Bde at Poonch was under heavy enemy attack.

04 Dec 71: At 1st light, Two Vampires (Manjit Singh & Bains) got airborne for T&R (Tactical & Recce) sortie in Poonch-Raja Rani-Hajipir Sector. We spotted large number of loaded Paki Army/civil trucks. We blasted them and reported back to base. Subsequently more strike missions were sent to support the Army.

05, 06, 07 Dec 71: We planned and executed attacks on Pak Bdes, Arty gun positions, Ammo & POL dumps, bunkers, vehicles opposite Poonch, at Potha, Dwarandi, Raja-Rani, Hajipir, Kahuta. 15 Corps Cdr, Gen. Sartaj Singh personally spoke to me for attack on Kargil post 13620 at 1st light on 08 Dec.

08 Dec 71: A two aircraft formation with self and Kaushik as pilots, took off for Kargil 13620. While approaching Dras, I called FAC (Tarzan), who replied "Keep off, keep off, two Mirages overhead", Shivers went down my spine. We spotted Amba Pass on our right, went over to Suru valley, flew low for endurance, spotted two PAF Mirages leaving, went in for 2×1000 lb, steep bombing attack from 23000 ft, conscious of FLOT, released the bombs a bit late. It was a washout. We reported back to GLO. At that time, Flt Lt Bajaj and Fg Offr Ramarao of 114 HU, took off from Kargil helipad, flew very low due to fear of Mirages, hit wires near Kaksar and crashed. Unfortunately, Flt Lt Bajaj died. Late in the evening, we repeated the same sortie at 1600h and got direct hits. Bde picked up Paki post R/T, "Dushman ka jahaz aata hai, jaata hai, apni Airforce mar gaee hai kya" Pak Post 13620 overlooking Kargil, was captured successfully and is held by us till today.

We Continued offensive attacks at Batalik, Marol, Olthingthang, Khermang, Chorebatla, Menthadalo, Treche, Chalunka, Turtuk, Thang, Gorkha Ridge, Piun, Siari, Khapalu—about 200 posts were taken over by our Army. Many of these posts were attacked by me during the last light hours, with 85+ dive attacks, which gave most accurate results. In Shyok valley, we pushed Pak back by 32 km and shifted the LOC accordingly. The aim was to take over Sakardu.

14 Dec 71: At 1st light, 4+2 Sabres pulled to attack Srinagar airfield. Though late, two ORP Gnats—Ghuman and Brother Sekhon scrambled. The Leader after unsticking turned right, No 2 was unsticking when the bombs fell just behind him. Sabre overshot Sekhon on his left and Sekhon latched on to him, fired at him. Jettisoned his own drop tanks, called Ghuman to come into the fight, pulled up, fired at the second Sabre. CAP Controller Pilot Officer Hooch David also asked Ghuman to come into the fight. Unfortunately one of the Sabres locked on to Sekhon and shot at him. Sekhon transmitted, "Hit on right shoulder, out of control, ejecting" aircraft rolled right. It was a low-level ejection, the aircraft hit the ground and unfortunately Brother Sekhon did not survive. This dogfight took place over Srinagar airfield at about 100-300 ft AGL. Cremation for Fg Offr Sekhon was done on the same day at 1400hr just behind the Stn MT Section.

121 Vamp Sqn attacked along 490 NM of the border from Sunderbani–Gali, Kalakot-Mendhar-Pooch-Hajipir-URI-Chakoti, Tangdhar, Tithwal, Kishanganga, Gurez, Kargil, Shyok, etc., etc. We carried out 64 offensive missions. Fortunately, there was no loss of life or aircraft except one aircraft which got strafed on ground in a softcover blast pen by F-86. In total, 64 PAF aircraft dropped bombs/ strafed ground airfield and a few attacks on Awantipur airfield.

18 Sqn was commanded by Wg Cdr Prince Raina. They defended Srinagar well and lost one aircraft.

114 HU was commanded by Sqn Ldr MK Mohanchandra and it lost two Chetak helicopters.

L-60 AD Rgmt lost one gunner.

Stn Accts Section got a direct hit of a bomb and lost two persons.

We at 121Vamp Sqn flew extremely well. The contribution of 121 Vampire Sqn helped India shift the LOC by 32 Kms in shyok valley in the Western sector where approximately 200 posts were taken over in Kargil. This was one of the main reasons for the Kargil war in 1999, that was once again won by India. For their contributions, the following personnel were awarded:

(a) Flt Lt Manjit Singh Sekhon VM(G), who flew 20 offensive missions was put up for VrC as well as MVC. VrC was awarded.

(b) Flt Lt Shavinder Singh Bains flew 14 offensive missions. VrC was awarded

(c) Fg Offr PPS Kawatra. VrC was awarded.

(d) Flt Lt SS Kaushik was put up for VrC, awarded Mention in Despatches.

It was a very satisfying experience for the 121 Vampire Squadron.

Veteran Air Marshal Manjit Singh Sekhon *was commissioned in the Flying Branch on 10 Nov 1962. He has flown many types of fighters, transport aircraft and helicopters. He has actively participated in both the wars with Pakistan. During the operations against Pakistan in December, 1971 he was commanding a detachment of a front line Fighter Squadron. He flew 14 missions at low heights in very difficult terrain of Jammu and Kashmir and caused extensive damage to the enemy assets. For his leadership and professional skills of the highest order, he was awarded a Vir Chakra during the 1971 War. He is now settled at Delhi and can be reached at airmarshalmanjeet@gmail.com and 9313997627.*

40 RECALLING – DEC 1971

Amal Kumar Sengupta

I am 84-year-old, Air Signaller, an active participant of 71 War and desire to pass on "Glimpses of IAF - Then" to the present generation, for whom Dakota aircraft may be an antique aircraft and they may probably not be aware of the capabilities of the aircraft and services rendered by her. A transport – Troops carrier, Air Ambulance and occasionally, VVIP carrier, all in one.

In 1971, I was posted to No 43 Dakota Squadron, stationed at AF Station Jorhat. The Sqn was commanded by Wg Cdr KC Sharma. Our routine task was to position the aircraft at Dimapur-Lilabari-Mohanbari to be loaded with dry ration for air dropping at various border posts of Army. We used to make two to three sorties in a day with crew composition being-Pilot, Co-Pilot, Navigator, Air Signaller for air to ground communication by international Morse Code – obsolete long back. On an average, an ejection crew of three to four people used to be onboard (to push out the load through the aircraft door) as Dakota had only side door and no ramp. I remember that the most spectacular load was MOH (live goats in a wooden case) Meat on hoofs.

This routine task took a sudden turn in November 1971. Reason is known to all. We started making frequent trips to the then East-Pakistan border towns. There were hectic flying-missions-mostly unknown to us. Later on, I was detailed with one set of crew to be positioned at Agartala for carrying out flying duties as and when ordered by Army Commanders (Akhora Range). Often, we flew short trips to bordering towns-Kamalpur-Kailashahar with high ranking Officers and Commando Instructors on board. Flying being very close to the border, it used to be hazardous-low-level flying to evade Radar detection and maintaining radio silence.

Here I had a chance to meet a few members of Bengali speaking Mukti-Bahini warriors. I came to know about the horrifying torture inflicted by Pak-Soldiers upon them and their families before they fled to this side for a greater cause. It is still painful when I think of the sorties carrying injured soldiers to the rear Base Hospitals.

50 years is a long time and memory plays its tricks at this advanced stage, so I will briefly give just a few important episodes as I remember-

(a) A lighter moment amid our hard days full of worries-tension-anxieties and that was when the then Honourable Governor with his family travelled in our aircraft. He used to carry green vegetables for his own use. Must have been very health conscious. We were looked after very well with lots of delicious food after a long days work. He spoke to us with love and affection.

(b) Another feather in our cap was that we had the honour to fly General JS Aurora from Tezpur on a short hop. He was so sympathetic to the crew that it was an inspiring and relaxed trip indeed.

Then came the glorious day, 16th Dec 1971, ceasefire declared and the war ended. A nation, Bangladesh was born. We rejoiced and rejoined our families. All was not well. One of our Dakota aircraft crashed in the valley the same day in the evening. Though it was a time for all to rejoice because of India's Victory over Pakistan, but hats off to the then Chief of the Air Staff, as he along with Mrs Lal arrived at Jorhat the very next day to condole the bereaved families and pay homage to the brave warriors. They did come back but in coffins. We lost Flt Sgt Thakur, Air Signallar of the ill fated aircraft, a colleague, a neighbour and a family friend.

My salute to the Martyrs.

Veteran MWO Amol Kumar Sengupta *joined the IAF as an apprentice in the year 1953. Later, during his service, he became an Air Signaller and flew as an aircrew in Dakota, Packet, AN-12 and IL-76 aircraft. He has more than 6750 hours of flying to his credit. He has participated in all the three wars i.e 1962, 1965 and 1971. He has been awarded the CAS commendation in 1979. He is now settled at Kolkata and can be reached at amalsengupta1106@gmail.com and 8777814730.*

41 1971 Indo-Pak War - 45 Sqn Dett. Pathankot

AJ Singh

Introduction

45 Sqn, had 3 detachments located on the western sector besides manning its home base, Chandigarh. The detachment which was manning Pathankot had pilots who had been pooled in from all over the Air Force. They were from Air HQs, Command HQs, Staff College and certain other units. I was one of from FTW, Hakimpet.

I was an instructor at FTW, Hakimpet, when six pilots were chosen to train in skip bombing on Vampire-52 aircraft. We trained in skip bombing using drop tanks filled with water. In Nov 1971 we moved to Chandigarh and trained in low level night navigation to eventually launch night skip bombing attacks on Pak army at night. During training the AOC, Chandigarh, came to know that I was fully operational on Mig-21, day and night. He ordered me to man the ORP at Chandigarh as there was no pilot in Chandigarh except the Officer Commanding. When the war broke out I was moved to 45 Sqn Detachment at Pathankot. We were 10 pilots who had come from different locations in the Air Force. Only two pilots belonged to 45 Sqn – Flt Lt Surjit Singh and Flt Lt Bhadsalve. Our Detachment Commander was Sqn Ldr D Keelor, VrC.

Criticality at Hand

During the first few days of the war, the army units in the Chhamb sector were complaining that as soon as our ground attack aircraft, SU-7, left the battle area the Pakistani aircraft would arrive and start attacking our troops. The then Station Commander, Gp Capt Katre (Later CAS) decided to send two MiG-21 aircraft to hold behind the range of hills, out of radar cover but in radio contact with the Forward

Air Controller – (FAC). When the FAC informed that the Pakistani aircraft were attacking our troops, the MiG-21s would surface and engage the enemy aircraft. This helped us a lot. But it was a shortlived happiness as the following incident took place soon after.

In the ORP we had put up a board showing the leaders and number 2's. Sorties were flown in turn. On the morning of 8th December, the then Station Commander, Gp Capt Katre, called Denzel Keelor and briefed him for a mission to be undertaken by the pilots of his detachment. Two aircraft were to take off and fly close to the the battle area, stay behind the hills avoiding radar detection, but remain in RT contact with the FAC. On instructions from the FAC, the aircraft were to head to the battle area and engage the enemy aircraft.

As per the board, it was the turn of Sqn Ldr Sonpar as leader and self as his number 2. When Keelor returned after the briefing, he looked at the board, picked up his helmet and started climbing the stairs and said " AJ follow me, we are going hunting". Sonpar expressed his desire to go as it was his turn but Keelor did not reply and continued heading to the aircraft. I did not know anything about the mission but just followed the leader.

As we got airborne I spread out and said tail clear. We headed towards Chhamb, the battle area. Before I could realise, we were over the battle area, flying at 100 ft above the ground. The FAC was talking to Keelor about army movements. We made a pass over the area and saw a convoy of Pakistani trucks moving towards Indian troops. The convoy was heavily guarded by truck mounted Chinese radar controlled ack-ack guns. Keelor reported the movement to the FAC and decided to make another pass over the convoy. I did not understand. Unfortunately, during the second pass we both got hit by ground fire. Keelor ejected and landed right in between the two armies. He was picked up by the Indian army and moved to an Army Hospital.

To Eject or Not To

My aircraft was badly damaged. The leading edge of the left wing had split open. The rod that controls the aileron had broken. The dorsal fin had been hit, knocking off the RT antenna and cutting of the hydraulic lines to the tail. As a result, I lost all hydraulic, and electronics to the tail section. I was about to eject when I realised that the aircraft was still controllable. I was flying with no hydraulic, no RT, no left aileron and with controls in manual. I headed for the hills and got down to 300 feet with one hand on the ejection handle. As I approached Pathankot airfield at 450 kts I lowered the undercarriage manually, I could not lower flaps. I landed down wind and touched down at about 420 kts. I managed to stop the aircraft by switching off the engine and braking. The tail chute did not operate. As soon as the aircraft came to a halt, I was surrounded by emergency vehicles. That's the time I realised what I had gone through and was shaken up. I was made to fly the very next day to regain my confidence.

Later on I went on to Command 17 Sqn and 102 Sqn.

I enjoyed my years with the Air Force, Commanded a forward Air Force Base, did two tenures with AEB and an Air Attaché posting abroad.

Veteran Gp Capt Apramjeet Singh *was commissioned in the Flying Branch in Jun 63. He is an A-2 QF1 and FCL. He actively participated in the 1971 war and was awarded the Coveted Vir Charkra. He had an illustrious career in the Air Force spread over a period of 33 years. He has Commanded two fighter Squadrons and a Station. He has been Air Attache at Rome. He is now settled in the USA and can be reached at ajsaulakh@gmail.com and 9958305029.*

42 My First Deployment and the Airman who went Missing

BP Singh

Young ACs in the War Zone

I am narrating an incident which happened after the ceasefire of the famous Indo-Pak war of 1971.

During the war, I was a trainee at 5 GTS, AF. In Jan 1972, we completed our training of Elect-II trade and I was posted to 230 SU as a young AC, fresh from the training centre.

I, alongwith one of my entrymates AC Suryanaryan (607552) was deployed to perform the observer duties on LLOP post No 13. This post was located at village Neshta, just a few kilometers south of Attari near Wagah Border. There were many such posts being manned along the border. Our control unit was 230 SU.

Our accommodation was in a single room in the village temple at Neshta. Our messing requirements were being catered for by an Army unit mess which was located nearby. We were paid members of this mess. A village located in Pakistan on the other side of the border had been captured by the Indian Army. Food for personnel on duty in that village was also being provided by the same mess. Thus, there was lots of movement of army personnel in the area in between the two villages, one in India and the second one in Pakistan.

Our post of duty was located on a rooftop of a house in the village, whose residents had moved out to some other town for safety during the war. Our duty was to keep a watch, visually for low flying objects (Aircraft and Helicopters) and to report to the control unit, using call sign through R/T set provided to the post.

How my Roommate Strayed into Pakistan

On 9th Feb 1972, then AC Suryanarayan was on duty in the morning shift. After having my lunch, I relieved him. He came back after lunch to hand over the key of our room and told me that he is going to the Pakistan village with the Army Havaldar and will be back by the evening. I did not have any objection to it, as we have been discussing it earlier. Frankly speaking, I too wanted to go and have a feel of walk in the enemy village. At about 4 pm, the Army Havaldar came back to me and told me "Apka dost Pakistan Chala Gaya". At first I did not believe, thinking how it was possible and he must be joking. But unfortunately it was not a joke. With the help of binoculars he started explaining to me giving reference of some trees in our village and another big tree in enemy's area and their post. I was not at all interested in listening to his explanation but was thinking of as to what will be the consequences, if he has actually gone over to Pakistan. He also told me that at the Pak post a jeep arrived and Suryanarayan was taken away. Now I thought for a few seconds and made a written note of what to speak informing about the mishap to the authorities. I switched on the R/T set, called the control unit and read the written note in one go. To my good luck on the other side on duty was Cpl Pandey, who had earlier briefed us about the R/T set, its handling and usage. He told me to keep calm and speak slowly. I narrated the event in detail to him. He instructed me to take the set and go back to the room and wait. He further informed that help will reach shortly. By the time I reached my room in the Mandir, this news had spread in the village, and the people (mostly ladies) gathered there in front of my room showing sympathy and worry as to what will happen to the Air Force da Munda, I being speechless.

At about 5 PM, Sqn Ldr Bountra, COO of 230 SU and Flt Lt G Singh reached there and I narrated the whole incident to them. They listened to me peacefully and consoled me. "Not to worry" they said. Further, they asked me to search his belongings and look for what all he may have carried with him. It was found that he had been with I-Card and taken some money with him. Sqn Ldr Bountra asked me not to go for the duty next day till somebody reaches to join me.

Thereafter, both the officers went to that Pak village. They met the Army Officer on duty and enquired from him as to why there has been no patrolling along the border line of control. They even briefed the higher ups in Army about this incident and the seriousness of the same. I learnt about all these proceedings later on - only after the arrival of another airman, Cpl DP Singh who joined me for working.

Further a CoI was ordered with Sqn Ldr Bountra as Presiding Officer. I had to face the CoI with verbal and written statements and also with so much questioning. Same time the incident was pursued by our IAF authorities with Pakistan authorities and after a month, the Pak authorities agreed that AC Suryanarayan was in their captivity.

Joyful Ending

In Jun 1972 there was an Exchange Parade at Wagah border which I attended with Sqn Ldr Bountra and other members, IAF(P) and Provost Police. To our happiness and big relief AC Suryanarayan came back. He was handed over to the custody of Provost. Further course of action is unknown to me. It is in my knowledge that he was in the service as JWO and has taken retirement. I pray to the Almighty and hope that he is happily living with his family and children.

***Veteran Honorary Flt Lt BP Singh** was enrolled in the Elect-II trade in October 1970. During the 1971 war, he was still an under-trainee and was due to complete his training in December 1971. The passing out got delayed due to the ongoing war. He eventually finished his training in January 1972. As per his original posting, he was to report to 27 Sqn. But the same got changed to 230 SU. He had had an illustrious career in the Air Force. He performed exceptionally well and superannuated on 31 December 2007 as an Hony Flt Lt. He is now settled at Patna and can be reached at babbansingh204@gmail.com and 9973115794.*

43 FALCONS OF CHHAMB

Gurdeep Singh

Run-up to the War

I was an instructor at Air Force Academy during the 1971 War. I had around seven years service and had flown Vampires, Toofanis, Mysteres and SU-7.

All of us know what had been happening since Feb 71 that year. As things started hotting up, the IAF swung into action. They decided to augment the pilot strength in all the Fighter Sqns. Hence, training institutions were instructed to part with the fighter pilots and manage the rest of the training with transport and helicopter pilots. I was away on leave and had just got married. I managed to report back on duty on 9 Oct 71, leaving my newly-wed wife, Maninder Kaur, a young girl, at Shimla, getting the first shock and taste of IAF life. We were told to keep our luggage packed and be ready to leave at a short notice. On 19th Oct 71, we were told to report to Begumpet for our onward journey to Palam. Everyone was excited with suspense, imagination, discussion, and guessing as to when the balloon would go up. Having seen token action during the 1965 war in the east when posted at Hasimara, I can say things were extremely well organised and planned this time. We commenced our journey from Begumpet in a Dakota somewhere around 8-9 pm. It happened to be Diwali night. All on board the Dakota we had the opportunity of enjoying an all-India Diwali, though from the air only.

The transit camp at Palam was humming with activity. On arrival we were issued with railway warrants to proceed to our respective old units from where we had all gone for the course etc. Accordingly, I reported to Adampur though with a little problem enroute regarding my likely deployment. From 20 Oct 71 till the commencement of war, we did a few familiarisation sorties to get our hands back.

The War Commences

Finally, the day arrived and on the evening of 3 Dec 71, war finally broke out officially. All that is well documented and widely known. However, what I am going to narrate is not generally known, although I told it to some journalists and radio and TV interviewers, Indian as well as foreign, when I was admitted at Army Hospital, Delhi Cantt after the ejection.

On the morning of 4 Dec 71 we woke up almost at 4 o'clock to attend the Met Briefing. Not that we had any proper sleep at night. The news and expectation as to what was going to happen, after hearing the news on radio the previous evening, had kept us half awake throughout whatever was left of the night. Once we arrived at Adampur Base Ops we found it to be humming with activity. We met pilots from TACDE (Tactics and Air Combat Development Establishment) AF (Ambala), then known as TCTDS, who had already undertaken night missions and landed at Adampur either for another mission or refuelling on their way back to Ambala. All attended the briefings—the weather was expected to be widespread fog over Indian as well as Pakistani airspace. Our CO and Flt Cdr were briefed separately regarding the targets to be attacked. The rest of us proceeded to our respective crew rooms for preparations for our missions.

Me and My Backache

Here I must mention that from 18 Oct to 4 Dec 71, while at Adampur, I had some backache problems and it was difficult for me to walk properly or even get into the aircrew van, which in those days was a rickety one-tonner. The rear platform of the vehicle was quite high and had no steps to get into. Initially, I tried some local lotions but they did not help. When I could not bear the pain any longer, I finally went to MH Jallandhar Cantt. They took an X-ray and to my utter surprise and horror found nothing wrong clinically. However, I continued to have pain and problems as earlier. I continued to fly too, although with difficulty in climbing the long ladder into the S-22 cockpit. Once I was in the cockpit or sitting in the crew room, it was OK but I had problems in getting up, walking, climbing stairs, etc. Once the MH authorities found nothing wrong, I could not say much. If I had refused to fly, it would/could have been taken as an act of cowardice and chickening out under adverse circumstances. Therefore, in spite of everyone knowing about it, but on my insistence, I was allowed to continue flying. In the sortie in which I ejected I still had the problem. Once the Sqn learnt about my ejection they were worried about my back and were 100 per cent sure that I would have injured my backbone. Amazingly, after I ejected, although I had other injuries, my back was cured totally. From that day onwards the joke in 101 Sqn AF or rather Adampur was that if you have backache problems, ejection is a sure-shot cure. However, I would not recommend it, as trying something new, the results of which you are not sure, is a gamble.

My Induction into the War

After the first mission by the IAF, it was now time to fan out in support of the Army. Our Sqn was assigned the task of supporting ground troops in Chhamb sector. So, on landing after the first mission, Flt Lt J Bhattacharya and I were assigned for a Close Air Support mission in the Chhamb sector. We went to our GLO who thoroughly briefed us on all aspects, targets to be attacked, precautions to be taken, alternative targets, etc. There we were fully briefed and raring to go once again. My memory about time fails me for to be exact but it must have been approximately about 9-9.15 am when I, as No. 2 took off from Adampur airfield, skirted Pathankot and the Shakargarh Bulge to approach the battlefield area of Chhamb. As is well known, on the night of 3-4 Dec, the Pakistanis had tried their armour thrust to cut off Kashmir from the rest of India and had succeeded in entering Indian territory; hence, the need for urgent air support.

On the dot and on time, we contacted the FAC Fg Offr VG Kumar, another pilot from Adampur base and well known to us. He tried his best to guide my leader but somehow he was not able to make contact with the tanks. We carried on orbiting trying to locate the targets. Although I had contact with enemy tanks and tried to guide my leader and the FAC but without any success. We had already spent enough time in orbiting and locating targets and were low on fuel without having achieved the main aim of attacking the Pakistani tanks. My leader asked me to overshoot him and carry on with the attack as I was in contact with the enemy tanks. In the meanwhile, the enemy had already seen our presence and got sufficient time to not only hide themselves in a grove of trees but also to be ready to take shots at us. Having overshot my leader, I turned around and pulled up for the attack. We had selected four rockets to be fired simultaneously from all four pods so that sixteen 57 mm rockets are released each time, which would have given us four passes with 16 rockets in each pass besides the gun passes, if required. I think it was almost simultaneous because as I released the rockets at the proper range more or less at the same time, I heard some thuds on my aircraft, which I soon realised were ack-ack gun hits from the same tanks that I had fired upon and destroyed (confirmed later on by Army troops as well as the FAC). I looked inside to check the after effects of those thuds. What I saw stunned me as numerous red lights were flashing and gauges were giving erratic readings, indicating engine failure and fire in the aircraft. I was obviously heading in a direction that would have taken me deeper into Pakistan territory. With intuition, sixth sense and presence of mind I turned towards Indian territory while pulling up to gain maximum height so that I could glide as much as possible into the Indian side. Ejecting immediately would have been asking for a sure place in a PoW camp if captured alive. After all, we are all trained to defend our nation while fighting the enemy, and if an eventuality arises must try to come back safely, which will not only be good for us but also a morale booster for colleagues. So there I was, having almost climbed to one km-plus and hopefully heading towards India as all the instruments were not behaving properly and I believed them with a pinch of salt. While I was trying to make RT calls to declare my emergency and intentions of ejecting, I was also attempting to revive the engine, which could take me to the nearest airfield of Pathankot for an emergency landing. Under the circumstances, going back to Adampur was asking for too much. I tried a MAY DAY call but it was futile as the R/T too had packed up.

Eject: Now or Never

In the process, while gliding I was also losing height having failed in my attempts to revive, etc. Suddenly, I found myself to be almost at tree height or rather lower. I told myself that it is now or never. No question of asking for any further clarification—just punch out. That is exactly what I did as I literally yanked back on the stick to pull the aircraft out of shallow gliding path as considering the height and downward angle, ejection would have been fatal. It almost was even otherwise. I levelled the aircraft at the tree tops and pulled both ejection handles as trained, with all my might not to err in applying the required force. The last I observed the ASI (Air Speed Indicator) was showing almost zero. I don't know what happened immediately after that. The whole process did not take much time as it takes place in milliseconds and for low height ejections like mine the parachute opens immediately and there is no free fall. After those couple of seconds that are blank in my life, I found myself safely under the life-saving tree canopy assuring me that everything functioned as laid down in the manual and expected by the manufacturers. Simultaneously, the aircraft crashed and with still plenty of fuel remaining caught fire instantaneously sending flames high up in the air, to the same height where I was hanging by my parachute and coming down. Everything was happening so rapidly. I was engulfed in those flames making it not only difficult but also rather impossible to see where I was going to land: besides my clothes also caught fire. I was getting intense heat on my face and my eyebrows got burnt, forcing me to close my eyes. Having ejected at a very low height and affected by fire, I had no time to put my feet together for a so-called class room learnt landing. Before I could realise it, I fell to the ground at a fall rate faster than expected because the fire and high temperature had burnt the parachute making it come down at a faster rate of descent. As I had landed, the fire spread out from the wreckage and I ran away to a safer place and far from the crashed aircraft. I soon realised that I had fractured my legs and was in no condition to walk.

I was in extreme pain but had to take action immediately to save myself from the fire. Besides, the aircraft was exploding with remaining ammunition firing/exploding in random directions, fortunately not towards me. Thank GOD for small mercies. It was bad enough to leave the cool comfort of the aircraft and be all alone on the ground that too in an hostile environment. (No doubt, they say the cockpit is really a safe place) After a safe ejection, it would have been unfortunate to be killed by our own ammunition. I unmasked myself, threw the bone dome away, and dragged myself away from the wreckage towards a few trees that I planned as my resting and recouping place and charting my further plan of action. I was thirsty and sweating in pain and wondered what was next? It was about 1000-1015 hrs when this happened. Contrary to what some people talk, no thoughts of my family came to my mind either before or after the ejection, although I had got married only on 27 Sep 71. I did not even see my leader's aircraft anywhere in the vicinity trying to locate me. Later, I learnt he had not seen my aircraft at all. It must have been approximately 15-20 minutes or so later when I suddenly saw an ambulance, typical one-Tonner of the Indian Army about 150 yards away. I thought I was lucky that a rescue operation has been very prompt, although I was unsure of the actual ground position and this vehicle could have been from any side (Although Pakistanis, I think, use a crescent on their hospital vehicles). Being injured and unable to walk, I needed someone to rescue me, friend or foe. Before I could realise it, the help which had come so suddenly, vanished and I could not see the ambulance any more. Was it a mirage or my imagination that I would be saved quickly and end the pain and suffering that was affecting me. Well, there I was, once again planning further what to do next. I was contemplating throwing the overalls into the fire (as we all were flying with civil clothes underneath. I even had a pair of scissors to cut my hair, if required, besides, of course, some Pakistani currency). In my condition, it was prudent to wait till dark which was a long way to come and hope like hell that I would manage to reach the Indian side as early as possible. A lot of permutations and combinations went through my mind, cancelling many ideas and coming up with new ones. I was not able to come up with a fool proof plan. The best was to wait, rest and think after the shock of ejection had subsided. I think it was within 45 minutes of ejection when I saw another vehicle—this time a Willy's jeep.

My Saviours

I learnt later that the ambulance crew had gone back saying the fire of the wreckage was widespread and that no one could have survived.

However, Capt Appayya, from the Engineers was adamant and perhaps keen to capture his first Pakistani pilot and took none of the nonsense and came himself to search along with another young officer and some jawans fully armed with weapons. I did not want to miss this, perhaps the last chance of rescue. Being a smaller vehicle, it drove close towards me and I tried to whistle and waved to attract their attention. It worked. They jumped out of the jeep after driving a little closer and in no time surrounded me with rifles pointing at me. A typical scene from a Western movie. There I was, helpless, lying half reclined on the ground with pain and weapons all around ready to shoot any moment. Some anxious moments passed that seemed like eternity, as there was a stunned silence except the booming of tank fire from both sides every now and then. I think both sides then decided almost simultaneously, and the captain took the initiative and asked me who I was. I replied, "INDIAN". No smiles, no emotions, no change in attitude or weapons lowered. Too soon to expect perhaps. Then again, some anxious silent moments passed and some conversation took place. I told the captain about the units around, I mentioned the Brigade in whose support we had flown, and told him the name of the FAC, Fg Offr VG Kumar from Adampur. How much I had convinced them, I did not know then.

Then suddenly, once again, I was asked whether I had a weapon., I was asked to throw it towards them, which I did. What amazed them was why the first chamber was empty. They were convinced with my explanation of accidental firing. Then I was asked for the map and other documents like code words, etc., which I threw towards them. Once this done I thought I would be rescued. However, nothing of that sort happened. This left me confused and wondering what was next. After some more horrifying moments, I finally took the courage to ask them who they were. I waited eagerly for a favourable answer. Ultimately, after a little delay which appeared to be the longest in my life, the Captain said "INDIAN".

I was happy to hear that and so was he as I learnt later. Why I have been mentioning him again and again is because he was shot later and had a bullet in his stomach. He had landed up not only in the same Army Hospital Delhi Cantt where I was but also in my room where there were three more patients. It was here where I spent from 6 Dec 71 to the second week of March 72 that we discussed and learnt the details that I would have never ever come to know.

However, in spite of all these clarifications, I was still there. Soon after, when I said I was in great pain and why we don't go to a friendly place, I was helped to be evacuated. Because of the pain I was suffering I asked him why he did not call for an ambulance as a jeep would have been highly painful for me. The Captain mentioned that Paki tanks were not very far away and if we waited any longer we would be sure targets for them. So I was and was cramped into the jeep along with all the others. They did their best, but those who know a Willys jeep will realise how much space it has for a patient with multiple fractures.

I was driven a short distance and placed in an underground bunker managed by the Advanced Dressing Station in the field (This, I think, was the most forward medical help available). They did not want to drive during the day because of the likelihood of being attacked again. This cross-type bunker was next to a tree where an Indian tank was parked and firing every now and then. Whenever it fired, the bunker shook and a little earth fell all around. I was sure that this tank would be an enemy target too. Inside the bunker, a jawan of the Med Corps ran around to help the injured, although I found no one else there. He appeared quite worried. He was kind enough to give me some water from his hip flask which had very little left as it is. No other medical aid could be provided as none was available. I had no choice but to wait until dark. One had no choice anywhere. (In the Army Hospital Delhi Cantt, I was later informed by the same Captain that I would have been shot if I had made the slightest suspicious movement) I am grateful to GOD who gave them the wisdom to think in a positive way to spare me and once again serve the Nation which I did until I superannuated. In the evening, along with some other patients, we were put in an ambulance and driven to Jaurian hospital. What a ride through the fields. It was no comparison to the smooth flying I was so used to. We reached the hospital at around 9 pm or so and the doctors quickly attended to me. Initially planks were tied to keep my legs straight. After some time they put plaster in the light of a Hurricane lamp. With no facility for anaesthesia, I was given simple and general medical aid. Only I know the pain I suffered when the doctor twisted my leg to straighten it. The plaster was so bloody tight that I was in more pain than even before. I was literally howling and told the doctor to please do something otherwise I would break it. He was kind enough to help me and make me a little comfortable. The night passed somehow. Some food was available.

In hospital (they had no x-ray facility there) I came to know that I had three fractures—one on the foot navicular, shin bone and a major one on my left knee–multiple internal fractures. All this because of my uneven landing with my left foot taking all the weight.

The next morning was another exciting experience. Until now I was declared 'missing'. Communication was poor. My Sqn mates were hopefully waiting for some good news, particularly they were worried about my backache and wondering what could have happened to me.

I still have not come to know as to how it happened, but it did. My wife was residing in Ferozepur Cantt after having shifted there from Shimla at the end of Oct 71..She had come to Jallandhar Cantt on 4 Dec 71 only because shelling had made life at Ferozepur extremely difficult. Her brother was somewhere in Amritsar sector as a young Captain in Signals. How he came to know I still don't know. However, he learnt about me and sent his batman to Adampur to enquire about my well-being. As IAF Base did not know about my fate, they were unable to comment and just said all was fine, he is busy flying. In any case, they did not want to say anything on telephone to unknown persons. This is generally the answer when you want to avoid saying the truth. Somehow, the night passed in acute pain with hardly any sleep. In any case, flying was going on not knowing whether it was the IAF or the PAF and some sort of heavy and small arms firing was taking place, so where was the question of sleep. Having come to a safer place, it was now time to think about family and friends and lots of thoughts went through my mind. Simultaneously, information reached the higher-ups that I was safe. Obviously Adampur Base was also informed and action was initiated for further rescue, and medical treatment that was urgently needed.

Move to Safer Havens

I was informed at night that a Mi-4 helicopter was being sent to evacuate the casualties to Udhampur Base Hospital. There were three or four of us. The chopper arrived and the plan was to keep rotating, shift the patients in and take off as quickly as possible. We were being shifted by Army jawans towards the helicopter when just then a PAF MiG-19 arrived on the scene and began orbiting overhead. I don't know if they spotted the chopper kicking up dust or not but as a precaution the Mi-4 switched off for safety. Imagine what the jawans who were lifting stretchers did! They almost dropped us on Mother Earth and ran for safety leaving us as sitting targets for the PAF although I wonder if the enemy knew about our presence at all. There we were helpless, lying on the ground fully exposed while the others ran into trenches. This is what happens when you have to depend on others. We had no alternative but to remain as we were. Fortunately, an officer came to our rescue. He bullshitted the jawans for abandoning the injured persons and forgetting their ethics. We were shifted to a slightly better and safer place. In any case, shelling by the MiG-19 would not have spared any of us, healthy or injured. I am thankful to the PAF for not spotting the chopper and going back when their mission was over because of fuel constraints.

As it flew away and before the next wave came, activity commenced, and we were hurriedly shifted into the chopper while its pilots were starting it. They kept to low level flying, following the contours of the hills and we landed at Udhampur Airfield. An ambulance was waiting, and we were quickly taken to the Base Hospital where an x-ray was taken and doctors attended to us. It was here that I was told the exact nature of my injuries, which still persist.

COMMINUTED FRACTURE MEDICAL CONDYLETIBIA, NAVICULAR AND CUBOID (Rt)

After a few days, three of us were evacuated in an Otter aircraft to Adampur, a refuelling point beside my base to tell them that I was safe and sound. The Otter landed some time at midnight and my Sqnmates and Flight Commander were there to welcome me. What a great feeling to be among my people in a friendly atmosphere. The stay there was short. I told my Flt Cdr not to inform my wife about my condition fearing unnecessary worry but she had already come to know, I don't know how. From Adampur we were taken to Palam airport in New Delhi and then to the Army Hospital which was going to be my home till the middle of March 1972. That was the end of war for me.

The final treatment was initiated and after an operation, I began recovering. I was in bed till 26 Jan 72 when I walked on crutches for the first time.

It was after about 24 hours when my wife, told in Adampur that I had been shifted to Delhi, came to see me. I was discharged from hospital on 14 Mar 72 and after two months of annual leave joined duty at AFA Dundigal and resumed flying again in Jan 1973 which I did for the next eight years. I am now living a retired life with all the fond memories of the years spent in the IAF and the wars I took part in. What a great life it was.

I would love to continue to be associated with the IAF for ever.

***Veteran Group Captain Gurdeep Singh** was commissioned in Flying branch on 01 Aug 1964. During the year 1971 he was a Flying Instructor. Along with certain other pilots he was attached to 101 Sqn, AF to participate in the 1971 war. Unfortunately, his aircraft was hit on the second day of the war itself and he had to eject. He has flown various aircraft including Vampire, Toofani, Mystere and S-22. He retired on 31 Mar 1995. Now he is settled at Jalandhar and can be reached at gurdeep_samra@rediffmail.com and 9464805045.*

44 NIGHT BOMBING OF DHAKA

Manbir Singh

During the December 1971 Indo-Pak war I was operating from Gauhati with No 28 Squadron. The Squadron was equipped with MiG-21FL aircraft. The war had started on the 3rd of December. We the pilots of No 28 and 4 Squadron operating out of Gauhati had put both the runways that is the ones at Tezgaon and Kurmitola at Dhaka out of action.

On the night of 7th December at about 8 pm I was in the Officers' Mess with other Squadron pilots when an officer came and told me that the Squadron Commander Wg Cdr BK Bishnoi wanted to see me in the ante room. I immediately went to the ante room. There I saw Wg Cdr BK Bishnoi and the Operations Commander Gp Capt MSD Wollen having some discussion. I saluted and stood there at the door way. I was asked to come in and was informed that I have to go on a night bombing mission to bomb the Tezgaon airfield at Dhaka in the wee hours. I was advised to have early dinner and go to sleep in the Air Crew room near the Squadron Headquarters.

Mission at Night: Mission 1

After having had my dinner, I went to the Squadron Headquarters and asked the ground staff to have an aircraft ready loaded with bombs at 2 am in the morning for the mission. I then went to sleep in the Air Crew room. I woke up to an alarm at 2 am on 8th December and washed my face. I had gone to sleep in my flying suit. I put on my flying boots, picked up my helmet and walked to the aircraft. It was a cold morning with the mist reducing the visibility. I could barely see a few yards ahead. I got to the aircraft and there I was greeted by the ground crew. They told me that the aircraft was ready for the mission. I walked around the aircraft to check out if all external systems were ok and that the bombs had been loaded properly.

When I lined up on the runway, I could not see runway lights beyond a hundred yards due to the mist. I wondered if all the runway lights were on. I enquired from the control tower if all the runway lights were on. The controller told me that all the lights were on. I then put on the after burner and released the brakes. The aircraft began to accelerate and as it rolled forward I kept it on the centre white line of the runway with the help of the landing light. I kept seeing the runway lights coming up as the aircraft accelerated to take off speed. As I took off at 0325 am and when I reached about 100 meters height visibility improved considerably. I could see the stars in the clear sky above and the half moon in the eastern part of the sky. I could see the hill tops in the south. I turned south towards Dhaka and levelled off at about 200mtrs above the hill tops.

I headed for the initial point (IP), a road and a rail bridge over a river at Ghoyashal. As I cleared the Shillong hills near Cherapunji I descended down to the plains of East Pakistan. I flew at 100 meters height and at 900 kmph. As the pressure altimeter was reading less than zero, I had to maintain the height with the help of the Radio altimeter. I could see the ground which was covered with mist and the mist could be seen clearly in the moon light. I could see the rivers with the water shining in the moon light. As I reached close to Ghorashal I could see the two bridges over the river loom large before me. Over the bridges I turned right and headed for Tezgaon airfield. Short of the airfield I pulled up to a height of 3000 metres and looked for Tezgaon runway. After an orbit I spotted the runway. Kurmitola runway was clearly visible in the moon light as it was not camouflaged. Tezgaon runway was camouflaged and was little more difficult to spot. I positioned myself in the correct place for an attack from north to south along the runway and armed the bombs before entering into a 45 degree dive.

I put the sight on the centre of the runway. When I reached 1000 meters height I released the bombs. After releasing the bombs I pulled out of the dive and turned hard left and upwards. I saw the bursting of bombs on the runway and the ack ack open up firing. The bombs created a barrage over the airfield. It looked beautiful like the fireworks in the closing ceremony of Olympics. The ack ack opened up after I had dropped the bombs and cleared the airfield area. I was safe as there was no air opposition. I returned to Gauhati and landed at 0412 hrs.

During the approach for the runway, I could see the runway clearly on the final approach but as soon as I reached a height of 100 meters and below I encountered mist and the visibility dropped to less than 100 meters. I landed safely and taxied to my allotted pen.

Mission 2

I flew a similar mission on 9th December morning. I took off at 0320 am and landed back at 0410 hrs. Again the ack ack at Tezgaon opened fire after I had dropped the bombs and cleared the airfield. There was no air opposition. I came back safe and sound.

Mission 3

On the night of 11th December I was briefed by my Squadron Commander to go on a mission to locate a Ghost runway 30 kms east of Tezgaon airfield. This runway had been laid out temporary to evacuate some important people from the country. This runway had been spotted by Flt Lt H Sardesai of No 4 Squadron. He had fired his two K-13 missiles on it. I got airborne for the mission at 0350 hrs and headed towards the target. On reaching the target area I climbed up to 5000 meters and orbited over the area to locate the Ghost runway. I even took the help of the radar at Shillong but could not locate the runway as the enemy had put off the runway lights. I asked the radar to vector me to Tezgaon airfield. The radar guided me to the airfield. I spotted the airfield and carried out a steep glide bombing attack. The ack ack opened fire after I had dropped the bombs and cleared the airfield. The bombs did not explode. I returned to Gauhati and landed safely at 0440 hrs.

***Veteran Air Cmde Manbir Singh** was commissioned into the Flying Branch on 10 Nov 1962. He is a fighter pilot with vast experience. He actively participated in the 1971 War and flew 27 missions during the war. For his outstanding performance during the war, he was awarded a Vir Chakra. He retired in 1994 and thereafter took to Commercial flying till 2002. He is settled at Pune and can be reached at manbir90@gmail.com and 8308813833.*

45 KILO FLIGHT AND THE BIRTH OF THE BANGLADESH AIR FORCE

CM Singla

Special Assignment for Me

September 1971: With war clouds looming, I was a Flight Lieutenant and one of the four flying instructors with the 112 Helicopter Unit of the Indian Air Force located at Bagdogra, West Bengal, which was on dawn-to-dusk standby daily. Ours was a training unit, essentially providing operational training to Air Force and Army pilots out of the Helicopter Training School before they moved on to their Chetak units; but we also provided helicopter support for sectors in our proximity. On 26 September, I was summoned by our Commanding Officer, Squadron Leader Naresh Kumar and told to move to Tezpur, Assam, the next morning. Hardly inclined to leave my flying unit and take up an assignment that could very well see me behind a desk while the war went on, I tried sounding my protests; but they fell on deaf ears. "An aircraft will pick you up at 0800 hrs tomorrow" was the unresponsive verdict I received. There wasn't even a word on my assignment; I was ordered to pack for 4-5 weeks and carry my bedding as well.

At 8 am the next morning, I boarded a Dakota. At Tezpur, I was personally received by Squadron Leader Mehtani, OC 115 Helicopter Unit. A VIP reception indeed but a no-frills one as I was escorted to meet the Air Officer Commanding of the Station who asked brusquely if I could fly the Chetak alone. "'Mama' Mehtani has a copter ready for you", he said on my affirmative response. "Take it to Dimapur. You will be further briefed there. You will get complete maintenance support for the Chetak on immediate priority. Questions? Carry on." In the Helicopter Unit, I obtained a map, VHF (Very High Frequency) and NDB (Non-Directional Beacon) frequencies, signed for the machine and for the first time flew it alone to Dimapur, Nagaland. On switching off at Dimapur, I remember that the rickety jeep that rolled up refused to re-start. Having woken up very early and been on the move the whole day, hungry and tired, I cursed and push-started the jeep back to life.

AF Dimapur was commanded by a Flight Lieutenant who had a staff of about 15 airmen. Their role was to provide support to Dakotas of AF Jorhat doing air-maintenance of troops in forward locations in Nagaland. I was given a cot in the ramshackle ATC building. Food that was spicy and oily came from the Airmen Mess. The rest of the creature comforts matched the cot and the food.

Training of Pakistani Pilots

I received a further briefing from the Station Commander Jorhat, Group Captain Chandan Singh, who landed in a Dakota the next day, 28 September, with Squadron Leader CM Choudhary, a Qualified Flying Instructor (QFI) on Dakota who spoke Bengali, for company. I was tasked to train three Pakistani pilots on the Chetak. Two of them, Squadron Leader Sultan Ahmed and Flight Lieutenant Badrul Alam, both Bengalis, had defected from the Pakistani Air Force and the third, Captain Shahabuddin Ahmed, was a civilian pilot. A hand-picked maintenance team led by Flight Lieutenant Ramakrishna had been assembled to give us necessary support. My brief was to get cracking immediately and make my three trainees operational within a week. This left me with far too inadequate hours for the task if I were to follow the IAF syllabus for day-and-night conversion. Ignore the rules of the IAF, I was told, complete the task. I got going pronto, grabbing writing material and commencing the preliminary ground training. I could have hardly imagined that, 28 September 1971, would later come to be recognised as the Raising Day of the Bangladesh Air Force (BAF).

I flew round the clock with them. Their age, mature fixed wing flying habits, distressed state of mind and barely acceptable living conditions made teaching and training a formidable task. Their attempts at hovering resulted in moving all over, frequently blocking the only runway. It was difficult to make them reduce speed on the finals. Nevertheless, we went on with no let-up and bordering on exhaustion, I was able to report on schedule that each of them was now comfortable flying by day and night.

"For your navigation phase", the Station Commander ordered, "I want to see you over Jorhat ATC at midnight tonight". I took off with a trainee in the pitch dark of the night with an 8/8 low cloud ceiling. About half way to Jorhat, it started pouring. The Chetak has only basic instrumentation with air-driven gyros. Flying blind without a visual horizon was bad enough, but entering the clouds, even in the plains, with zero instrument landing capability had resulted in disasters in the past. I kept reducing my altitude and speed, maintaining my heading. Naturally, instead of the trainee, I had the controls, yet I suddenly saw tree branches rushing past the copter. I had descended below the canopy of the trees! That was enough; I did a gentle 180 and safely returned to Dimapur in pouring rain. Not surprisingly, I was pulled up for not being seen and heard over AF Station Jorhat at midnight.

Armoured Version of Chetak

We barely got a day off to rest when on 08 October I was summoned to Jorhat. One Chetak had been brought in by transport aircraft. Its serial number is recorded as 364 in my log book. It had two rocket pods of a Mystere fighter aircraft mounted on either side. They carried seven rockets each, capable of being fired in pairs/salvo. The selection switch for pair and salvo and the firing switch were mounted on the captain's control column. A side-firing twin barrel machine gun was mounted on the floor. The sliding door on the left had been removed. The Station Commander flew with me in the co-pilot's seat to Dimapur.

Armourer fitters were flown in and so were loads of rockets. I was asked to teach my trainees to fire rockets by day and night accurately. Such a thing had never been done in the Air Force and I had no clue; and I told the Station Commander as much. Harmonisation of the pods, gun sights, ground attack tactics and target practice were unprecedented and had to be improvised. "Who will guide me, Sir?" I asked. "You will learn", he said smilingly, "I am confident." This was first of the several pioneering flying tasks that were to be entrusted to me later in my career.

We now had two Chetaks—an armed one and a passenger version. We were issued a sten gun each. We practised firing it and then were given two loaded magazines each to carry with the weapon while flying.

The rocket pods were synchronised, ring and bead gun sight installed. On the test flight, I noticed that with the extra load and aerodynamics burden, the helicopter behaved sluggishly. During night, I found that the gun-sight had been mounted very low and was so bright that I could not see a target through it. These defects were rectified despite the resource crunch and a rheostat fixed on the stick gave us the realigned gun sight operational viability.

Practice Rocket Firing

Since we needed targets to practice firing RPs (Rocket Projectiles), a Dakota was made to drop three parachutes with bundles of hay slung under it. The parachutes flung over the dense jungle canopy were to make targets for us to fire at; unfortunately, all three parachutes went clean through the canopy of trees. I suggested that three airmen could para-jump on to the neighbouring grass-topped hill slopes and nail the parachutes. But then, it was unsafe for para-dropped men to land on steep slopes. Neither could we land a copter on such slopes. So I went into low hover and had the airmen jump out; and once they had nailed the parachutes I picked them up in a very low hover. We now had excellent targets. I found myself enjoying the game; free of rules, regulations and red tape. I evolved the aiming procedure, elevation of commencement of the dive and the height above ground for release of rockets and procedure for pulling away. We soon burned and re-laid several parachutes and I reported that all my three pupils could now fire RPs with reasonable accuracy by day.

Transfer of Helicopter to Bangladesh

Squadron Leader Sultan Ahmed and his countrymen were now asked by the Station Commander to design an emblem for painting on the armed Chetak and give the helicopter a name and number. This was an exciting moment for them and after lively deliberations they decided that the helicopter's vertical stabiliser be painted with a red roundel having a map of Bangladesh superimposed on it in green. They chose EBR (for East Bengal Rifles) as the call sign of the copter. The IAF roundels were removed overnight and the armed Chetak donned the Bangladesh Colours. By all accounts, it was the first aircraft of the BAF and in all my subsequent log book entries IAF Sl. No. 364 was substituted by EBR.

Further Assignments for Me

My mission accomplished, I was ordered back to Bagdogra on 15 October. Back to routine, I found life boring. On 27 October, I was on an assignment flying some VIPs around Barrackpore and Dum Dum airport in Calcutta when my CO telephonically ordered me to take an Indian Airlines flight and get back to Bagdogra. I was required back at Dimapur. Though other instructors had volunteered, I had been asked for by name. I was back at Dimapur on 01 November.

Night missions were being planned and I was to learn and teach night firing of RPs to my Bengali trainees. Night firing was not to be guided by phases of the moon. The ability to fly and fire in dark nights was to be mastered. Visual sighting of a target in the dark posed a severe operational limitation. Nevertheless by end-November we were operational day and night.

On 01 December I was asked to fly down to AF Jorhat by myself. Group Captain Chandan Singh wanted a night strike to be launched within a couple of days from an abandoned airfield near Agartala. Could my trainees navigate, strike accurately and return? he asked. I replied 'yes' except for the returning part. Returning to an un-lit point on a dark night without the necessary device could be disastrous. Even if I had a hand-held RT set, we might not be able to lead them in should the course they were steering go wrong in strong winds that were likely to prevail. He suggested that we light up the point with petromax lamps covered by a perforated tin. Would it suffice, more so if we cover and uncover the lamp repeatedly? I felt confident it would. On 02 December I flew to Kailashahar—an abandoned airfield in Tripura bordering East Pakistan—along with my trainees. The strike was to be launched from Teliamura. The Group Captain also arrived during the day with complete ground support. On the night of 03 December, Squadron Leader Sultan and Flight Lieutenant Alam got airborne with a full load of rockets and fuel. The checks and procedures, well imbibed, got them to keep the navigation lights on making them absolutely visible. I got on the hand-held set and got them switched off. They were now invisible—though were audible. Their target was the fuel storage tanks at Narayanganj. As they were not expected and therefore, they received no opposition. The mission was accomplished. On return, locating the helipad and landing went without a hitch. Early next morning, I retrieved our element back to Dimapur.

War Begins

War with Pakistan was declared that day, 04 December 1971. By then our miniscule unit, designated Kilo Flight, was quite well organised with manpower, spares, ammunition, tentage, and mobility. Now that war had been declared, on 06 December, the Station Commander issued instructions that I fly all armed missions as pilot-in-command. We were given Pakistani currency and personal weapons. I moved our two helicopters, the armed and the passenger Chetaks, to Kailashahar. Thereafter we would live in tents surviving on food from the nearest Army units.

Ground attack and close support missions started in the right earnest. Group Captain Chandan Singh was directing my flights and flew with me as a passenger from time to time to gauge enemy status and our efficacy. I flew three missions on the night of 06 December. On the first night of the attack sorties, I realised that not until we were looking directly at the muzzle flashes of enemy rifles and machine guns would we have any inkling of being under fire. The muted thuds that we heard were direct hits on our Chetak, I learned, and not colliding bats. Flying from Kailashahar, we engaged targets in Kalaura, Maulvi Bazar and Shamsher Nagar.

The next morning I looked at the bullet holes. The bullets had gone through our fragile cowling. There was no armour plating of any kind for the vital engine installations, pilots or the gunner on the copter's floor. I told the technicians to number each bullet hole and also paint the name of the place where we had been hit. This was done, but later when the machine took frequent hits the exercise was abandoned. On the first few sorties, I remember handing over my wallet and watch to our Engineer, Flight Lieutenant Ramakrishna, just in case. Later, when the frequency of flights increased, I discontinued the practice. Pakistani currency was always carried, but the sten gun, cumbersome as it was, ended up being tied to the pilot seats.

We established the helicopter airworthiness norms early. After checking the bullet holes and manageable vibrations of the machine, Ramakrishna and his team would do some patch repairs. Then he would ask me, "Will you fly her?" "Yes", I would say. "Then she's serviceable". Despite several bullet holes in the cowling, main and tail rotors, we never grounded the copter and flew it every day, so much so that Army personnel used to come to our camp to look at our flying sieve.

I flew 11 missions on 07 December. For the first day's flight, I was given fighter cover. Soon after getting airborne we established RT contact. After a few minutes, the fighter escort lost visual contact with me that could not be re-established despite our mutual efforts. Perhaps it happened because he was high and fast and I was low, slow and in camouflaged colours merging with the green earth. The effort was given up eventually. A couple of days later I was assured and highly relieved to know that the IAF had established complete air superiority over East Pakistan.

A Regretful Mission

Operating out of Kailashahar, we attacked enemy positions in Darbart, Brahmanbaria, Daud Kandi, Narsingdi Road and so on. By the night 07 December, there were signs of the Pakistan Army retreating from Kalaura. I was given a site on a river bank by our army where Pakistanis were expected to cross en masse. Sure enough, the river water was clogged with boats of different sizes. I hit the biggest boat with a pair of rockets–only to be shocked to find they carried no army transports or troops; the crowds on board appeared to be civilians. My co-pilot confirmed this. We aborted the attack and reported the fiasco. To this day, I regret harming those civilians that night.

Commencement of SHBO

IV Corps of our army was pushing Westward. Their formations were to move on Shamshernagar–Maulvi Bazaar axis as also on the Kalaura–

Sylhet axis. We had been supporting their advance and during an intense night mission, my helicopter, EBR, took several hits. Early next morning, Ramakrishna said that the damage to the machine was beyond permissible limits, but she was serviceable if I shall fly her. Rockets were loaded and I took off for Shamshernagar airfield in East Pakistan that was now with our Army.

Soon heli-borne operations were launched. Commencing one afternoon, Gorkhas were being flown into enemy territory in waves by Mi-4 helicopters. On landing, the copters and soldiers came under heavy enemy fire. I expended all my ammo, re-loaded and came again ahead of the next wave. Light was fading and I feared hitting our soldiers. Firing at a distance from the landing zone did not really help our men and machines. Despite the vulnerability of our soldiers in the landing zone, further induction had to be stopped, as it turned dark. Any amount of explanation that attempting further induction could claim lives of soldiers as well as air crews in accidents would not pacify a Gorkha officer who desperately wanted reinforcements. Exasperated, Group Captain Chandan Singh had to tell him off saying, "All right, SHBO (Special Heli-Born Operations) will not happen now. You can pull out your pistol and shoot me".

By the second week of December, IV Corps was racing westward. One morning, about 0600, the Group Captain had me flying him over Sylhet airfield to ascertain whether it had been vacated by the Pak Army. Orbiting overhead, the airfield looked deserted; so he asked me to land at the dumbbell of the runway. I was approaching to establish hover and was perhaps 10 feet above ground at 10 knots forward speed when a machine-gun opened up from a bunker nearby, its roof visible barely two feet over the ground. I managed to pull away, of course...or else I wouldn't be telling this story today. The fool could have taken us alive along with the copter if only he had waited! I suggested a salvo of 14 rockets to take care of the bunker, but was asked to hurry back; perhaps to report and prevent a disaster! We ended the day with a pleasant dinner with fish in the menu, paid for in Pak currency, as my co-pilot had me land near a river where fishermen had kept their day's catch alive.

The Surrender

On 16 December, the day of the surrender, I flew into a desolate Dacca airfield with Squadron Leader Choudhury. Joining the scavenging for whatever one could from the assortment of stuff strewn around on the potholed tarmac, I too picked up a belt of a Sabre aircraft cannon shells. At Dimapur it was broken into smaller lengths and shared. I still have my piece.

End of a Satisfying Role

We flew back to Agartala at night and talked with a big feeling of relief. Our comrades in uniform had broken a big threat into two and created a new nation. On 18 December I was instructed to return my trainees to Dacca and to handover the bullet-ridden, armed Chetak to them and fly back in the other Chetak. I shook hands with Squadron Leader Sultan, Badrul Alam and Shahabuddin Ahmed in Dacca–the capital city that was theirs now. Shahabuddin wrote his Dacca address on a Pakistani currency note and invited me home. I still have it. Squadron Leader Sultan, by consensus among the three, refused to hand over the sten guns. We spent the night in an Officers' Mess in Dacca. Next morning Sultan saw me off with a crate of Scotch.

The Awards

For our role in the war, I was awarded a "Vir Chakra" and Sultan, my co-pilot, "Bir Uttam" by the free Bangladesh government. We thus formed a unique crew to be decorated by two different nations.

Veteran Air Cmde CM Singla *was commissioned in the Flying Branch in 1962. An alumnus of Modern School, New Delhi; National Defence Academy and Defence Services Staff College, he has been a Category A Flying Instructor and an IAF and DGCA helicopter aircrew examiner. He actively participated in the 1971 war and trained Bangladeshi pilots on helicopters. He was awarded a Vir Chakra for his exceptional performance. He served in the IAF for almost 28 years before seeking premature retirement in 1990. Post retirement he has been the Chairman and Managing Director of Pawan Hans Helicopters Ltd. and has held other civilian assignments at the Executive Director level. He lives in Gurugram and can be reached at cmsingla@yahoo.co.in and 9811851958.*

46 LITTLE CONTRIBUTION BY A MEDICAL ASSISTANT

Jai Bikerma Jit Singh Sodhi

During the 1971 war, I was an LAC and was on the posted strength of 3 Wing, AF. By virtue of my trade, Medical Assistant, I was working in the Station Sick Quarters (SSQ). One fine morning I boarded an AN-12 aircraft at Palam along with a few more airmen of different trades. The aircraft headed towards Srinagar. Our task was to airlift the causalities who had been gathered together from various forward areas due to various injuries like frost bite, compound fractures and bullet injuries etc. These soldiers were on SI/DI list and were to be brought to Delhi for treatment at Base Hospital Delhi and Army Hospital Delhi Cantt. There were nearly 200 causalities and some of them were on drip. I, being a Medical Assistant by trade, assisted them during the two hours journey from Srinagar to Palam. It was a very satisfying feeling for me, as I, as a young LAC with around five years of service contributed my little bit to the war.

I still remember that flight and the pain on the faces of the wounded soldiers.

***Veteran Sgt Jai Bikerma Jit Singh Sodhi** was enrolled in the Medical Assistant trade in May 1966. He served for 20 years in the service. He mostly worked in the Station Health Organisation contributing his services to the upkeep of the stations. He retired from the Air Force in May 1966. He is settled at Amritsar. He can be reached at kaurkulvinder06121972@gmail.com and 9915896877.*

47 Operation Cactus Lily - The Bangladesh War 1971

World's First Night Heli-Borne Drop at Sylhet

RM Sridharan

Humble Beginning for the Young Flying Officers

I had already spent over two years at 110 Helicopter Unit at Kumbhigram when the clouds of war became imminent with the massacre of Bengalis in East Pakistan and the mass exodus of refugees into Eastern India.

My operational training culminated with my categorisation as a C White Pilot, competent for all kinds of heli-borne and other related role based operations, both by day and night. This categorisation was with most of the 20 pilots posted in the unit and all this happened just a day before the war broke out. We pilots were delighted at our CO, Sqn Ldr CS Sandhu and Flt Cdr, Flt Lt PK Vaid's decision to utilise only those pilots who were on the posted strength of the unit and not the few experienced MI-4 pilots, who had just returned from Russia after MI-8 training. This was a great morale booster for us young enthusiastic junior pilots, just waiting for combat war action.

MI-4 in Action Op Cactus Lily, 1971

MI-4s in the 1971 War

War broke out in the early hours of 3 Dec 1971 with a pre-dawn air strike in the Western Sector that sparked off the conflict. As per our Unit War Plan, we reached the unit premises in our overalls and Pistol Holster Webbing, awaiting further instructions from our CO & Flt Cdr. The war instructions were very clear as the bulk of the unit helicopters with air and ground crew were to move to HQ 4 Corps located at Teliamura on war detachment with them. The remaining air and ground crew would disperse the reserve helicopters in different locations, before finally joining up with the main unit as and when required. The eastern element of the Pakistan Air Force had been virtually wiped out but the air threat had not been completely neutralised. Thus, the rest of the unit had to be dispersed and kept in readiness at different locations. All the pilots were issued with revolver pistols with six rounds for our self-defence and we kept them in our webbing holsters. We stowed our kit and bedding in our respective helicopters as we began dispersing to different safe locations.

At the Met briefing, it was stated that the weather would be clear and fine for the next few days in our area of operation. I dispersed to different locations on three days until finally, Fg Offr Kruts Krishnamurthy and I set course for Aijal in Mizoram with a set of ground crew and flight Gunners as load masters. We set course for Aijal early in the morning and landed at the 1 Assam Rifles helipad around breakfast time. Our unit operated throughout at this helipad mainly for the Army. We had a special affiliation with 1 Assam Rifles as we generally stayed in their beautifully located Officers' Mess. That night we spent at the Mess and while listening to the radio giving all the war news from different areas, I received a message to take off for Teliamura for further briefing there.

I got airborne just after lunch. There was a huge ground at Teliamura, which is in the State of Tripura, a short flight from Agartala, the capital of Tripura.

After landing at Teliamura, we were called to the Ops Room of 4

Front L to R: OBE & DOC
Back L to R: NAMBI, NL & LAMBOO

Corps for a briefing. Here, I came to know that a heli-lift of 4/5 Gurkha Rifles Battalion was being done by our unit from an airfield at Kailashaher to a ground at Sylhet. I was instructed to move to Kailashaher with air and ground crew to augment our unit force. I got airborne late that afternoon and set course at treetop level for Kailashaher which was a small airstrip being used by Indian Airlines for hopping flights to Agartala. We landed around sunset in fading light and poor visibility.

By the time we switched off the helicopter and reached our makeshift crew room at the small airport complex, I was told that all the helicopters of the last formation of the second wave led by our Flt Cdr Palokha Vaid were on their way back. Earlier, the first foray was led by CO Charu Sandhu who inaugurated 110 HU'S SHBO operation for 4/5 GR to Sylhet with two Vics of three helicopters each. Subsequently, Palokha Vaid took another two Vics after a Mukti Bahini of a Kilo Flight Allouette flown by Sqn Ldr Singla strafed the Pakistani positions as our helicopters and troops encountered a lot of ground fire at the landing ground. The Forward Air Controller, Fg Offr SC Sharma and his helipad team with kerosene goose necks were dropped by the second wave for our night operations the next day.

I had only done SHBO by day in Mizoram and Nagaland from proper helipads with trained army battalions. However, this Gurkha Battalion was untrained but quickly became operational with professional and enthusiastic briefing by our Flt Engineers/Flt Gunners and Pilots and the first day of the SHBO went off quite well with the troops and our aircrew full of enthusiasm and josh.

My Induction into the War Zone

Next day, we were all set for action. I was excited awaiting my turn to go into battle stations and enter the war zone. I had to wait until about 1000 hrs on 8th Dec for my first sortie of SHBO to Sylhet. Flt Cdr briefed us about our sortie. He asked me if I was confident to take on No 3 in the formation as that would involve a little extra time on the ground at Sylhet as the mortar had to be wheeled out with some extra ammunition. Both No 1 flown by Flt Lt Jayaraman, Jaya and No 2 by Fg Offr Murtuza Ali, Lamboo, had done two sorties on Day 1. Both helicopters could only carry 14 troops. The briefing in short was to start with No 1 giving a call and the other two acknowledging with clicks. Line up one behind the other and take off. After take off, the other two will take position on the starboard, with Lamboo and me on the port behind Jaya. All went as briefed and I was slotted in at No 3 on the portside of Jaya. The formation was flying as low as possible with no obstructions in the flat terrain in the then East Pakistan. In a few minutes, we had settled inside enemy territory. We had been told that there was no aerial threat and concentrated in keeping both 1 & 2 helicopters in visual contact. In the distance after about 30 minutes of flying I could make out the river that flowed around Sylhet. Formation Leader Jaya called the FAC SC who reassured us by saying that the helipad was clear and there was no firing. I spotted the big building across the river that was a landmark for the formation. Jaya lined up in the centre of the big ground as I remained to the left of some trees just short of the landing spot. All the three landing points had similar approaches. On the final approach to Sylhet, my co-pilot, Sukhi Hundal, blew the helicopter horn to keep the troops on stand-by and in a couple of minutes No 1 touched down with a bit of dust and then No 2 and finally my helicopter was on the ground. As soon as the troops disembarked, both 1 & 2 in the empty state would turn right and back and clear Sylhet LZ. Because of the gun, I took a few seconds for the troops to clear the helicopter. SC on the ground was by now warning us about firing from the left. So there was live action on the LZ. Once clear of the enemy area we increased our speed and keeping low altitude were back on course for base. The flying time to the base was another 35 mins and I concentrated in keeping both 1 and 2 in sight. It had been a successful induction for me into SHBO for surprise induction of 4/5 Gurkha troops to Sylhet.

My Baptism

The Gurkha boys in all the three helicopters were full of josh and shouted their war cry just before leaving the helicopter. I had felt so proud for carrying out my first war sortie successfully as we touched down at Kailashaher and parked the helicopter on the grass beside the other unit helicopters. After landing, Sukhi and I did an external check of our helicopter and found a couple of bullet holes on the tail boom which were minor as per our Senior Technical Officer, Flt Lt Shankaran, Shanks. Perhaps we were hit while on the ground at Sylhet while our FAC was warning us. Thereafter, I returned to my Flt Cdr and I briefed him about the sortie and told him it had gone off well. Formation leader Jaya gave his Thumbs Up to Flt Cdr Palokha for the sortie well done. The baptism by fire had been achieved in the first sortie and all the butterflies in the stomach had been calmed.

That day I did two more sorties in No 2 & No 3 positions in the Vic formation by day. In the first, we had to land and pick up troops from Kalaura where 4/5 GR was located in battle. Both these sorties also went off quite well with my helicopter again being struck on the third and last sortie, this time on the main rotor. Fortunately, all the damage was minor and did not affect our helicopter serviceability which remained at 10 serviceable all through at Kailashaher.

Day SHBO ended late in the evening. Preparations were now being made for history to be made as it had been decided to continue the **SHBO by NIGHT FOR THE FIRST TIME EVER IN INDIAN AIR FORCE HELICOPTER HISTORY**.

I had earlier flown two sorties in the night; both with Flying Officer Jagdeep Singh. The sorties were uneventful. For the next night's SHBO sortie, I had CO Charu Sandhu as leader with Fg Offr Reddy BLK as No 3 and self at No 2. This sortie was quite similar to the first one except that the moon was shining nice and bright. This was a great help for night navigation. This time there was a flurry of calls from FAC SC to exercise caution as there was plenty of ground fire from Pakistani positions while we were approaching. I landed watching the CO's No 1 helicopter to my left. This time the goose necks were mostly off while landing and subsequent take-off. The troops again were very quick in leaving the helicopter and the sortie was without any unusual happening. The heavy Pakistani ground fire at Sylhet did find my helicopter on the tail boom which did not trouble our technicians. Our CO and Flt Cdr were very happy with the performance of the entire unit. Late at night when all the helicopters were back and the first night's SHBO operation had been completed, we gathered in our makeshift crew room at the Kailashaher ATC. Our CO was extremely happy and so was our Flt Cdr for a most successful heli-lift of 4/5 Gurkha Rifles by day and night. The unit had lifted 254 troops and equipment to Sylhet to airlift the battalion so that the Gurkhas, as planned by Gen Sagat Singh, Cdr 4 Corps, could take over the Pakistani garrison in a swift and lethal strike.

Back Row Standing - Chandu, Jaya, Dogga, Johnny, Mitra, AD, Yogi, Dubby, Gads, Solly. Front Row Kneeling - Self, Chippy, Bob, Nambi, Lamboo, Bhatta, BLK , Obe !!

Proud Moment for Me

I had participated as the junior-most unit pilot in this historic night SHBO to Sylhet with no formal training of night Operations on unprepared landing grounds. I was very proud to have been part of such a historic event which played a very crucial role in speeding up Operation Cactus Lily in the war for the liberation of Bangladesh. The speed of operations by 110 HU with 10 helicopters and crew without any loss to man and material earned high praise for the unit under **Sqn Ldr CS Sandhu and Flt Lt PK Vaid**.

Subsequently, the unit was awarded the President's colours which is very big honour for any unit. Both the CO, Sqn Ldr CS Sandhu and Flt Cdr Flt Lt PK Vaid were awarded VrC for their exceptional performance during the war.

***Veteran Air Cmde RM Sridharan** was commissioned into the Flying Branch on 21 Jun 1969. He is a helicopter pilot and was a part of the Helicopter Guys of Silchar" during the 1971 war while being on the posted strength of 110 HU. He held many key appointments during his 34 years of service with the IAF including Command of a HU, Command of two big Stations. He is a keen tennis player. He is now settled at Pune and can be reached at rammanoharsridharan06@gmail.com and 9890384253.*

Special Note: Air Cmde RM Sridharan had forwarded to articles but only one has been published.

48 Recollections of 1971 War

Sankaran Subramaniam

Background

During the 1971 War, I was on the posted strength of Air Force Technical College, Jalahalli. I was a young Flt Lt. One fine day while I was taking a class, I got a message to report to the Chief Instructor. That was in Oct 71. On reaching there, I found some more instructors. We were told to be ready to move at 48 hours' notice.

The 48 hours notice was actually shortened to 8 hours. All of us, who were to proceed, were taken to AFTC Officers' Mess for the night halt. Next day, early morning, we were taken to Yelahanka where a Dakota was waiting for us. The Captain of the Aircraft clarified that the priority is to take Armament trained personnel and MT Tradesmen only. I was lucky to be included. We reached Palam in the late evening. There was a reception committee. I was told to report to the SMSO'S Branch at HQ WAC, IAF.

I reported to Wg Cdr Chakraborty, Command Armament Officer who took me to meet Air Cmde Amrit Lal Sehgal SMSO, WAC, IAF. I was instructed to visit all the bases in WAC where Gnats were located, carry out serviceability checks of all the guns in use as well as those in the stores. It was quite a good experience where I learnt a lot and shared my knowledge with the technicians in the field.

At the War Front: No 4 MEMU (Now 1 FBSU): Later on, I was asked to report to 4 MEMU located at Amritsar. That was on 1st Dec 71. I reached Amritsar by train on 2nd Dec 71 and reported for work on 3rd Dec 71. There were two detachments at Amritsar, one of Gnats and the other of SU-32. Based on my background and experience, I was asked to look after the armoury. At that point of time, it was being looked after by Cpl Chandra. The Officer i/c for the Maintenance at the Base was Flt Lt SS Kurpad who had also come on attachment from HQ TC.

MWO Soma Sundram and a few more armourers had also come from units based under Training Command.

Same day in the evening i.e on 03rd Dec 71, I was trying to settle down in my make-shift accommodation when I heard the air-raid sirens. I came out to see three Mirage ac flying low and releasing bombs on the runway. There was a 4th Mirage following them probably taking photos to see the extent of damage caused to the runway. All this happened very fast and we saw the four Mirages returning west. Pakistan had made a pre-emptive strike.

Subsequently, we went to the runway and found that the bombs have made four deep indentations. The damage inflicted on the runway was neutralised by our CPWD brethren by using quick settling concrete and the runway was operational by 10 pm. While the CPWD people were at work, another raid of two or three B-52 bombers came. They dropped some bombs and the ack-ack guns also retaliated, one bomb fell around 500 yards from where I was standing. The armourer was smart. He pulled me to a freshly dug trench. Subsequently, the Station was on full alert. I was asked to issue revolvers to all the officers and small arms with ammunition to entitled persons. The same was done following all the laid down procedures.

Capture and Dispatch of PAF Pilot: On 5th Dec 71, at around 2 pm, there was an air raid siren and ack-ack guns coming into action. There were two F-104 Sabres flying very low. Sure enough, one was hit and the pilot ejected. There was lot of excitement. The pilot was captured by the locals. Wg Cdr Johny Greene and another pilot came to his rescue. He was taken to the Officers' Mess for interrogation. The pilot had a small colt pistol which was collected from him and handed over to the Station Commander. Later in the night, the same day, the pilot was escorted to Delhi in an IL-14 aircraft. There was an option to send an armed escort. On my advice, the Pakistan pilot, who was now a PoW was mildly sedated also. This was purely a safety measure so that he does not overpower the passengers and hijack the aircraft.

Demolition of Enemy UXB - Unexploded Bombs: Coming back to demolition, during the 1971 war at Amritsar airfield, known as 4 MEMU we had about 27 enemy air raids but nil casualty; both human as well as airplane on the ground. Yet we had to deal with about 25 enemy unexploded bombs of 500lbs and 1000lbs capacity. We had a Bomb Disposal Unit at our base but the Warrant Officer in Charge somehow pleaded inability stating that his team would do only buried bombs as surface bombs are to be done by Senior Armament Officer, that is me. Well, I did not feel like informing anyone that I was equally a novice in bomb- disposal as I had no practical experience at all. Yet I decided that I would do the demolition all by self based on the theory that I was conversant with. The PAF aimed at the runway mainly that too with normal HE, HC bombs of 500lbs and 100lbs only. In one such raid, one 500lbs and one 1000lbs were lying on the shoulder of the runway as blinds—in the technical sense the fuse system did not function. We had to improvise pits to cart the bombs slowly by tying and dragging them with manila ropes and make an enclosure of sand bags. As they were on the shoulder of the runway with a distance of about 700 meters between the two, it was decided to do a simultaneous demolition with safety fuse with time interval of 5 minutes. The Operations Commander made it clear that he would not stop flying for this and I could do the demolition only on cessation of flying by around 1715 hours which is fairly dark during December in Amritsar. Well, you all know the rules say that only an armament officer can initiate the demolition. So, I went to the first bomb [500lbs] in the jeep with MTD {Cpl Mishra} asking him to be calm and keep the engine running while I lit the safety fuse. The fuse was lit and I ran to the jeep and asked the MTD to proceed to the next bomb that is a 1000lbs. Mind you it is getting dark besides cold, and the MTD got excited in that he slammed on the gear and the jeep got stalled and would not move. I had a Hobson's choice of aborting the demolition or wait for one or two attempts by the MTD to coax the jeep to move. After about one minute delay and two more attempts the jeep moved and we proceeded to the next bomb and lit the fuse without any problem. We took shelter in the ORP area and waited for the explosion of demolition. Well one came well, could be the 1000lbs but the other was a bit subdued and not so loud. We thought possibly it was just a 500lbs bomb that too far away from the place of our shelter-so we left it like that. Regardless, we waited for the cooling off period and inspected the site of demolitions and found both bombs were not there.

AOC-in-C HQ WAC IAF Desires to See the Crashed 20mm Gaddling Gun of PAF:

That Gaddling Star Fighter F-104 gun with its belt of live 20mm ammo was retrieved from the crash site. Air Officer Commanding-in-Chief HQ WAC IAF Air Marshal Minoo Engineer was quite impressed with the shooting of F-104-Star Fighter, more so on the retrieval of its Gaddling gun. He directed that it should be sent immediately to his office for his view. When the verbal message came to me, I prepared the gun, freed it of its ammo belt, just dusted off the debris but not cleaned as I wanted to show it in its recovered position. I carefully kept aside the belt of around sixty 20-mm HE ammo.

We asked for MT authority for moving the gun by road and also P-authority for my move to escort the gun. I was very keen to present the gun to the AOC-in-C myself. Fortunately, my request was accepted by SMSO, Air Cmde Amrit Lal Sehgal. It was around 12 or 13th December noon when we could move from Amritsar in an IAF Three-tonner with the gun and my Warrant Officer and two airmen. The journey by road was supposed to be about 12 hours. By sunset we reached Panipat. It was getting dark. The staff desired for a tea break for which they looked up at me! I had barely fifty rupees or so with me. We reached a dhabha and ordered some samosa and tea. The bill came to about Rs 19.50. As I was clearing the bill some 7 to 8 Sardars came to us asking what is this all about. My Warrant Officer explained—hardly had he finished when an aged sardar, with full of free-flowing white beard asked,

'Beta apka officer kithai hai?"

On being pointed out to me, he came close to me, almost hugging,

"Sahibjee, such bolo, hamara Harimandir kaisa hai?"

I replied,

"Bilkul theek hi saab, aur Pakistanis ke
liye Golden Temple ke ooper flying karne ko manna kiya hai"

He was so pleased that he tightly hugged me again to a delightful chorus of other sardars. One among them whispered something to the senior sardar. He straightened up, flared his nostrils,

"Dhabawala bulao aithe"

Saying that he pulled some wad of currencies from his side packet,

"Rakhoo beta, ye poora paise aap logon ke khaane ke liye"

I declined. By the time someone brought the Dhabawala also who almost prostrated to me saying: 'Galti ho gaya, saabjee, apke khanna ka poora paise vapas karange'.

I simply, yet sublimely was impressed by this spontaneous patriotism of resident Punjabis. Later I came to know that in Panipat there are a few famous gurdwaras and good number of sardars are staying there. We reached Palam around midnight. We left the cargo at Palam armoury-everyone was curious and helpful. Yet I reminded them that I would come next day morning to present it to AOC-in-C. I proceeded to HQ WAC Officers' Mess to a room which was allotted to me. On reaching there, I found that some other Officer was occupying the bed allotted to me. Despite mid night, the instant he realised that I had come from Amritsar he vacated my bed post haste, offering profusely "you must relax, sleep well" so saying he disappeared. I slept like a log. Next day morning the gun was brought from Armoury to HQ WAC IAF office and kept for view by AOC-in C. SMSO and his entire staff were all there briefing their boss. The rituals over, I was asked to report back to MEMU in the same three tonner. But I opted for a rail journey.

Few Unbelievable Anecdotes at No 4 MEMU During Indo-Pakistan 1971 Hostilities: Squadron Leader EV Thomas {hereafter will be called EVT} was a very senior Tech/Armt officer, then held the post of Deputy Command Armament Officer at HQ WAC IAF. He was like an Old Monk- with instant inclination for that famous—Roger Uncle Mike or *Rambha Urvashi Menaka* -that he enjoyed himself on the floating stage as much as possible. He visited 4 MEMU arriving by train that reached Amritsar late night. HQ WAC was very liberal in hiring civil transport at the discretion of Station Commanders. Yet our Maintenance branch being what it is or what it was, was hesitant to utilise this sanction fully. To cut the long story short, my MTO said that no transport could be made available to pick up Deputy Command Armament Officer from Amritsar Railway station to airfield that night-perforce EVT has to wait till the next day morning for the routine run. I was helpless and reclining in the Armoury which was my office of late, when Sqn Ldr EVT burst into my office cursing me for not arranging a transport to receive him. I profoundly regretted my inability stating that the MTO had expressed difficulty. He stated that he would like to see the MTO tomorrow and informed that he had to speak to the Station Commander Group Capt E Fernandez who arranged for a transport to pick me up. By then an air raid siren came and persons were all huddled into a trench. I somehow gave up that drill, knowing well that in any aerial bombing, survival is a matter of chance and not choice. If the bombs fell over- even when you are in a concrete bunker-survival is all Inshallah-God willing. So EVT - a care too hoot type - stayed in the armoury along with me. We had been talking of the war scenarios, especially armament problems. I informed him that to remove the unexploded bombs [that are usually 500lb or 1000lbs] from its various locations in the airfield to a predetermined pit we need strong manila ropes to pull them [*those days we had not heard of fork lifter, leave one who would operate them!]* We had to buy the rope on local purchase as there was no stock in the armoury. Unexploded bombs were frequent occurrences and for each bomb disposal—set of manila ropes had to be bought which along with the bombs were obviously demolished. But for giving money to buy the ropes the Accounts Officer wanted a voucher for the previous issue/purchase. I was at a loss to comply with this.

I also informed him that the Warrant Officer in charge of Bomb Disposal contended that they were all meant to demolish buried bombs only and that for surface bombs the Station Armament Officer only had to dispose.

When EVT heard this-he became unusually calm. He asked me to take him to meet the Accounts Officer. We went next day at dawn as two more bombs had to be demolished. EVT had drawn a revolver on his arrival unknown to me. We were in the Accounts section. I had barely raised the point of advance, the accounts officer asked for settlement of previous amount. EVT made a surprising move - he took out his revolver and aiming and addressing the Accounts officer, he said, *"You young man, know that I am your Command Armament Officer-I order you hereby to give money whenever Sankaran asks for without any condition. If you say NO - I have full authority to shoot you here itself. Now do what I say."*

The young accounts officer trembled in knees, opened his vault paid me Rs. 300, not even asked for signature. Self and EVT made a quiet exit. Surprisingly no further query on this matter was raised later or forever. EVT later professionally helped me to demolish the two bombs and returned to HQ WAC. Next day I got two messages:

(a) For demolition of unexploded bombs, advances should be given as and when required- without conditions-voucher action for settlement of accounts can be done later.

(b) Warrant Officer in charge of Bomb disposal will assist Station Armament Officer whenever asked for disposal of surface bombs as well. A policy directive is being issued.

So much about EVT

I have fond memories of the 1965 and 1971 wars. I would continue cherishing them. It was great to be a part of this beautiful service.

Veteran Wg Cdr Sankaran Subramaniam *was commissioned in the Tech/Armt Branch of the Indian Air Force on 30 Jan 1963. During the 1971 War, he was an instructor at the Air Force Technical College. He was initially attached to HQ WAC, IAF and then moved to Amritsar. He contributed immensely during the War. He had earlier also participated in the 1965 War. He was the junior most officer to have been awarded a Vayu Sena Medal on 26 Jan 1966. He retired on 28 Feb 1990. He is now settled in the USA and stays in California state. He can be reached at sanks38@gmail.com and 7358012702.*

49 When Pegasus Winged over the War Zone

AN Verma

Comm Sqn: Background

Pegasus is the winged white horse in Greek mythology that sprang from its mother's blood as she was beheaded. Its soaring flight is considered an allegory to the immortality of the soul. No wonder Air HQ's Communication Squadron (Comn Sqn or VIP Sqn in common parlance) adopted it as its mascot. With its special aircraft and fussily chosen air and ground crew, the Squadron is justifiably proud of its routine primary duty of flying dignitaries. The very nature of its primary duty requires it to maintain a safe distance from battle zones in times of regular war. However, it has not always been so. India has fought only three declared wars since independence. The 1971 Indo-Pak War in which India obtained an abject surrender of a humongous 93000 enemy troops, stands out in the history of Comn Sqn for the very unusual role it played in it. It was the first time during a war when instead of resting in a safe haven the Squadron deployed a part of its fleet in the war zone for operational duties, very different from its normal role.

Half a century has passed since then, but the proud moments still linger in memory. The account here is based on my first hand experiences as one of the junior-most aircrew in the Sqn at that time, without recourse to official documents and historical records. By March 1971, the influx of close to ten million refugees hounded out from East Pakistan by the Pakistani Army had become an unbearable burden for India. It is common knowledge now that Prime Minister Smt Indira Gandhi was keen on an urgent military offensive but was advised by the then COAS, Gen Manekshaw, to wait till the heavy monsoons in the Eastern wing of the subcontinent faded away. Mrs Gandhi's acceptance of the ideas gave India many months to bring its armed forces in top gear to fight a war at a time of their own choosing. We in the Comn Sqn were obviously not privy to such lofty decisions, although in the course of our duty we did receive a polite thank you and a smile from the suave Prime Minister or a thumping on our backs by the extrovert legend called Sam Bahadur. We considered this as quite normal.

Preparatory Phase

However, the decision to prepare for a decisive war could not remain a secret for us in the Comn Sqn due to the rapid increase in our commitments to fly the three Service Chiefs and other top brass of the three Services to bases all along the extensive border from the Western Coast to the Eastern flank. Even distant Car Nicobar and Port Blair did not remain untouched by the increased activity. In the ensuing summer months, as the dry dust raised by scorching winds of Naliya, Barmer, Uttarlai, Nal, Bikaner, Jodhpur, Jaisalmer, etc., settled on the flying overalls of many of us, others amongst us found Chandigarh, Ambala, Bhatinda, Sarsawa, Adampur, Pathankot, Amritsar, etc., no less scorching and dusty. In the Northern Sector, there was a sudden spurt in our flights to Jammu, Srinagar, Awantipur, Leh, etc. The thought that this huge geographical area under the Western Air Command then was under the direct operational control of a single commander is awe-inspiring. No wonder the name of Air Marshal Minoo M Engineer who commanded the WAC for four very eventful years (1969-73) was the most visible name in the Flight Authorisation Book of the Comn Sqn during those preparatory months. Other top brass of the three Services also left no stone unturned in ensuring full operational preparedness. The Avros and TU124s of Comn Sqn could often be seen parked on the aprons of airfields at Vishakhapatnam, Cochin, Calcutta, Madras, Cuttack, and even Port Blair. We started getting more occasions to fly low-level sorties, even at night, while so far this had been a requirement only of the Aircrew Examining Board. My own first experience of navigating an Avros at not much higher than treetop level in a dark night with all external radio and radar aids switched off and with the AOC-In-C, Air Marshal Engineer sitting in the left-hand seat in the cockpit on one such flight still lingers in the mind for its thrill even after half a century.

The rising tempo of such flights left no doubt in our minds that the 'D' Day was approaching fast. We found the naivety of Pakistani supremo Yahya Khan hilarious when he imagined he had sprung a big surprise late in the evening of 3rd December 1971 by launching air strikes at our bases at Ambala, Agra, Amritsar, Bikaner, Halwara, Jodhpur, Jammu, Bhuj, Srinagar and Uttarlai besides our radar units at Amritsar and Faridkot. When our fighter aircraft gave a befitting reply the same night and early next morning we felt a surge of pride for having been an important aid for the three Services to prepare for this very day.

Avros in Maritime Recce Role

What now came as a surprise for us in the Squadron was the utilisation of our Avros in a role very different from the routine. Going by my personal experience, I kept wondering about our destination when we were told one late afternoon on 12 November 1971 that some of us had to leave our families that very evening to proceed for an unspecified period to another base that would be disclosed to us the next day. The very next morning, i.e., on 13 November 1971, a couple of our aircraft took off for distant Charbattia on the Orissa coast. We were to carry out maritime reconnaissance over the Bay of Bengal in areas specified from time to time. The recce had to be both medium level and low level, visual and electronic, with the help of airborne weather radar in the Avro. We were to maintain a sharp lookout for all surface craft while patrolling in the designated area across the mouth of important naval bases near Vizag and Madras. Descending to low levels over the rising waves of the sea even in dark nights whenever we got the slightest hint of an echo from the sea surface on our radar screen, we covered large areas of the Bay of Bengal extending a couple of hundred nautical miles into the sea along the Eastern coast.

The credit goes to India's inter-services intelligence which had warned that Pakistani submarines were ordered to move out from Karachi on to our West coast off Kutch and Bombay on 14 November

1971 and that one with a range long enough to reach Chittagong base in East Pakistan had been assigned the mission of hunting and sinking India's aircraft carrier, *Vikrant*. Thus, even before PNS *Ghazi* could start trying to locate INS *Vikrant* in the Bay of Bengal, the search for this submarine had already begun by Comn Sqn's Avro aircraft. The Pakistani version of the sinking of PNS *Ghazi* puts the blame on its accidentally hitting hard rock as it dived deep, while the Indian version gives credit to the dropping of torpedoes from INS *Rajpoot*. On 9th December, the Indian Navy proclaimed that it had destroyed *Ghazi* on 3rd December and the few intervening days in announcing this had been spent in collecting irrefutable evidence of the same. No wonder my own flying logbook shows that we had carried out repeated maritime recce sorties usually of four hours' duration, both during day and night on 3, 4, 6, 9 and 10 December 1971. (Other aircraft of the detachment covered 5, 7 and 8 December.) Reports submitted by us must have been compiled by the Indian Navy to link it with the reports of the two naval divers who confirmed seeing the *Ghazi* with gaping holes at the bottom of the sea with all its crew of 90 on board.

The Surrender

Our complete naval and air superiority established in the Eastern sector by 11th December 1971 and total encirclement by our Army left no choice for Lt Gen AAK Niazi but to surrender with his 93,000 men before India's Lt Gen J S Aurora. For our detachment of Avros too, the war in the Eastern sector was over. We flew back to Lucknow to join the rest of the Squadron from where we sneakily flew our usual sorties until 16 December 1971 when the official end of the war was proclaimed.

Epilogue

The signing of the Shimla Agreement was not the last activity connected with the War for the Comn Sqn. The visit of the Defence Secretary and other diplomatic dignitaries to Islamabad to conclude the exchange of PoWs gave our Sqn an opportunity to land at Rawalpindi airport on 23 July 1973 and again on 31 July 1973. By some coincidence, I navigated our TU124 to Rawalpindi on both the occasions and by a greater coincidence, I was the only one amongst a five-member aircrew who came on both these flights and who could converse fluently in Urdu. No wonder I received a lot of attention from our Pakistan Air Force hosts led by Wg Cdr Abdul Moneem Khan of their No 6 Hercules Squadron.

These last lines of a wartime saga might sound incongruous, but I will not shy away from admitting that a certain pathos hit me when Wg Cdr Khan gave me a telephone number of Bhopal and requested me to contact his Nani (maternal grandmother) and convey to her that I had met him and that he was in fine fettle. He longingly mentioned how he had been her favourite grandchild. His inability to talk to her during the preceding many months of turbulent Indo-Pak relations was as painful to him as it must have been to her. I said, "Hopefully the coming years will see improved relations between our two countries" and he added "Insha Allah." We had no inkling then of what another misguided General would do in Kargil many years later only to find his soaring ambitions sink like the *Ghazi* and another one called Bajwa ***"baaz nahin aayegaa"*** another two decades later.

Veteran Wg Cdr AN Verma *was commissioned in the Flying Branch as a Navigator on 16 Oct 1965. He had an illustrious career and served for nine long years in the prestigious Air HQ Comm Squadron. He retired in the year 1987 and took up freelance writing. He has plenty of books both in English and Hindi to his credit. He is settled at Noida and can be reached at arungraphicsverma@gmail.com and 9811631141.*

50 The Moment of Immense Pride

Zakerya Bhai

The last quarter of 1971 was a significant period for all serving defence personnel when war clouds were hovering over Indian skies. The threat of external aggression from Pakistan was well conceived and a general alert code named 'Cactus Lily' was declared for all the operational units. We were all infused with high spirits in anticipation and stayed committed to perfecting flying 'Standard Operating Procedures', working extra hours.

During this period, I was posted to 48 Sqn of American-built CII9G Fairchild Packet aircraft as a young Flight Lieutenant. I had the opportunity to fly over the high hills of J&K, to Leh and Fukche, the highest airfields in the world, and to the Eastern Naga and Mizo hills for Air Maintenance sorties. We had been flying to every part of the country including the Car Nicobar Islands.

I recall with nostalgia some of the important and challenging sorties that have carved a deep and indelible impression and become a lifetime treasure.

Para Dropping in the Enemy Territory

The most memorable mission was the "Pathfinder" dropping mission at Tangail near Dhaka, well inside enemy territory. The Pathfinder was the 1st transport aircraft to fly over enemy territory with commandos on board to be dropped at a predetermined spot. Their mission was to capture a particular bridge to facilitate the advance of our ground forces towards Dhaka. The flying was in uncertain conditions under the threat of a possible enemy attack.

On 11 December, we had positioned our Pathfinder aircraft BK507 at Dum Dum airport, which was the base for the dropping mission. We were in flying overalls with no rank badges and had some Pakistani currency and chocolates in our pockets, our service number engraved and hanging in a chain around our necks. Our briefing was very clear—total radio silence was to be maintained at all costs. Actual photographs of enemy territory were given to us for navigation and an escape route was provided to come back after the drop.

Just before proceeding for the mission, all the aircrew assembled in the airport lounge; it was a touching scene when the ladies of AF Station Barrackpore came to bid us farewell and good luck with prayers in their hearts and tears in their eyes. I was touched by their affectionate talk, a few words of motherly advice, kind and morale-boosting words, words of praise for our high spirits, though secretly they were all worried, knowing fully well that we were going on a challenging and dangerous mission.

After the final intelligence briefing, we took off with the commandos on board heading towards our destination. We were perfectly on the predetermined route to Tangail Dropping Zone. Small arms firing was done by the enemy that was there to "receive" us short of the Dropping Zone; this was as predicted. We ignored them as we were out of their range and continued with our mission.

Throughout, we were scanning the skies for Pak fighters but there were none. My heart sang a salutation for our fighter boys who had established complete command of the air. They had even preceded a sortie to ensure an undisrupted commando drop by us.

Right over the Dropping Zone, the green light flashed and the commandos jumped into the unknown territory equipped with their arms, ammunition and 'reserve' for mission accomplishment. We tracked them visually to confirm that their landing was at the correct spot.

Later in the evening, we learnt that not a single commando had sustained any injury of any kind, and still later, we were told that they had accomplished their mission as well. It was a moment of immense pride and satisfaction as the job had been done with clockwork precision.

General AAK Niazi Onboard our Packet

It was a privileged sortie from Calcutta to Nagpur that gave us the rare opportunity to fly General Niazi and other 'PoW' Generals of Pakistan on 6th Jan 1972, in our Packet aircraft BK515 that had been modified with an additional Orpheus jet engine. General Niazi came to us, shook our hands, and went around our Packet showing the other Generals the modification done by the IAF for extra safety and operational capability. He jokingly commented, "Lovely bird! It will be a good experience to fly in this plane". As per regulations, they surrendered their batons to be kept safely with the luggage and took their seats. We took off at 6:50 am and three hours later landed at Nagpur airport which was wearing the look of a military base, with army personnel cordoning off the entire tarmac area.

Alighting from the aircraft, Gen Niazi thanked each one of us before entering one of the cars of the long convoy that was to take them to Jabalpur Cantonment.

In Dhaka as Victorious Soldiers

We landed at Dhaka on 24 Jan 1972 on a mission to fly back sophisticated Chinese military equipment used by the Pakistanis against the Indian forces. One Wing of the Pak AF Officers' Mess was occupied by Bangladesh Air Force Officers, and we stayed in the second Wing. Taking an abandoned van, we went around the airfield, which had been badly damaged by Indian firepower. The dispersal area where all the Sabre jets, the pride of the Pak Air Force, were parked in damaged condition looked like a graveyard of their prestigious planes.

Many anti-aircraft guns, huge ammunition dumps and heaps of empty cartridges were scattered around. We went to the ATC tower where an IAF Officer had been tied up during Indian bombing raids. We walked on the busy streets of Dhaka in our flying overalls and were greeted by the locals who shook our hands in gratitude for having liberated them from Pakistan. We went to Sheikh Mujibur Rehman's residence where we were received by him very warmly. We had a touching experience when we went to a locality where Indian Muslims had been practically confined to their houses living in the fear of attracting the wrath of the local population. They requested us to persuade the Indian Army not to leave their area. They gave us letters and messages for their relatives living in India. Later, after returning, I personally ensured that every letter reached its destination in India.

Today, as I look back and recall the 1971 Operation, I realise that war can proffer all hues of variegated emotions and experiences—excitement, thrill, vulnerability, stoicism, defeat, victory, surrender, joy, and sorrow. However, nothing is as sublime and peaceful as living in a prospering place.

***Veteran Gp Capt Zakerya Bhai** was commissioned in the Aeronautical Engineering Branch on 04 October 1965. During the 1971 war, he was on the posted strength of 48 Sqn, AF and actively participated as an Aircrew. Subsequently, he changed track to TROPO and was a part of the original lot who was trained in the USA. Thereafter, he was instrumental in setting up of the TROPO communication units in the Air Force. He is the recipient of VSM. He has the unique distinction of handling an offshore project for the ONGC as its Chief Engineer during the period 1981 to 1986. He retired from the Air Force in 1993. He is settled at Nagpur and can be reached at zakerya3112@gmail.com and 9923131252.*

আত্মসমর্পণের ঐতিহাসিক দলিল

INSTRUMENT OF SURRENDER

The PAKISTAN Eastern Command agree to surrender all PAKISTAN Armed Forces in BANGLA DESH to Lieutenant General JAGJIT SINGH AURORA, General Officer Commanding in Chief of the Indian and BANGLA DESH forces in the Eastern Theatre. This surrender includes all PAKISTAN land, air and naval forces as also all para military forces and civil armed forces. These forces will lay down their arms and surrender at the places where they are currently located to the nearest regular troops under the command of Lieutenant General JAGJIT SINGH AURORA.

The PAKISTAN Eastern Command shall come under the orders of Lieutenant General JAGJIT SINGH AURORA as soon as the instrument has been signed. Disobedience of orders will be regarded as a breach of the surrender terms and will be dealt with in accordance with the accepted laws and usages of war. The decision of Lieutenant General JAGJIT SINGH AURORA will be final, should any doubt arise as to the meaning of interpretation of the surrender terms.

Lieutenant General JAGJIT SINGH AURORA gives a solemn assurance that personnel who surrender shall be treated with dignity and respect that soldiers are entitled to in accordance with provisions of the Geneva Convention and guarantees the safety and well-being of all PAKISTAN military and para military forces who surrender. Protection will be provided to foreign nationals, ethnic minorities and personnel of WEST PAKISTANI origin by the forces under the command of Lieutenant General JAGJIT SINGH AURORA.

(JAGJIT SINGH AURORA)
Lieutenant General
General Officer Commanding in Chief
India and Bangladesh Forces in the Eastern Theatre

16 December 1971

(AMIR ABDULLAH KHAN NIAZI)
Lieutenant General
Martial Law Administrator Zone B and
Commander Eastern Command (Pakistan)

16 December 1971

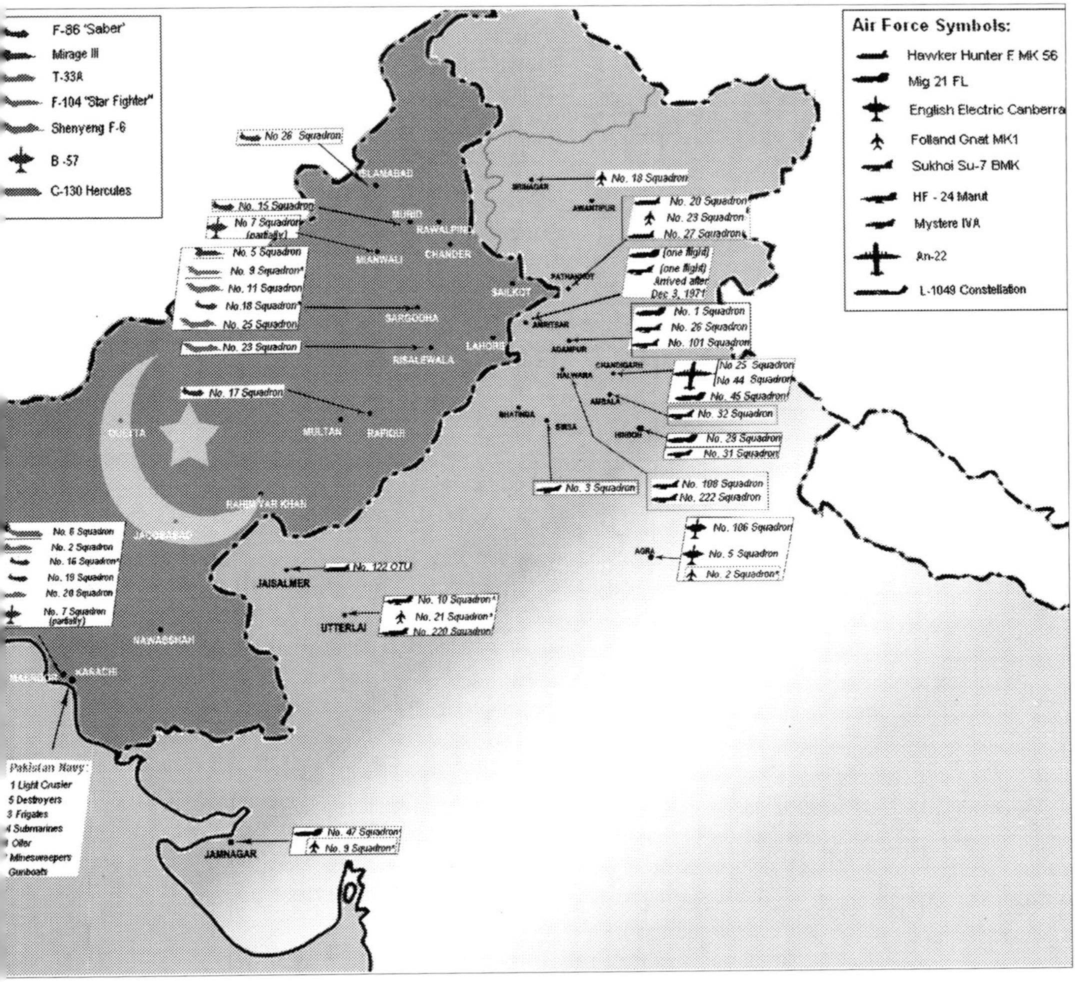

Pakistan Western Front: Dec 1971 Plan and Deployment

Defence Minister Felicitating Pilots of 22 Sqn after Battle of Boyra: 1971

Packets Drop at Tangail

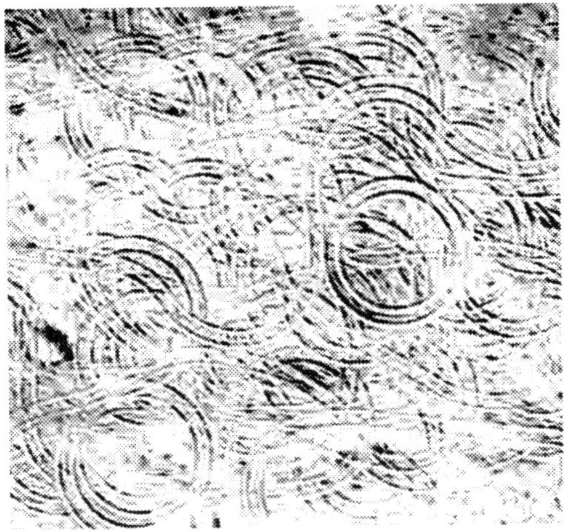

PAK TANK TRACKS

CRATERS CREATED BY AIRCRAFT ROCKET FIRING AND STRAFING

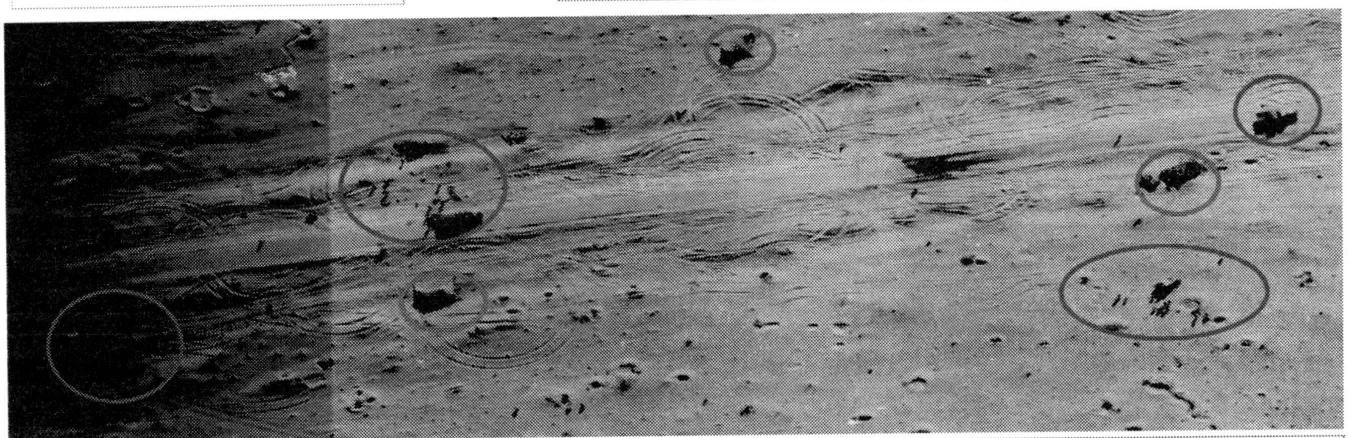

O- ABANDONED CLASS 'A' VEHICLES CAPTURED BY INDIAN ARMY

O- ABANDONED CLASS 'B' VEHICLES

Zoomed in View

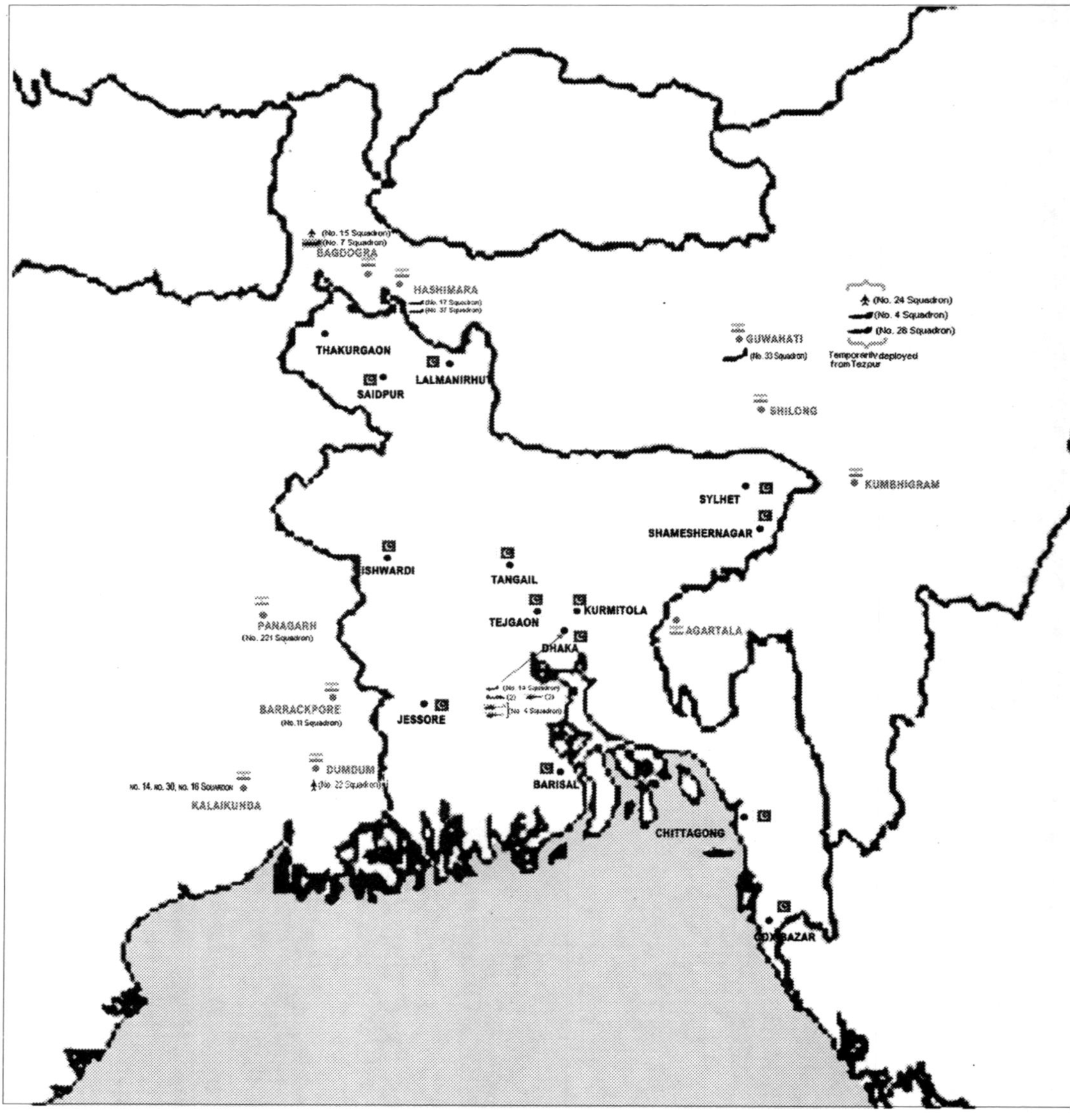

Eastern Front Plan and Deployment

Tejgaon Airfield Attacked

Lahore Railway Station Bombing

Attock Oil Refinery

ABOUT THE EDITORS

Veteran Air Marshal Jagjeet Singh was commissioned in the Aeronautical Engineering Branch on 03 January 1977 after obtaining his BE Electrical degree from Thapar Institute of Engineering and Technology, Patiala. He is a Postgraduate in Electrical Engineering and also holds a Postgraduate Diploma in Management. He served for 39 years in the IAF and superannuated on 31 December 2015. He has been the Senior Vice President of AFA from 01 Jan 2017 onwards. He can be reached at aircmdejagjeet@gmail.com and 9910948444, 9868940200.

Veteran Gp Capt Shailendra Mohan was commissioned in the Equipment (now Logistics) Branch on 23 December 1964. He is an MA in Literature and MSc in Defence Studies. He is a graduate of the Defence Services Staff College. He has served as Senior Logistics Officer of three operational bases and as Dy CLMO of HQ WAC. He retired as Director of Mechanical Transport at Air HQ. He was awarded commendations by AOA and CAS. Presently, he is the editor of AFA Magazine (Eagle's Eye). He can be reached at shailmohan@gmail.com and 9811078880